Copyright © 2020/2021 Larry Schroeder All Rights Reserved

All Rights Reserved. No part of this publication may be reproduced or transmitted in any form or by any means, mechanical or electronic, including photocopying and recording, or by any information storage and retrieval system, without permission in writing from the author or publisher (except by a reviewer, who may quote brief passages and/or show brief video clips in a review).

Disclaimer: The Publisher and the Author make no representation or warranties concerning the accuracy or completeness of the contents of this work and specifically disclaim all warranties for a particular purpose. No warranty may be created or extended through sales or promotional materials. The advice and strategies contained herein may not be suitable for every situation. This work is sold with the understanding that the Author and Publisher are not engaged in rendering legal, technological, or other professional services. If professional assistance is required, the services of a competent professional should be sought. Neither the Publisher nor the Author shall be liable for damages arising therefrom.

The fact that an organization or website is referred to in this work as a citation and/or potential source of further information does not mean that the Author or the Publisher endorses the information, the organization, or website it may provide, or recommendations it may make. Further, readers should be aware that the websites listed in this work may have changed or disappeared between when this work was written and when it is read. Disclaimer: The cases and stories in this book have had details changed to preserve privacy.

ISBN: Paperback 978-1-64873-142-6
ISBN: Ebook 978-1-64873-141-9
ISBN: Hardcover 978-1-64873-143-3

Printed in the United States of America

Published by: Writer's Publishing House
writerspublishinghouse.com
Prescott, Az 86301

Project Management and Book Launch by Writers Publishing House

Cover and Interior Design by Creative Artistic Excellence
Marketing: lizzymcnett.com

Facing Fear

The True Story of Evelyn Frechette

By Larry Schroeder

Acknowledgments

In my more than thirty years of research writing Facing Fear, I have met some incredible people who helped move this process along more than I could have ever imagined. One person, who prefers to remain nameless, spent one whole afternoon with a complete stranger talking about her life encounters with Evelyn. We sat and talked over lunch, in her kitchen. I do not believe the book would have been completed without her help. I just wanted to say thank you from the bottom of my heart.

The next person shall remain nameless as well, but his stories were from John Dillinger's point of view. In the same fashion, his information helped a great deal as well. I will always be grateful for his assistance.

John Fricke was instrumental in sending me the information on Walter Wilson. His help became invaluable over the years.

My next acknowledgment goes out to Kathy Tic Easland and Sharon Tic Plasky, Evelyn's step-granddaughters. Kathy and Sharon came to my event at Little Bohemia and it was exciting to meet with them. We have shared many meals regaling the stories of their great-grandmother. None of this would have been possible without your help.

More thanks must go out to the following people: Leroy Clark, Rita Bohm, and George Hoffmann. It is with my deepest sincerity to thank all of these people publicly for their help.

Author Biography

My journey writing Facing Fear started in the mid-80s. During that time, my career took me on a daily drive from Wausau to Green Bay. The trip was like watching paint dry after a few months. I needed something to keep my mind occupied on the drive. So, one afternoon a short time later, I stopped at a local gas station for fuel and to stretch my legs. It happened to be on the Menominee Indian Reservation. While filling up the truck, some local kids ran up to me asking if I knew Evelyn Frechette. It seemed odd at the time, I had no idea who she was or why they would be asking. They proceeded to tell me she was John Dillinger's girlfriend and was born on the reservation. Since I had lived in Wisconsin most of my life and spent time in that area of the county, the Dillinger name is fairly common. However, that was the extent of my knowledge. The interaction left me curious and I started researching this person born in

the early 1900s. Needless to say, her story got my attention. This thirty-year research project has finally come to fruition. But before going any further, the story of naming the book outlining Evelyn's story must be told first.

At night, I would go downstairs to the basement to work on my research. Our house was three stories with the basement half underground, in a remote location along the edge of the woods. Back then, we did not have computers so all my research was written in notebooks or on index cards. I had gone downstairs after dinner to write, while my wife went about her nightly routine. I was sitting at my desk and the only light on in the room was the small desk lamp. It was quiet and dark; I could see the faint house lights illuminating across the edge of the woods through the window above my desk. Shortly thereafter, I heard a voice echo 360 degrees around the room. At first, I thought it was my wife coming downstairs. But when I realized there were no footsteps, I leaped from my chair and scanned the room, when I heard it again. The voice was clear, a quiet but firm tone. It echoed, Facing Fear. In the few seconds I stood there, it repeated several more times.

The incident almost scared me to death. I took off across the dark room, nearly breaking my leg running upstairs. My wife heard me charging across the house as I entered the bedroom. She looked shocked to see me panting, as the sweat poured off my face. I have always been very active, an athlete. In my youth, I competed in cycling and speed skating. So, to see me out of breath was unusual. Once I started to relax and explained what happened, she did not seem surprised or even alarmed. She just simply said, "I guess Evelyn is trying to tell you something."

The title was perfect; the occurrence connected me with her on a spiritual level, unlike anything I had ever experienced. So, in essence, Evelyn named her own book. As I have learned, she faced fear every day of her life. I am not sure why Evelyn sought me out to tell her story to the world, but I am honored to have been the one she chose.

Table of Contents

Acknowledgments 3

Author Biography 5

Prologue 12

Introduction 30

Chapter One: Trials of Youth 49

Chapter Two: Genocide 78

Chapter Three: Precious Child of God 94

Chapter Four: My Dream Ended 125

Chapter Five: Life with Johnnie 139

Chapter Six: The Big Escape 164

Chapter Seven: Our Florida Vacation 173

Chapter Eight: Alone on the Road 194

Chapter Nine: No Contact 211

Chapter Ten: Charged with Murder 227

Chapter Eleven: A Back-Country Road 247

Chapter Twelve: Sentenced to Prison 264

Chapter Thirteen: Life in Prison................278

Chapter Fourteen: The Fatal Shooting 295

Chapter Fifteen: Agonizing Pain........................310

Chapter Sixteen: I'm Free 353

Chapter Seventeen: I Grieved! 388

Chapter Eighteen: The Spying 408

Chapter Nineteen: Time Heals All Wounds...........417

Chapter Twenty: My Baby's Gone 436

Chapter Twenty-One: The Spying Has to Stop......448

Chapter Twenty-Two: You Can't Go Back 470

Chapter Twenty-Three: The Women of My Past...484

Chapter Twenty-Four: War Games 570

Chapter Twenty-Five: A New Age Is Dawning......587

Chapter Twenty-Six: True Love Comes More Than Once 605

Chapter Twenty-Seven: I Brought My Toothbrush 620

Chapter Twenty-Eight: Pacific Ocean Here We Come 639

Chapter Twenty-Nine: Holidays with the Family ..652

Chapter Thirty: I Said Goodbye 664

Epilogue 674

References 693

Prologue

My mother used to say, "When you know who you are; when your mission is clear and you burn with the inner fire of unbreakable will; no cold can touch your heart; no deluge can dampen your purpose. You know that you are alive." Her immortal words will always be a part of my soul.

I can still remember that day, the agony in her face. I could only imagine how she must have felt, watching me disappear out of sight. It was the first time I'd seen her cry since Daddy died. At the time, I had some idea of the horrible events taking place on the reservation, but no idea how bad things were until I headed off to the boarding school in Flandreau, South Dakota. The experience exposed me to the real world beyond the confines of my childhood home. Now, I am not saying life on the reservation was easy, it wasn't. We faced hatred and bigotry every day as travelers made their way around the country. Although not everyone was bad, I remember one such gentleman and his wife; their acquaintance touched my soul, and allowed me to keep hope that not every human on the planet wanted all Native Americans dead. Or confined to a cell like a criminal.

As a young teenager, my thoughts transformed to becoming an adult with a life of my own. One such evening brought my longings to a head when a traveler named E.P. Bridgman stopped for the night. He and his wife were living in Keshena on the Menominee Reservation and moving to their new homestead. His belongings consisted of a cookstove, table, a few chairs, bedding, simple clothing, and a brood of chickens. Their wagon was pulled by an ox team owned by an Indian man they hired to move them. The homestead was about 30 miles away.

As he regaled us with his stories of their journey, most of the passages were overgrown with wilderness that had to be cleared before they could pass. He said if they traveled 1 to 2 miles it was a good day. After they fought the gnats and mosquitos all night, they headed for the mud hole to water the oxen before heading on their way. Mr. Bridgman was bound for a small town called Polar. In all, three families were headed in that direction.

Their departure left me desperate to find my own path away from Neopit. It's amazing how adolescence misrepresents life. I watched them with a longing desire to see the world. It made my choice to leave and get an education from a boarding school in South Dakota a good decision. Although, many of my family members did not approve of me leaving the reservation to be educated by Western culture. In those days, the hatred between settlers and Native Americans was violent, to say the least.

Since I was born long after the early Indian raids began, my only memories are of the elders telling stories of our past. The carnage was horrific. My words could never do the whole event justice. But as I understand, the problems began when the European settlers traveled to the Americas in the

1600s, wherein some cases, White women were kidnapped by various tribes. In most cases, it was only to diversify the bloodline. However, unlike history recalls, the women were never injured and were well-cared for once they settled into their new tribe. They were married off to younger Native American males. The mistreatment issue came into play when the European migrants considered marrying outside their race offensive. So, to instill fear among the colonies, rumors were spread to make them fear the Native people. As the word seeped into the Native American tribes, they found it horrifying to kill women and children while raiding villages. Mistrust raged on both sides and the war between our people began.

    It escalated for centuries, but as the struggle for control over North America began, the U.S. needed help against the Spanish, so they employed the Native Americans to fight our enemies. However, as relations calmed between England and Spain, help from the Indians was not necessary, and a plan was enacted to civilize the tribes. Native Americans became an obstacle in the way of expansion. It was a common belief by then that if the Indians would act like a normal European Caucasian person, assimilation into Western culture would be easy. When the plan did not work with the tribes, they became hostiles and considered dangerous. Such a shame when all we wanted to do was preserve a heritage that had lasted for centuries. Just as the settlers wanted to procure their culture, we wanted the same for our people. The Quakers saw this as a rivalry, which slowed the number of souls who could be converted to Christianity. We never wanted any of the violence brought against us, but when we fought back to protect our race, we were slaughtered by the thousands. If I am not mistaken, was that not the reason why European settlers fled England?

Unfortunately, the battle was far from over. In 1838, the government announced the Indian Removal Act which was meant to move willing Indian tribes off their land; however, when opposition pressed against them once again, we were then called a great hindrance. From there, as I understand, the wars became bloody massacres for both sides.

One battle that is surrounded by false beliefs is Custer's Last Stand. Near the Little Big Horn River on Sioux and Cheyenne land, in less than an hour we won the battle against over 200 soldiers. The Great Plains was the last Native American area left to gain control. It was well-known that America was running out of room, and the government needed the land along the Great Plains. So, the decision came down to forcing Native Americans off the land or to exterminate us by whatever means necessary.

After the soldiers lost the battle, the government contracted with the railroad companies to slaughter buffalo herds by the thousands in an attempt to starve us out. It was also encouraged that hunters do the same. I have seen pictures of the rotting animals scattered for hundreds of miles. The thought makes me sick to my stomach. As tempers grew, tribes retaliated by attacking settlers and railroad workers regardless of gender. In our eyes, we share this planet with both animals and humans, and to devastate Mother Earth in such a way was savage.

Over the next several years, anyone seeking revenge against the Native Americans was free to do, as necessary. The result was complete annihilation. However, that plan did not work, or I would not be telling this story. On what we celebrate as the Fourth of July, the US Army was dead set on hunting down and killing all of us Indians. Crazy Horse was one of the last Native American Chiefs to surrender.

At that point, rounding up the remaining Natives was not difficult. We were either forced onto reservations or killed. That is when the boarding schools for Native children were built by the government in an attempt to 'civilize' us. However, if that was the end of the war, it would have been wonderful; nonetheless, that was not the case.

A loathing distrust for the Native Americans had reached a boiling point. Both sides hated each other, and rightfully so if you believe all the rumors. The *New York Times* reported the battle of Little Big Horn as, "Troops, killed like a slaughter pen." I have seen newspaper clippings of the event, but none as horrific to the force raged against the Native Indian tribes around the Americas. We are not perfect either and had our own wars with different tribes, but none were dead set on the annihilation of our race. I remember one such story the elders told for years when I was a kid. An old Army barracks was remodeled into a boarding school, and three of the children were Little Chief, Horse, and Little Plume. They were forced into the school where speaking our language was forbidden, after which their names were changed, they were given haircuts, and forced into a military uniform. They were trained to exhaustion without proper nutrition or rest. Within two years of arriving at the Indian school, the three boys were dead, and the worst part— no one cared. They just rounded up more, and if they died, it was one less Indian alive on the planet.

Eventually, there were more than 150 schools based around the US. All of them with a mission to 'civilize' the Natives into God-fearing, soil tilling, White brothers. General Pratt pushed for reform at any cost, so the method of assimilation began. Indian children were forcibly removed from their homes and taken far away to transform them. If only the cruelty stopped at that point, yet sadly it only got worse.

Before I continue talking about the boarding schools, there is one very important topic that needs to be addressed. It further explains the reason Native Americans had every right to retaliate against the government for its unfair treatment. When World War II broke out, the country was in desperate need of metal to build weapons, vehicles, ammunition, and anything the military needed to fight in the war. As if matters weren't bad enough, the country was desperate for food, gas, clothing, and oil. All of these were being rationed extensively. Therefore, to alleviate the problem, several women started their own gardens to feed local families. I believe that over 40 percent of the vegetable gardens were grown by women. They were called 'victory gardens.' In total there were 20 million of them spread throughout the countryside. Many of the Native American women helped due to their extensive knowledge of farming and harvesting food. We did not have the luxury of buying groceries in a store. Nonetheless, the war raged on and the military struggled to break the enemies' code or send coded messages without being broken. During World War I the government recruited Native Americans to transmit messages to other forces in tribal languages, so the orders were kept secret. This was the reason we were asked again to help fight in the battle. Of course, we complied with their request. Our respect for the land we loved and the communities built a sense of patriotism and desire to defend the US. Our livelihood was at stake as well.

One such person stands out in my mind; he was a civil engineer in California. I remember his name being plastered in the newspaper at the time. He was a Marine named Philip Johnston, but he grew up on the Navajo reservation.

He said, "This conflict involved Mother Earth being dominated by foreign countries. It was our responsibility to defend her."

As he spoke fluent Navajo, which is very difficult to learn, he was a perfect candidate. Now, most of our language was unwritten, so there was no documentation on learning it from a book. When Johnston approached the military about his idea there were fewer than thirty non-Navajo who could speak the language; hence, his reasoning for being such an attribute to the fighting soldiers. The first recruits were sent to boot camp in May of 1942 for training. The Navajo code was formally developed and used to transmit messages while in combat. Their codes were never broken. Their presence was a vital role in the US winning World War II. Our traditions were passed down through the generations without writing everything down on paper. It is just another example of how unjust the treatment of my people became when our very presence saved many lives and helped win a world war.

As much as we did to help the government fight during World War I and II, the hatred continued to grow and spread across the Americas. It was a one-sided way of looking at things. Intimidation and fear were very much present in our daily lives. At the time, I wondered if it would ever end. I could never understand why Western culture was so unaccepting of something new or foreign to them. Yet they did not have a problem using the Native Americans to get what they wanted, then throw us away like trash.

    Life on the reservation intensified over the years, especially after Daddy died. All of a sudden, my mother was a single parent raising five children. One night before I left for the boarding school there was an incident in the town. It was common for the men of the reservation to work during the week, and then go buy alcohol on the weekend and spend the night drinking and sleep most of the next day. Our society was devastated by the invasion of Western culture. Not only were we forced to give up centuries of traditions, but also our very essence and the things that made us Native American. However, the men would never harm a family member, or another person, unless provoked. I cannot say that about everyone, especially some of the Caucasian men.

Typically, as children, we were in bed sleeping by eight. But no one in my family was allowed outside after dark–unless to use the outhouse–and then it was no dawdling because it could be fatal. One such incident reminded me of just how dangerous it was going outside after dark. The screams will forever be present in my mind.

One of my classmates, a young girl up the road, was attacked on her way home by some despicable men who traveled onto the reservation looking for some excitement. Well, let's just say we have different definitions of excitement. Anyway, she was grabbed and tied to a hitching post across from one of the shacks in town. They stripped off her clothing and proceeded to gang-rape her for hours. Many times, there might have been up to twenty men at a time taking turns.

I laid in my bed listening to her screams for hours. When it finally got the best of me, I covered my ears with the pillow. The gangs were well armed and used deadly force to disengage anyone trying to break up their actions. My mind raced praying for someone, anyone, to come forward and help her; however, my pleas went unanswered. She was found the next morning, naked, beaten, covered in blood, and hanging over the hitching post where they left her. I, still to this day, see the image of her brutalized body. Shortly after the incident, another girl was kidnapped in broad daylight and gang-raped in the same fashion. She was found dead in the woods several days later.

Life in Boarding School

I prayed that choosing to leave and finish my education in a boarding school would save me from such insidious acts, but nonetheless, the brutality continued. As I grew up with loving parents, I was not accustomed to domestic abuse. We dealt with the attacks from men mostly of the Western culture; although, not from any family members. It was all about to change drastically.

When we arrived at the boarding school, we were stripped of our clothing and sent to bathhouses. Everyone was placed in kerosene and our genitals were scrubbed with lye soap. I had to walk on my tiptoes for a week, it was excruciating. Then our hair was cut; the boys' heads were shaved, and girls had a bowl cut. We were given solid-colored dresses (usually grey in tone with some lace on the edges), black leather boots, and undergarments. The girls who were developing breasts had to wear a corset.

At first, except for the abuse, it seemed to be fairly safe. Until one night, when a nine-year-old girl was raped in her dormitory bed. Many of the girls were so scared that we jumped into each other's beds as soon as the lights went out. The sustained terror further tested our endurance, as it was better to suffer with a full bladder and be safe than to walk through the dark, seemingly endless hallway to the bathroom. I remember one male teacher, and everyone knew of his escapades, but did nothing. We would cringe anytime we entered his classroom.

I wish I could tell you the abuse stopped at the rapes; however, that is not the case. The school's disciplinary practices left a lot to be desired. A young boy had his ear yanked so hard, it almost pulled off his head. Anyone who resisted being civilized was tortured in a multitude of ways. The most common was starvation. On average, our daily calorie intake was 160 to 400 calories, so let me compare the statistics. Almost eighty years later during the Holocaust, Auschwitz prisoners were to rationed 1,300 calories a day. Yet we survived all attempts to annihilate the Native American Indians.

As we fought to survive the boarding schools, even more, devastating atrocities were taking place around the US. The militias carried out most of the slaughter against my people, while enjoying the financial support from the government on a state and federal level. The Eel River Rangers had become so prolific that they killed Indians daily, then reported their deaths to the California head of Indian Affairs.

When asked for proof, each man would provide a brass toe tag to prove the kills. Again, we wondered how much worse it could get.

By the middle of the nineteenth century, "Buffalo" Bill Cody slaughtered more than 4,000 bison in two years. Bison were a centrepiece of his Wild West Show, which was very successful both in the United States and in Europe. It thrilled the spectators into thinking it was an honored tradition to destroy the Indian culture. Once our food source was eliminated, most of the remaining tribes starved to death. An unconscionable act.

The last point I want to address happened after things settled down between the races, the boarding schools closed, and we were allowed to go home. Since most of the children were kidnapped at such a young age, they had forgotten their culture. When they tried to find records of their families, the government had erased all entries. The children essentially became a non-person. It destroyed what little hope they had left.

Time passed, and so did the hatred. Nonetheless, we fought every day with the hopes of one day living in peace with the Western culture on our homelands. It took centuries for the bigotry to ease; although, for some, it may never subside. Like one Christian mission that made its calling to civilize us by whatever means necessary, because we were an ignorant race who must be shown the way to heaven.

Introduction

On one November evening while at the Olympic Lounge in Chicago Illinois, Evelyn Frechette met a man about thirty years old. The gentleman was introduced to her as Jack Harris. 'Billie' (Evelyn Frechette) felt an instant attraction.

"I'll never forget that. It happened the way things do in the movies. I was twenty-five years old and I wasn't any different from all the other girls that were twenty-five years old. Nothing that happened to me up to that time had amounted to anything. Then I met John, and everything was changed. I started a new kind of life," said Billie.

He grinned at her with the cute cocky half-grin and said, "Where have you been all my life?" His name was **John Dillinger**. She was hooked.

Evelyn said, "There was something in those eyes that I will never forget. They were piercing and electric, yet there was an amused carefree twinkle in them too. They met my eyes and held me hypnotized for an instant."

Early Years

Born Evelyn Frechette, known later in life as 'Billie", it is thought she coined the nickname in honor of her father who died. She was just seven years old. But others think she chose the name after the death of her son in 1928.

Evelyn's father was William Frechette, a Frenchman who married a half Menominee Indian named Mary Labell. Billie was born on September 15, 1907. When her father died in 1913, it left Mary to raise her four sons and daughters alone.

Menominee Family Winter Home

The Menominee Indian Reservation is in the state of Wisconsin, with a rich history dating back ten thousand years. At one time, the Tribe took residency in the area known as Wisconsin, and parts of Michigan and Illinois. Before the Treaty in the early 1800s, the tribe occupied a land base estimated at ten million acres. By the time their negotiations ended with the United Government, they were down to two hundred thirty-five thousand acres.

Menominee Camp

The Menominee Tribe's origin begins at the mouth of the Menominee River, just sixty miles east of the present reservation land. Their rich heritage consisted of five clans: Ancestral Bear, Eagle, Wolf, Moose, and Crane. Very few tribes can confirm their origin base is so close or near the present reservation.

According to the Menominee Indian Tribe, "Menominee Dreamers foresaw the coming of a light-skinned people in large boats that would come into the bay of Green Bay and change our lives forever. This prophecy came true in 1634 when the

French explorer Jean Nicolet arrived at Green Bay (La Baye). Nicolet was looking for a route to the East.

Soon after Nicolet's arrival, the Menominee would become involved in the fur trade and a once independent people would now become dependent upon trade goods and a new way of life. The Menominee have survived for over ten thousand years of existence in this area, and are indigenous to the State of Wisconsin. We have managed to keep a fraction of our ancestral territory for a home which is now our reservation. We continue to have strong leadership and it was this type of leadership that has taken us through much adversity. We continue to speak our language and practice our traditions and our traditional religion. Spiritually, we continue to speak with our creator through tobacco, prayers, and other offerings. We will continue to survive because we are a sovereign nation, a nation that refused to be pushed from our territory, a nation that will remain strong and independent.

"The Menominee People were integral in Wisconsin becoming a state. We have had hundreds of Sesquicentennials. We gave up lands through agreements called Treaties and in the 1848 Treaty, we refused to leave what would become Wisconsin our ancestral home. This is our story. We will remain Menominee until our language is no longer spoken. We are 'Kiash Matchitiwuk' the Ancient Ones" (Wisconsin, 2019).

The current government seat is located approximately forty-five miles northwest of Green Bay, Wisconsin. The Tribe includes five main communities: Keshena, Neopit, Middle Village, Zoar, and South Branch.

"Today, the Tribe remains a proud and resilient people living on the most beautiful lands to ever grace this earth. The Tribe's members enjoy pristine lakes, rivers, and streams, over 219,000 acres of the richest forests in the Nation, and an abundance of plant and animal life. The Tribe cherishes its natural resources and considers itself to be very fortunate to have them, but the richness of the Tribe's surroundings is often overshadowed by the many social ills Menominee people suffer. Like many other Tribes in this Nation, we are greatly dependent on funding provided by the Federal Government to help us address and overcome these difficult challenges, and we are especially dependent upon funding provided by the Bureau of Indian Affairs and Indian Health Service.

"Although the Tribe has over 8,700 members, less than half can reside on the Reservation due to the lack of employment opportunities, available housing, and an aging infrastructure that is incapable of sustaining current demand, let alone take on additional residents or economic development opportunities. It is the Tribe's sincere hope that, with the help of Congress, the Tribe can transform the Reservation and Menominee County back into a place Menominee will return to for occupational, economic, educational, housing, cultural, and other opportunities."[1]

When Evelyn's father died, her mother remained on the reservation close to family and friends. She attended Saint Anthony's Mission School until she reached the age of thirteen.

St. Anthony's School

"In 1872 the Parish opened and the school consisted of four classrooms. Each room held three to four grades. The school was run by the School Sisters of Notre Dame.

"In 1873 Mother Caroline purchased two lots on Fourth Avenue and built a home for the Sisters.

---

[1] School, S. A. (2019). St. Anthony School. Retrieved from : https://stanthonymilwaukee.org/history

"In 1881 St. Anthony Church was erected. An addition was built in 1889 and 1895. 112 children received First Holy Communion.

"In 1906 Sisters erected a larger convent south of the church. The Parish Hall was built in 1907.

"In 1920 the school building was condemned and a new one was built and dedicated by Archbishop Messmer."[2]

Evelyn attended the Mission School until she was thirteen, after which she moved to South Dakota where she finished her schooling. The establishment was a government boarding school for American Indians. Evelyn was always a model student. She stayed at Riggs School for three years and then moved to Milwaukee to live with her aunt.

---

[2] School, S. A. (2019). St. Anthony School. Retrieved from : https://stanthonymilwaukee.org/history

Evelyn Frechette – The Early Years

Neopit circa 1909-1912

Briggs Indian Boarding School

U. S. Teams, Neopit, Wis.

U.S. Hotel, Neopit, Wis.

Neopit Cemetery

Neopit Power Station

Drills to civilize

Native children gardening

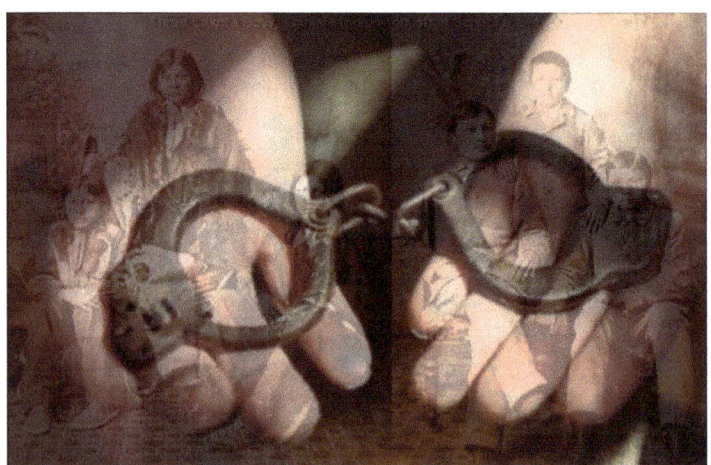
Child handcuff

Chapter One:

Trials of Youth

The moment my feet hit the dirt in Flandreau, I felt a loneliness creep in, unlike anything I'd ever experienced. My decision put me in a place filled with unimaginable hatred. In the main lobby of the administration building was a picture of Army Lieutenant Richard Henry Pratt with a plaque stating his immortal words, "Kill the Indian, save the man."

The words burned a hole in my heart that would not soon heal. They have followed me around since I was thirteen.

Before we continue on the journey of being a Native American in the 1920s, I want to backtrack for just a minute and explain in more detail my life at Riggs Boarding School for Indians.

The whole premise was to 'civilize' us at any cost. If anyone refused, they were exterminated. I found the sentiment unsettling.

I rode the train from Neopit, Wisconsin to South Dakota. All the Native children were hauled in a converted livestock car.  We did not have seats and it smelled like death. As we debarked from the train, I waited quietly on the platform while the other children filed singly off the passenger car.

As the group of children gathered, I noticed several of the younger ones were terrified. It was an experience we all shared. My heart went out to their pain. I shuddered to think of how they must have been feeling; at least my age allowed me some wisdom to understand what was happening. Since it was always good to be with my people, I made my way over to the children and attempted to calm their fears.

While the train emptied, a large caravan of buckboards approached behind the train depot. Several soldiers paraded alongside the depot station. The sight brought welling terror to the surface. They carried period rifles and gun belts armed with plenty of bullets. The young ones clutched my leg in fear of what would be coming to all of us very soon. I knew my decision to leave home would not be easy, but in the long run, it was the only way to make a better life for myself.

They rounded us up like cattle and we were shoved into the back of the wagons. Any outbursts were met with swift punishment. However, I followed my mother's instructions, "Evelyn, keep your head down and do as you are told." Some of the

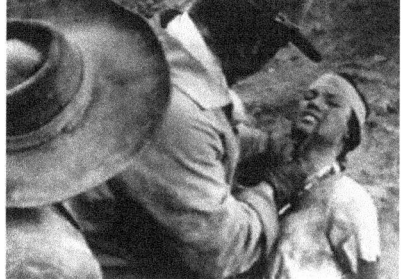

boys tried to assert their authority, but the men acted with vengeance against their actions.

The ride out to Riggs Indian School was about an hour. All of which my backside cried with agony. When we arrived, several of the staff members stood out front with clothing, scissors, and shoes. The girls were escorted to the bathing room in one of the buildings far away from the rest of the compound. I say that because it was nothing more than a prison. On the first day of our arrival, I still remember them yelling, "Filthy savages, dirty ignorant Indian."

If labeling us an ignorant was not enough, our clothing was burned in the furnace room. I watched the one last memory of my heritage disappear in the roaring flames. It would be years before I had dealings with any Native Americans outside Riggs school.

My biggest challenge was communication; from the time we arrived at the school, it was forbidden to speak our native language. I was grateful to have learned some English while I attended St.

Anthony's Mission School. The nuns were strict, but not uncaringly brutal. However, I cannot say it was this way for all the other children who only spoke their native language.

When the sun rose our first morning, the day started with drills at dawn on the front lawn. We marched to learn discipline and follow the rules of society for a government completely foreign to us. If we owned our own land on the reservation, then why did we have to assimilate? All of which could have been better achieved with some compassion for the horrific events we endured.

As my time at Riggs taught me, I was skilled at taking care of others. The young ones found my presence soothing and came to me for comfort on many occasions. It kept them calm and manageable, so the staff left us alone. I do have to admit the comforts of having clean bedding, clothes, shoes, and regular meals were reassuring. Nonetheless, it did not wash away the cruelty.

One thing I remember vividly was the fact we were only allowed to read the Bible. According to our teachers and staff, we had to accept Jesus to be civilized. We believe the Earth is sacred and all the inhabitants are meant to be respected; not just the ones with a certain color or breeding. In the evenings after dinner, they allowed one hour of reading time before bed for the children who could read. Our nightstands held a Bible for each child.

The education we received at Riggs was mediocre at best; yes, we learned to read, write, and do arithmetic, but at the cost of our sanity. Many of the children could not deal with the horrific abuse, and  either perished or were killed. I did not suffer as some children, maybe because I am mixed race. My father was French, and my mother was half-French and Menominee Indian. Nonetheless, the nightmares continued for many years after I left that place. In the end, I graduated with a trade diploma in nursing.

I was eighteen when my stint ended at Riggs, and it was none too soon. Carol, one of the staff members who had over the years grown a conscience, grabbed my shoulders and pulled me in close to her chest. The human contact eased the pain for a moment. I appreciated the gesture. It felt good to know someone in this place cared about my well-being. I had suffered in silence for many years.

Once the initial shock wore off, I asked them to reply by asking my sister if I could come and stay with her in Chicago. The request was accepted and my plans to leave this school were well underway.

I had completed my time at Briggs and was eighteen, ready to take on the world. Most of the girls that I had mentored over the years were grown into young teenagers and dealing with the environment on their own. Although, the influx of new students never slowed down during my stay. The only thing I can say is the torture had diminished over the years, which was a blessing for everyone involved. However, nothing kept them from reminding us of our stupidity, and that we were a waste of human flesh. When someone tells you these kinds of things for years, it is hard not to believe them. Especially for the younger children who were scared for life. My people went from a proud, brilliant race to alcoholics riddled with depression. The whole affair removed a part of our souls that can never be replaced. It left us broken.

My last night at Riggs seemed like a dream. I was finally leaving this prison and was given a fighting chance in Western culture. In the school's eyes, I was reformed, meaning my fate belonged to Jesus. In all aspects, it was alright. I had accepted the enlightened frame of mind, but would always love my people and culture. It was a sentiment that I kept deep within my heart.

One of the other children—well, young women—at the school named Aponi. Aponi was her given name and not the one they forced on her. We had become very good friends over the years. She and I were leaving at the same time, and since my family was so far away, it left me stranded for transportation. So, her parents let me ride with them to Mankato, Minnesota, which was half-way between South Dakota and Chicago. When you're young you don't always plan things out, you just go with the flow. I figured it would be easy to hitchhike the rest of the way.

We finished out the rest of the week, and on Sunday morning after mass, we were released. Her parents arrived the night before and made camp just outside the school perimeter. Since their hatred for the school reigned high, they stayed at a distance. It was better for everyone.

Aponi and I stayed up most of the night talking, and after the last bed check at 10:00 p.m., they pretty much left us alone. We talked and giggled like school children. It is a fond memory that has stayed with me all these years, one I choose to remember. It helped wash out the agony.

We finally fell asleep just before dawn, cuddled in the same bed. The breakfast bell rang at dawn, and everyone had to be up and ready within fifteen minutes. Since food was highly rationed, they did not care if you ate or not. I wanted to eat with the other children one more time, as I would most likely never see them again. Aponi did not care, she wanted out, but as a favor, she stayed with me. It was a room filled with tears and hugs, and even a few of the teachers bid me adieu with sincere regards. Then, it was time to leave this place forever.

We were escorted out the gate, where Aponi's parents were waiting. She had written about me many times, so it was as though I was another child to them. However, most of the communications were lost, or not delivered. It never stopped us from writing anyway. The gesture made us feel better and brought them close to us in our minds.

Our journey lasted several days, as expected. Most of the roads were dirt and very rough, but at least we did not have to clear our path. On a good day, in our case, we could travel up to thirty or forty miles. We took two breaks: a mid-morning restroom stop, and noonday for lunch. Then we quit about dusk for dinner and made camp.

The alteration in our surroundings was thrilling. Both of us were so happy to have left our imprisonment; words cannot describe. In total, our trip took about a week. We had two problems: the wagon lost a wheel, and one of the oxen hurt its leg. Aponi's mother had a poultice to wrap the leg, and by the next evening, it was fine. All I remember was sleeping under the stars, free, no men creeping in at night to get their thrills or worrying about getting switched for whatever. I knew what freedom was in the dictionary, but nothing could compare to experiencing it in person.

We kept up a hard-steady pace to reach Aponi's parents' farm. It was mid-summer and that meant the crops were ready for harvest; work on a farm never stops.

By the time we reached Mankato, I was done with that buckboard for a while. Believe me, there was nothing comfortable about them. No matter how smooth the road, you bounced around like a rag doll; especially if you were a kid and got stuck in the back.

We finally reached the ranch mid-afternoon on the seventh day. Once we unloaded everything and got the chores done it was well after dark. Aponi and I were just grateful to do chores and move around. It was the first time we had a full gourmet meal in years; fresh bread, meat, and a vegetable were decadent. Her mother was a great cook, not as good as Mom, but I am biased.

Aponi had been my best friend for years and leaving her in the morning was going to be hard. She wanted to come with, but her parents were getting older and needed the help. I understood, but it was time for me to step out on my own. My sister had arranged a job for me in Chicago. Since my education trained me for nursing, I would be caring for elderly patients in their homes. Some of them were bedridden and needed help with their care, shopping, and housework. The pay was not bad and at least I was free, however, it did not stop the nightmares about my life at Riggs Indian School. The night was a dangerous time to be a woman in that place; luckily, Aponi and I were never attacked or raped. Nevertheless, it did not stop us from hearing the screams during the night. On several occasions, some of the girls would disappear for months on end, and then one day show up out of the blue. They were forbidden to speak of their absence and were never the same. We were all scarred from our time at the school, but others will never get over their terrifying experiences.

Summer in the Midwest is beautiful, but the heat can really be horrific. The humidity can be as high as the temperature, so if you have to travel, it's best to leave at dawn and rest during the midday heat. Since it stays light until nine o'clock, you can travel in the evening as well. I said my goodbyes to Aponi and her family. Her mother packed me a week's worth of food and gave me a satchel for carrying belongings. I had new shoes and a warm jacket for the cool evenings or bad weather. Her father got me a ride with a friend for the first couple hundred miles so that only left just over another two hundred.

We hit Madison, Wisconsin early on a Tuesday morning. Samuel, the man who drove me, bought me breakfast and gave me a few dollars, so I could at least take a shower at the local YMCA. The experience was exhilarating. I had never been to a big city. However, Samuel warned me of the dangers and told me not to stay in town alone any longer than necessary.

    I understood his concerns and tried to respect the advice, but city life was fascinating. The day was half over by the time we ate, and I had a shower to clean up. So, I walked through town looking at all the sights and even went into a grocery store. After I paid for the shower, it left me about two dollars, so I bought a soda. The man in the store even showed me how to open the bottle. You might think that is funny, but soda bottles are carbonated and the only way to keep in the fizz was to put a small ball inside as a cap. Then when you wanted to drink the soda, you hit the bottom with the palm of your hand, hence soda pop. I was the kid who got caught with their hand in the cookie jar that day, a memory I have always cherished.

I drank my soda in front of the ice cream parlor and watched the people coming and going. It was quite fun. As evening set in, I headed for the outskirts of town to spend the night. Since rides were few and far between, it meant doing a lot of walking, because not everyone who stopped was trustworthy.

On the way into town, I noticed a spot close to the road but out of sight from any passerby. It seemed as good as any to spend the night. Aponi's mother packed me some jerky and homemade bread slices. It made a good dinner. Since we were rationed to one main meal a day and a smaller portion at dinner, this was more food than I'd had in years.

The nights still cooled off somewhat. It felt good compared to the hot sunny afternoons. I made a small fire and curled up to get some sleep. Sleeping outdoors was natural to me, and at times I even preferred it. It made me feel closer to my family. Since both of my parents were gone, and I had not seen my siblings in years, I felt alone in this large cruel world. As the sounds of nature lulled me to sleep, I cannot describe the feeling of what it meant to be away from that boarding school.

At dawn, I felt the sun's rays warm my face. Since my journey had just begun, I moved quickly to get on my way. If I was lucky, someone would stop to offer me a ride.

Just a short walk from where I camped was a nice stream, so I could wash my face and get some water. I had a small canteen to refill and enough food for a few more days. If my predictions were correct, it would be enough. I'd be in Chicago shortly.

The freedom of being able to just walk was a joyous feeling. It reminded me of the times I went with my father to hunt or gather food in the fields. Most of the time he took my brothers, but sometimes, he let me come along. It had been many years since Daddy died. I was eight years old and I still remember the day Mama told me of his death.

I stood in the middle of our one-room shack looking up at my mother listening to her solemn words conveying the cold reality of the truth about life and death. As her words expressed the sorrow that my daddy had passed away during the night. My thoughts were drowning in agony over the loss. It was one of the most distressing moments of my existence. One second you are learning to walk, then run, followed by going to school, and the next someone you love dies in the blink of an eye.

My mother continued attempting to console me, but as a child, death was an unknown event, of which I had no idea of the real meaning. The only certainty I had was that my daddy would never again be an active member of my life. As her muffled words elaborated on the incident, she was distracted by a knock on the door. In an instant reaction to flee the situation, I ran to the corner of the room, clutching my ears to quiet the sounds of cries filling the small room.

As my sobbing continued, I remembered Daddy had given me a handkerchief the prior day, before we left for school. It was mid-fall and the early morning crispness of the air made my nose run. A simple piece of cloth gave me some solace to calm my apprehensions over the circumstances. The fragrant aroma of the hankie brought a fleeting memory of Daddy's sweet kisses, whisking me off to the makeshift bed on the floor closest to the wood stove in the center of the room. But, the rest of that story is for another day.

The walking gave me time to reflect on life, and how it can change from one minute to the next. I had walked about eight miles down a small country road, hoping someone would come by and offer me a ride. However, there is an old saying, "Be careful what you wish for." I learned that day to never again ask for something before I had completely thought it through.

I heard a vehicle coming down the road behind me and just knew it would be a ride. My feet were getting sore and I really wanted to rest them. As it drew near, I could hear yelling from the car window. My heart instantly stopped, I wanted to turn around and look, but something told me to keep walking. It kept getting closer; I could hear the tires against the dirt road and the sound of the engine was louder. My first instinct was to run, get off the road, but if they were honest people, I would lose my chance for a ride. So, I kept walking. As they approached, I heard four different voices: they were young men. I panicked.

At that moment, any option to run, hide or disappear was non-existent. My heart raced, and I could feel the beads of sweat dripping down the side of my face. I tried to remain calm and just ignore them, hoping they would just speed past me. A few seconds later the car sped past and I took a huge sigh. I was safe. They ignored me and moved on.

I watched the car drive up the road going very fast, but then it stopped and started to backup. I could not believe my eyes. I froze; my body would not move. The fear rushed over me like nothing I had ever felt.

As the car approached, the passenger leaned out the window, yelling, "Hey, Indian woman, you're mine."

The driver slammed on the brakes in front of me, and the man on the passenger side got out first, while the driver put the car in park. I went numb, and time stopped. The only thing I could think of was please don't kill me and leave my body lying on the side of the road like the men left that young girl lying over the hitching post down the street from my childhood home. The sounds of the terror in her screams have haunted me for years.

"Hey, do you think you have the right to show your face in our world? You should be more careful where you wander," the one man yelled. I just stayed quiet.

"I'm talking to you Indian!!!!" he shouted. I shook my head.

"Well, that's better. But don't worry, we are here to teach you a lesson. Once we are done with you, you'll know your place once and for all." They all laughed.

The men scrambled between each other, while the one grabbed my satchel and threw it in the ditch. "I got her now boys, who wants the first crack?"

"I will go before you all get your dicks in her first," the driver yelled. I can still see the hatred in his eyes, cold black pools of evil.

He grabbed my hair and yanked my head backward as he ripped off my clothing. The other one tied my hands behind my back and threw me on the ground. When I hit, my head slammed hard, leaving me somewhat delirious. My breaths were short as I tried to regain some composure. It was hard to breathe. I thought I was going to die. As each one thrust, I gasped for air. I only got a break between one getting off me and another one jumping on.

The driver hooted and hollered, "Yes, look guys, we got our very own Indian." They all cheered.

I laid there on the side of a public road, mostly naked, my clothes were torn to shreds, being raped, and no one stopped to help. I felt the hours pass, while they gulped their beer and took turns defiling my body. All in the name of forcing us to become 'civilized'. At one point, the pain was so excruciating, I believe I passed out. Although, in hindsight, I think that is what saved my life. Once they thought I was dead, it was not fun anymore.

It took hours for me to regain some strength, but I managed to crawl away from the roadside into the bushes out of sight. Thank God, they left my satchel intact. It had landed out of sight, or I am sure they would have taken that as well.

In those times, we did not have money to buy a lot of clothing, so instead, we carried a sewing kit, needle, and thread. It was almost evening before I could move, but the nights got chilly and I needed to get my dress fixed before dark. My coat made a good cover in the meantime, while I gathered some wood to start a fire. Alongside the road was a small stream that allowed me to wash out my undergarments. The blood still flowed steadily, but I carried items for these occasions. We used sponges to help hold the blood; however, the pain was so intense that putting anything between my legs was impossible.

By the time I was done washing, the fire was hot enough to dry my clothing, after which I used some torn strips to wash in the stream. My plans changed quickly when I realized how good the cold water felt, so I just sat down for quite some time. It also helped stop the bleeding.

As the sun started to set, I scrambled my way back to the fire, and every inch of my body ached. I could barely move. I had a huge goose egg on the back of my head and the thoughts raced as to how I was going to get to Chicago now. The last thing I wanted to do was hitch a ride with anyone, and it would be days before I was strong enough to walk, not to mention my food supply decreased quickly.

The next morning, I said some prayers when the sun's warming rays hit my face. I had hoped it was all a nightmare, but sadly that was not the case. Nonetheless, I felt much better and most of the pain was gone, and even the bleeding slowed to a tolerable level. I guess, God does not stop all bad things from happening, but he provided everything I needed to carry on.

Since staying put was not an option, I decided to try walking. If nothing else, I'd go along and stop when I got tired and rest. A few hours later, my prayers were answered. A wagon filled with Native Americans came by and stopped to help me. I explained my situation and they agreed to give me a ride and share their food. I had been blessed after all. The lesson taught me if you give in to the hatred it is the same as losing. The only way to prevail is to be strong and prove your worthiness to God.

It was, however, the first and only time I ever slept in the back of a buckboard. The woman gave me a blanket and her bag for a pillow. I slept like a baby until we stopped for the night. Their generosity was endless. I will be forever in their debt. It was the only reason I made it alive.

1101 N Clark St. Chicago, IL

Two days later, we hit Chicago. My sister had given me the address and I would have found my way, but the couple refused to leave me alone in a strange city. So, they took me right to her doorstep. We bid farewell, and it was the last time I ever saw them. They were most definitely angels sent from heaven.

I remember being scared, knocking on my sister's door. We had not seen each other for years. "Evelyn… I have been so scared. I am so happy to see you," she burst out. I smiled and felt instant relief. "Come on, get in here."

Anna was always my favorite sister; we were always very close. "Ann-" I began, but she interrupted.

"What happened to you?" She saw my dress when I took off the coat. I burst into tears.

"I was…" My words stopped. I could not say anything else.

"RAPED! You were raped, when?" She saw the terror in my eyes. I nodded. "Come sit down, I will get you something to eat, and how about some tea or coffee?"

"Yes, please," I choked out.

While Anna was gone, I fell asleep on her couch. I woke the next morning with a blanket, warm and safe. Anna had written a note and put it on the table. She had gone to work, but left me food in the refrigerator. Since I had not eaten much in days, food never tasted so good. Plus, she had mastered most of Mama's recipes, so it felt like she was here to hug the pain away.

It took weeks before I was fully recovered physically, but the emotional scars stayed with me forever. The only thing we can do is learn to live with it, and over time the pain subsides somewhat.

City life took some adjustment; nonetheless, it had many advantages. Anna had a job already lined up with my training as a nurse. Many of the people in our neighborhood were housebound for one reason or another and needed a nurse to care for them. I enjoyed the work; it was rewarding. It felt like I was appreciated for once. The older ladies were always giving me clothing, furniture, and jewelry. Since I had never had new clothes that weren't homemade, it was a real treat.

Several months after my arrival, I went to see one of my patients, her name was Beth. When I arrived, she was sitting in the living room as normal but had a wonderous look on her face when I walked in.

"Beth, are you okay?" I asked.

"Evelyn, you're looking radiant this morning. If I did not know better, I'd say you were pregnant." My heart sank.

I stopped dead in my tracks. "Oh," I gasped.

"What, honey? Come sit," she requested.

I sat down next to her. "Beth-" But she interrupted.

"Honey, you can tell me, it's alright," she cooed.

"I was raped on my way to Chicago." I waited for the lashing.

"You were what? Raped? By whom?"

I heard the disgust in her tone. "Some men who stopped while I was walking on the side of the road."

"Walking on the side of the road? Why were you hitchhiking? That is dangerous for a young girl."

"Yes, I know, but I had no money. It was the only way to get here from South Dakota." I could see the pain in Beth's eyes, much like my own.

She proceeded to tell me of her best friend that was raped at a young age, like me, only she died from her injuries. By the afternoon, we both sat in tears, healing each other with our faith in life.

I left Beth that evening, feeling refreshed and empowered to face the future, whatever it might entail. The next morning when I arrived at her house, an ambulance was parked on the street.

The policeman stopped me at the door. "Miss, you can't go in there."

"I just work for Beth, is she alright?"

"I am sorry, she passed away a few minutes ago."

I was devastated; although, a few months later a letter arrived for me. It was from Beth, explaining how much she enjoyed our conversations and to always make lemonade when life serves you lemons. However, I knew she had been right that maybe I was pregnant. My body was changing, something was different, I just did not know from what.

Chapter Two:

Genocide

I had spent several years yearning to find myself in a world bent on killing the Native Americans. Then when it started to feel as though I fit in, the unthinkable happened. Not only was I raped because of my cultural background, now I was pregnant with a child from that horrific event. Nonetheless, the reason for my pregnancy and many other young girls' during that time was unacceptable. It did not matter how we became with child, the only thing that Western culture looked at was, we were not married. Unwed pregnancy was a sin in the eyes of the Lord. As I look back on the situation, nowhere does the Bible say that it's alright to defile a person, man or woman. But, as I learned quickly, the only way to survive was to assimilate and keep moving forward, no matter what was happening. In my mind, faith is believing in the unknown.

The death of Beth hit me hard, she was so much like my mother. Being able to have that maternal connection with someone again kept my heart light and filled with hope. It had been many years since I had seen the rest of my family. They were scattered around the country, and after my mother passed away, we lost contact.

Anna was a true blessing. She kept me from losing my mind after Beth died and the reality of being pregnant hit me. I always wanted and thought about having children, like any young girl. The dream of a fairy tale wedding, being swept off your feet by the man of your dreams, and having a large family was alluring. However, it did not seem like that would be possible; although, hope was the one thing no one could ever take away.

In the short few months after the rape, my pregnancy was starting to show, and hiding the issue was no longer possible. Anna had been bugging me to go see a doctor, but dealing with the condescending behavior of the doctor's staff had me gun-shy. Since Anna had been in the city for many years, she had some good connections and learned how to survive in the open world. She came home one afternoon and told me there was a care facility for unwed mothers. So, we made an appointment at Beulah Home and Maternity Hospital. It seemed the best course of action at the time, as I would be needing some medical treatment very soon, and with not having any money, the options were limited.

My first appointment was for Friday afternoon when Anna got off work and we could go together. She did not want me there alone in this strange land. Since I had never been to a real hospital, and being pregnant, the doctor ordered several tests and did a wellness exam. It was an alarming experience. If anyone got sick on the reservation, we went to the medicine man, or he came to us.

After several hours of being poked and prodded, the doctor diagnosed me with syphilis. It was in the early second stage, but he said he should be able to treat it. I panicked; we had heard the horror stories of many people, even Native Americans, dying an agonizing death from the mercury treatments. However, with a shot of Treponema pallidum, a variation of penicillin was supposed to cure the infection.

The whole scenario left me mortified. I was pregnant, had syphilis, and now most likely my child would be born with this horrendous disease. The doctor gave me a mortality rate for the baby of lower than fifty percent; I struggled to stay in a healthy frame of mind. Anna did her best to keep me motivated; nonetheless, it was a horrible time in my life.

We went home that evening and had a celebration dinner. Anna thought it might cheer me up after the recent news. At the time, it was hard to see the positive side of the situation; however, looking back, at least the prognosis was not terminal. Otherwise, I would not be writing this book. The following days passed and reality settled in that the only option was to deal with what had happened and get on with my life.

It was late summer and the normal time for rain to refuel the land after the high-temperature days. Although, forecasters were predicting a very dry season. The devastation could already be seen across the prairies. Crops were dying in the fields and planted farmland was turning to a

dust bowl. This was the one time I missed being home on the reservation. We may not have had the luxuries someone can find in the city, but we could always feed ourselves. It was heart breaking to watch people begging on the street corner for food or standing in line at the food banks for a weekly ration. We were given ration tickets that must be shown when you picked up your weekly quota. Anna, gratefully, understood the concept of food storage, since we grew up gathering food to survive the Wisconsin winters. It becomes part of your blood and stays with you the rest of your life, and Western culture condemned the Indians for our lifestyle. We at least took care of each other in the good times and especially the bad. I  remember one incident like it was yesterday: the homeless had a rough time in a normal environment, but with the rationing and winter setting in hard, it became unbearable for many. I was working at a local diner on the early morning shift. It was hard to find a job in those days, and we took whatever was available. Since we were Native American, most businesses would not even hire us. However, a few people were beginning to see the devastation among our people and developed compassion. Anyway, the restaurant was only a mile from our apartment, so I would walk since taking a taxi was expensive. An alley along my way was a favorite for some of the homeless. It was near another restaurant and the owners would put food out at night for them to eat. Plus, in the bitter night air, the cops stayed at the police station unless called out, and they could start fires to keep warm. At any given time, there might be fifteen to twenty men huddled in the alley.

My work week started on Tuesday and ended on Thursday. As I walked past the alley, a younger male was curled up in a ball on the ground, uncovered except for a light jacket. I noticed the grey ashen color of his skin and knew exactly what happened. Once you see death, as I have, it stays with you forever. He must have either been sick or injured and died right in the alley. Granted, seeing someone dead was commonplace in my life, but on the reservation among my people, we take care of our loved ones after death. We have burial ceremonies and cherish their memories. It may not be with a church and Bible; nevertheless, we don't leave them on the street for days before we take care of their remains. His body lay there for three days before the police brought the coroner. I can still see the expression of agony in his eyes. He haunted my dreams for years. Anna had been living in the outer world for many more years than me at the time and had grown accustomed to the sight. I shuddered at the idea of getting used to seeing death in that fashion.

When you are pregnant, each day is a new adventure. It starts with the morning sickness, to the constant restroom breaks, to the weight gain, and then finally the food cravings. These alone are enough issues, but adding syphilis to the mix made my pregnancy agonizing. The doctor prescribed the medication and told me to get plenty of rest. To which I abided for the most part, but as time progressed, between my illness and pregnancy, I was sick all the time. Before the medication started working, syphilis caused these ulcerated sores to form on your genitals, and in a woman's case, was just on the inside of their vagina. It is excruciating to move in any fashion. The topical ointment burned so bad it felt like I had been scrubbed with lye again. I would be curled up in a ball on my bed for days. It broke my heart to see Anna working day and night to support us, while I lay around. She never felt that way, but it made me feel helpless. The only saving grace was that we were in the center of the building.

It kept the apartment much warmer, instead of losing our warmth to the outside air. By my third trimester, the syphilis had all but healed and I was starting to feel normal again, except finding work now was nearly impossible. Anna had taken on some house cleaning duties for some neighbors in the area, and she talked them into letting me help with the understanding we could finish the job quicker. I was grateful to get out of the house and move around. I had never been bedridden; it gave me a whole new outlook on life.

    My third doctor's visit went better than expected. I was even able to hear the baby's heartbeat. What an exhilarating experience. The doctor had a Pinard horn that you pressed against the stomach to hear the heartbeat and it would amplify the sound. I must admit, that until then, it was easy to keep my emotions in check, but after that visit, a connection developed, unlike anything I had ever felt. I instantly understood the pain my mother felt when I rode away in the buggy that day. Other than advising me again about the baby's chances for survival, there was no way of knowing the results until it was born. I know that sounds harsh to call your baby 'it,' but in that day and age ultrasounds did not exist. Anyway, I accepted the diagnosis and pushed to remain positive. The stages of my pregnancy smoothed out, the syphilis was healed, and no more morning sickness; however, the smell of hot dogs still made me ill.

I remember the first time the baby kicked. I was lying in bed on my right side and I felt this fluttering on my side, like a bug crawling up your arm. At first, it startled me, until I realized it was the baby moving. By the time I was in my seventh month, he would start at about 4:00 p.m. and ride the circus wheel until about 8:00 p.m., then quiet until morning. During the last month, I am not sure the movement ever stopped. It was a fond memory that I often look back on when I am feeling down.

Anna worked at a local bakery during the day, and at the diner in the evenings. She would come home long enough to eat and get about an hour's rest, then back to work until about 10:00 p.m. In the event I went into labor while she was working, I spent my time on the couch so I could be near the phone and call for help. Unbeknownst to me, babies like to be born in the middle of the night, or early morning. It was a blessing since she was home. The winter had started to wane and was slightly warming for spring.

I had been dreading the delivery since many of the women in our tribe died during labor. But, as Anna pointed out, I would be in a hospital. It was somewhat comforting; although, when you have never experienced something, it can be frightening. We counted the time between contractions and called for an ambulance when the time was right. The labor seemed to be progressing as the doctor instructed; nonetheless, I had an uneasy feeling. I had learned to trust my instincts over the years. They kept me alive many times.

The ambulance arrived and carted me off on a stretcher. "I'll be right behind you, Evie," Anna shouted.

"Okay. I love you," I said. The driver closed the door and we were headed to Maternity Hospital. It was about a ten-minute drive.

My doctor was standing inside the ambulance doors when we arrived. He greeted me with a smile, and I felt instantly calmed. He had a soothing air about him.

"We are going to take good care of you, Evelyn," the nurse said. I nodded in agreement.

All total, the labor lasted about sixteen hours, 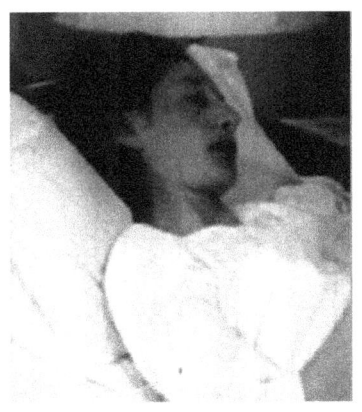 and it was unlike anything I had ever experienced. The nurses took the baby and cleaned him up after he was born. They gave me a sedative. In those days it was customary for the mothers to be away from their babies for almost a day. I feared in my case it would be quite a different story.

The next morning, a nurse came into my room with a pan and sponge. She wanted to clean me up after the birth. When I asked to see my son, she calmly explained the doctor would be in soon. My heart stopped; I knew it was bad. As the doctor professed, the birth defects were severe. Anna came in after the nurse had finished and presented the news. She did not want me to hear about this from a stranger. We begged and pleaded for them to at least let me hold him one time. The doctor reluctantly agreed.

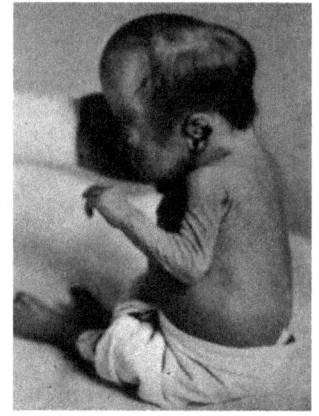

"Evelyn, are you okay?" Anna asked.

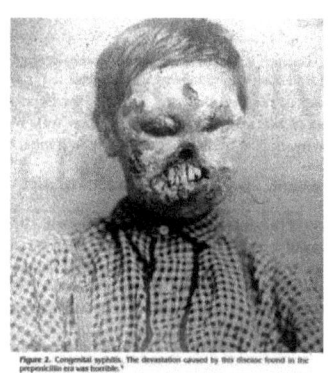

Figure 2. Congenital syphilis. The devastation caused by this disease found in the pre-penicillin era was horrible.

"I don't know, Anna. I wish Mom was here, she always knew what to say," I said.

"I know, me too."

The nurse returned a few minutes later with a little bundle of joy. I took one look and fell in love. Regardless of the horrific scene during which his life had begun, I was holding a small person. One that was not only created but developed inside my body for the last nine months.

I remember the delicate softness of his skin. He seemed to coo with my touch. He actually knew his mother. But mostly, I recall his brilliant blue eyes, just like Daddy.

"Are you going to give him a name?" Anna said.

"Do you think that I should?"

"What does it matter if it's right or not? It will help you remember him. Besides, nothing can change the fact he is your son. Don't you remember when Mom lost that baby? They named him."

"Oh, I forgot… Yes, then, he looks like a Billy."

"Good, Billy it is."

This seemed to ease my fears. I spent one hour with my son that day. A few hours later, Rev. Edward L. Brooks came to see me. I mention his name for a good reason, which I will explain shortly.

"Hello, Evelyn, my name is Reverend Brooks. I will be caring for your son on my farm. We specialize in caring for children with severe birth defects. I cannot imagine what this might be like, but I can assure you the Lord will provide. I think you should say goodbye to your son; delayed goodbyes only make matters worse." His words crushed my soul. The idea of leaving my son and never holding him seemed impossible.

"But...." He interrupted.

"I do not mean to sound harsh. It is just the best for all parties involved. We will be leaving in the morning for Michigan. I wish you a speedy recovery." I heard the words, but time stopped.

I could not imagine my life without Billy. No mother with a conscience can just walk away from her baby willingly. At times, I can still feel his delicate skin, even the way he smelled. But nothing could ever compare to his incredible blue eyes. The hospital released me two days later, and it was the last time I ever saw Billy.

Over the next several weeks, I stayed in a deep sorrow filled with anxiety. I even tried to call the Brooks Farm in Michigan, but they would not tell me anything about Billy. My heart ached, and I prayed for his precious little soul.

Chapter Three:

Precious Child of God

From the moment I survived the rape, my life had changed forever. However, the sadness, in a strange way, made me feel alive. Even though the pregnancy was tied to a horrific event, one that no woman should ever have to endure, I still felt love for my child. After everything I had withstood, this one event caused catastrophic memories that haunted me until the day I died. You must understand, the feelings I had were never against my son; he was a precious child of God. My recollections dealt with the way women were treated in that era. We were less than human, more like an animal that must be controlled, especially minority females. I hated that idea and fought every day of my life to endure, one lesson I learned from both my parents.

The Native Americans have a rich and wonderful culture; I was proud to be Indian. It was the closemindedness of society that never ceased to amaze me. If you are different, of an unknown race, culture, or belief, somehow it makes you less human. In my era, it was due to whether or not you were a Christian, yet the Bible specifically says, "Do unto others as you would do unto yourself," or "Judge not or you will be judged." Is it just me, or do these words mean something I don't understand? Granted, I am not a highly educated woman, but I have a good grasp of the English language. Lord knows it was beaten into us for many years.

The long months after my son was born left me saddened. It was hard to even function some days. I struggled to get up in the morning, and no matter how many times someone told me everything would be alright, nothing eased the pain. I cannot explain why it devastated me so much; maybe it was my inability to care for him. When we left the hospital, it made me feel as though I was abandoning Billie. My age probably brought about more intense feelings than if I had been older. Nonetheless, I wanted to feel the love for someone, like my parents felt for their children. Even though we were poor, and the world wanted us dead, being with my family on the reservation made us feel safe. Once I was forced to leave the only home I had ever known, it made me understand just how lonely and dangerous it is to survive in Western culture.

After my father died, we were bounced around for many years, never being allowed to find a safe place to live. Then when I finally arrived in Chicago, after being raped and enduring a pregnancy, it was difficult to maintain hope for a bright future. My sister was a blessing. She made life bearable, but unless you have experienced rape or pregnancy, it is impossible to understand how I felt. In my mental state of mind at the time, all that mattered was finding love. Anyone who had a hint of strength or a 'bad boy image' grabbed my attention.

It took me a long time after arriving in Chicago to make friends, especially since the first year I was pregnant and then the recovery lasted for months. My days consisted of either trying to stay warm, looking for food, or working every odds and end job I could find. Some days, we would go from one business to the next working a few hours here and there. It kept our heads above water and a roof over our heads, but that was the extent. I may have been in a big city, but the living conditions were not much different from on the reservation. Our apartment building was very old and drafty, and at night we could hear the rats inside the walls running up and down between the floors, not to mention the cockroaches. They were as big as June bugs; you could actually hear them running across the floor at night when someone turned on the lights. My sister and I kept our place immaculate; however, when you are packed inside a large building with everyone else, it's impossible to keep them out of your place. Our food had to be stored in airtight containers in the highest cabinets possible. We limited our storage because of the bugs; although, the depression made that reality anyway.

By 1930, the state of the economy was horrendous. Between the drought we called the 'dust bowl' and prohibition, life in the US took its toll on

everyone: race, culture or gender did not matter. The *Chicago Tribune* pushed papers out daily with headlines about how the unemployment increased weekly. I remember that by 1932, almost 4,000 workers a week lost their jobs. Then by the end of 1939, almost 9.5 million were still out of work; however, the economy brought huge opportunities preparing for the post-war demands. It granted the population some financial stability.

After prohibition, the blues and jazz musicians flocked to Chicago and the city

fell in love. The theater scene was the only business to thrive over the next twenty years. It was the only solitude many of us had trying to survive in this big city. We would save for weeks, even months, to see a theater show, or hit one of the cabarets. At times, people would forgo food to see a live show.

One story hitting the headlines that stayed with me over the years was the kidnapping of Charles Augustus Lindbergh Jr., a twenty-month-old baby. It was a heart-wrenching event to read about in the paper. He was taken from their second-floor nursery in Hopewell, New Jersey. As the story flooded the countryside, my emotions erupted. I had  lost my son a few years prior, and I knew what his parents were enduring. Per the ransom note, the wife, Anne, paid the money, almost 70,000 dollars I believe, only to not have their son returned. The search went on for days, until he was found four miles from their home on May 12, 1932. A truck driver found the body. He had been partially buried and been dead for almost two months. The papers called it the 'the crime of the century'. I cried in pain for his parents, the agony was completely exhausting. However, as time passed, people were right: you never get over the loss, it just becomes bearable to deal with daily.

Shortly after the media slowed down on the Lindbergh case, life calmed and we learned to find food and just survive. Inside the city bustled with women, as many of the men left in search of work; unfortunately, most of them became homeless after their farms were foreclosed by the banks, so they built shantytowns, called Hoovervilles. It reminded me of the reservation, small shacks bunched together in small lots just outside the city limits. In that same year, Chicago was celebrating its one-hundredth anniversary, and just since my arrival it had grown incredibly. I even began to see an influx of minorities, which surpassed the white households by 1934, but that is a topic for later in the story. First, I want to tell you about the second love of my life, after my son, Billie.

My sister Ann and I had been cooped up for months. The warm weather of summer was starting to break through the bleak dampness of winter, and everyone had spring fever. So, we planned an outing to one of the theaters in town. I think we had three dollars between us. It felt like a million in those times. Anne got us tickets for *Cat and the Fiddle*. It was my first theater show, and I was very excited. We  pulled our crepe dresses from the closet and period hats: a black lace veil lay gently over one side of the brim. Then we put on our lace-up mid-heel Oxfords, they were perfect for dancing in the evenings. Of course, our dresses were a perfect twelve inches from the floor. Once we were dressed for the occasion, it was time to hit the town. I felt like a kid at Christmas. Since my arrival in Chicago, the only thing I'd seen and experienced was heartache. We were ready for some fun, no matter how dismal our future looked.

The show started at 7:00 pm; it was kind of dangerous to walk the streets of Chicago at night, but we didn't care. I remember seeing the line outside the theater wrapped around the corner with people waiting to buy tickets. As we walked past the bystanders, it made us feel like royalty. The ticket master took our stubs and moved the red velvet rope. I remember brushing my fingertips over the velvet as we walked inside, it was smooth, exciting.

I can't say that the musical had an ever-lasting impression on my life, except that it was an exciting place to be in the midst of a country in chaos. After the show, Anne and I went to one of the local cabarets and had one drink. We listened to the jazz band and left just before midnight. Upon leaving the establishment, I met the man I considered to be the love of my life, but let's just say young love has a lot to be desired.

Welton Sparks was an exciting renegade. The perfect mysterious handsome figure, every young girl's dream is that a man will ride in on a white horse and  sweep them off their feet. He was almost six feet, with dark hair and brown eyes. He had a scar that ran between his eyebrows, and a loaded facial expression. I instantly fell in love. As we all learn, love can make you do stupid things, no matter the consequences. The country was in the midst of several devastating situations that were making life unimaginably difficult. I longed for the same things every young girl wants: someone to take care of them. We only talked briefly but made arrangements to meet the next evening in town for dinner. The night turned into an incredible evening. I walked on cloud nine for the next twelve hours.

Anne and I walked home like two giddy school girls. It reminded me of the warm summer afternoons walking home from through the fields of wildflowers. We would sing and dance along, skipping across the yellow pastures. If I remember correctly, I did not sleep a wink that night, thinking of the handsome young man I had just met. The only thing I knew for sure, we were both native to Wisconsin. It felt wonderful to finally meet someone from my home state, especially in a city filled with strangers.

In those days during the depression, money was beyond tight. If someone had five dollars, they were considered rich. As a matter of fact, the abandoned child rate jumped dramatically during those three years. Most of it was because either one parent left to find work and the other one got sick, or they turned the children over to the state because they could not afford to support them. However, most of the country felt the effects until the beginning of World War II. But, as Native Americans, we had never known such luxuries, so the restrictions meant nothing to us. Our way of life became non-existent after Western culture took over the Americas. The fact that we even survived at all was a miracle, one in which I believe Jesus played a big role.

As the sun rose the next morning, it brought a new lease on life. The dull drum of trying to survive had a new meaning. Anne and I rushed home after work that day and prepared for our dates. Welton had asked if he could bring a friend along for Anne. His name was Art Carrington. We rushed out the door, dressed a bit more casual, but nonetheless divinely.

"Good evening, Evelyn, you look great. This is my friend Art," Welton stated.

"Good evening, this is my sister Anne." I held out my hand.

"Nice to meet you, Anne," Art said.

"Well, shall we go inside?" Welton asked.

"Yes, I am starved," I replied.

"Good… order whatever you want, dinner is on us." He smiled. I instantly knew he was the man of my dreams. *Oh, young love… if I'd only known then.*

The waitress came over. "Hey, Evelyn, how are you?"

"I am good. Have you met my sister Anne? And this is Welton and Art."

"Yes, we have met, and nice to meet you as well," she replied. The waitress usually worked the day shift, but since keeping able bodies employed was difficult, we worked whatever hours were available. "Thank you, I will be right back with your drinks." She smiled. I knew she would grill me tomorrow at work.

Anne asked, "So, Welton, what brings you guys to Chicago?" Welton looked hesitant to answer.

"I--- we got laid off at the mine and set out in search of work in one of the large cities south."

"Have any luck yet? Most of the men in Chicago left to find other mining work elsewhere," Anne asked.

"No not yet, but we are still looking. In the meantime, we are taking odd jobs wherever possible."

"Yes, both Anne and I have three to four jobs each just to make ends meet. They keep us on short hours."

"Well, tonight let's just live it up. Forget our troubles and just have fun." Anne and I nodded. The night went off without a hitch. We ate dinner and hit one of the cabarets for drinks later.

Between dancing, we talked and got to know each other a little. At the time, it was like meeting an old friend years later. Welton had a sadness, a fundamental fissure that erupted every so often. However, we shared that emotional mentality somewhat. As with me, Welton lost his father at a young age, only I stayed with my mother for many years. Welton ran away from home and never returned. I related, it felt like having my son close by, he was a child inside trying to find himself. We were two misfits struggling in a world filled with unimaginable chaos.

Our relationship developed quickly. When people are forced together in disorienting times, you can bond with someone completely out of character from your normal acquaintances. We were looking for love, someone to take care of us.

Welton and I were inseparable over the next month. He moved in with Anne and I. It was wonderful having someone else to help pay the bills. The question of how he got his money never came up, and I did not ask. We had fun just like he promised. Art and Anne got along great as well. The four of us did everything together over the next couple of months.

In June of that summer, Welton asked if I wanted to go on a romantic weekend getaway with him. He supposedly had business in Michigan City, Indiana. He did not have to ask me twice. I had never traveled, so I jumped at the chance. We packed a small bag with some drinks, a cooler with sandwiches, then climbed in the car and headed for Indiana. On our way out of town, we picked up Anne and Art along with Roy Little. I had never met him, but he seemed like a nice kid. I remember being cuddled up next to Welton on the seat, and he put his hand on my thigh. We turned up the radio, when it worked, and life was good.

It took most of a day's drive since the top speed for our car was about forty miles per hour. But we did not have a care in the world. I had the wind blowing in my hair and freedom laid at my fingertips. Since Welton said we had to pass as a married couple, he checked us into the hotel under Mr. and Mrs. James M. Malone. I giggled at the chance to be married. Art and Anne registered under Mr. and Mrs. Jack Riley. Roy stayed alone in a separate room. As I said, we were young and stupid.

After we got settled, the boys told us they were going to go and get their business matters handled and be back before dinner. So, Anne and I headed for the pool. June in the Midwest is hot, and the humidity is higher than the temperature. It was another first for me to go swimming in a public pool. We laughed and giggled all afternoon. We brought out the sandwiches I had made, so Anne and I ate lunch poolside. By evening the boys were back, and we played around to well after dark. Since the pool closed at 8:00 p.m., they chased us out.

The next morning, right before dawn, someone came pounding on the room door. "Open up, it's Michigan City Police. Welton Sparks, you are under arrest." I nearly jumped out of my skin.

Welton darted for the dresser drawer, but before he got it opened, they busted down the door. I covered up and kept silent. The police handcuffed Welton, put him in the police car, and then came and arrested me along with him. By the time I got out to the car, they had already arrested Anne and Art, along with Roy. We spent the night in jail, it was horrifying. I had visions of the Riggs Indian School when I was young. Only at least this time, I was not alone and only eight years old.

The next morning, Art and Welton were extradited to Illinois for their parole violation. Anne and I luckily had the car and their belongings. Welton's wallet had enough money to get us home. Anne had to drive since I did not have a license. Most people would have walked away, but as I said, we were desperate and in love. Our cases were dismissed since we had nothing to do with their prior crimes.

After the men were booked into Cook County Jail, the push would be on for them to get married. In our defence, life alone was unimaginable. So, the idea of getting a cash stipend for an indigent spouse seemed appealing. Plus, the men had more advantages in their commissary account being married. However, I did have to sign over my ward of the Menominee Reservation allotment.

So, the marriage was arranged on August 3, 1932, and overseen by Chaplin Ware. We entered the jail wearing our perfunctory smiles. I admit the vague hope felt good. It gave us the courage to glow in the positive attention, if only for a moment. The Chaplin allowed the couples to exchange their vows and kiss the bride. In hindsight, it turned out to be a bleak day. Certainly not the wedding I imagined. Welton and Art were sentenced to fifteen years in Leavenworth for mail fraud. He exchanged his name for inmate # 42165. My only correspondence was signed, Mrs.

Welton Sparks. My marriage never amounted to much, and I lost track of him right away.

Evelyn Frechette

More of Early Years

Menominee Reservation

Menominee Camp

Menominee Medicine Lodge

Menominee Reservation

Menominee Cemetery

Neopit, WI 1907

Riggs Indian Boarding School

Native American Children in Boarding Schools

Native American children being victimized because of race

Evelyn Frechette - Neopit

Main Street, Flandreau SD 1930s

Native American Boarding Schools

Chapter Four:

My Dream Ended

My dreams of living a fun-filled life with Welton Sparks ended almost as fast as they started. The decision to marry, looking back was regrettable, but at the time, the choice seemed necessary. It is difficult to explain how hard life was during those days. Between the great depression, the dust bowl, and now the beginning of World War  II, the country was literally in chaos. People were desperate, many from starvation which can make anyone do crazy things, and others just wanted to take advantage of the weak. Whichever way you want to look at the situation, nothing came easy. All we did was take it one day at a time, living life to the fullest extent.

Now, consider life as a woman, then add a minority female, and in my case an Indian woman. Granted, some things within the government were settling down with the vast drive to eradicate us;  however, it only served to build more hatred among society in general. We learned to keep our heads down and mouths shut. It is one era of my life that I would never want to relive. Until that point, it was difficult to just find some meaning to what we were doing. The future seemed bleak, especially in an environment filled with strangers that only want to die. Yes, I had some family, but it did not change the minds of the average citizen. When I think back now, there were only a few instances that made me smile, and where my heart gleams with joy. But, more on that soon.

In the meantime, after Welton went to prison and I received my first stipend check, it felt like I had a million dollars. However, with the unemployment rate sky high, finding work was hard enough. My sister had been doing  occasional work in the American Indian ceremonial dance programs. They helped pay the bills, but in my mind, they were another way for the Western culture to exploit the Native Americans. When the government forced us onto reservations, they forbid any sort of so-called 'Indian Activity' to occur. Our secret dance ceremonies were prohibited, except in the case of entertainment for an audience. In these cases, the attire was made by Western citizens, according to them it was close enough to our cultural history. Of course, so was the dance choreography.

But the days passed just as the times. I was finally settling into city life in Chicago; however, some rituals never seemed quite right, such as funerals. A few years after arriving in Illinois, a friend of my sister's passed away and we were invited to the funeral. I can honestly say, it was the most depressing function I have ever attended. As Native Americans, we celebrate life with death. I remember when my father died, we all took part in his burial ceremony.

Every tribe has a sacred burial ground outside the main camp for the bodies of our loved ones. The graves are dug in a rectangle shape about four feet deep, then we build a wooden slatted cover to go over the grave. After the ceremony, each person is buried in the grave and covered with cloth. We use large rocks and more fill to protect the body from animals. Each grave is always oriented along the east-west axis. On the end of the wooden dome is a hole and shelf so the soul can escape, plus food for their journey in the afterlife. Our Midewiwin priest carves a grave marker with the clam totem to mark the site. It has an animal, bird, or fish carved upside down to denote death. After this, we go home and have a ceremonial meal to celebrate their journey into the next life. The death of our tribe members is an honored ceremony, they are in the next phase of their passage in life.

    Yes, we cry and feel sorrow over their loss, but we don't fear death. Native Americans celebrate death. I struggled with many Western rituals, they seemed so chaotic. Although, it matched their actions on wanting to eliminate the Indian people and culture. As the years passed, the government was still rounding up Native children and sending them off to the boarding schools; however, I believe their treatment was improving somewhat. Except many of the children who graduated from the schools were released and left to fend for themselves. If they happened to wander back on the reservations, many of them never found their families or parents. In fact, for generations, no one even bothered to trace their family trees. So, the ability to locate their families was impossible. It led to severe homelessness and impoverished circumstances.

A few years later in 1924, the government passed the Citizenship Act allowing the Native Americans to become United States Citizens. By its provisions, all Indians were automatically made legal citizens. What they failed to disclose was that it voided our federal allotment. Many tribal lands were taken through fraud and state sales taxes. The federal protection was eliminated and our land was sold out from underneath them. The poverty, lack of education and illness ran rampant on reservation land, and the government failed to follow through with their promises.

I can remember some of the boys in the school with me joking about the missionary teacher, pointing out pictures of Jesus with long flowing hair, but we had to cut our hair because it was uncivilized. We had no rights on an economic or legal basis. The average annual wage for a Native American in those times was less than two hundred dollars. Unfortunately, our reprieve did not come until the start of World War II when the country turned to defend us from our enemies. Funny how when our way of life was being affected, all of a sudden, they needed the Native Americans to help fight the war.

After the budget for the Bureau of Indian Affairs was cut, racism began to play a part in the hostile response by wealthy businessmen who lost their chances to plunder Native American resources. We soon were seen as un-American because our people refused to be assimilated, and just lay down to the Western cultural beliefs. However, it was not until the 1960s when political attacks opened the door for the civil rights movement. In the meantime, we got up every morning, and dressed and worked like anyone else. I was twenty-four already, had a baby, got married, lost my baby, and my husband was in prison. Nonetheless, we made the best of things under the circumstances.

Between the federal stipend and my odd jobs, I was starting to somewhat see the light of day. The way we saw it if there was a roof over our heads and food in the cabinets, life was grand. Most of my regular waitress jobs were eliminated due to food shortages. The favoritism did not just apply to the

Christians; anyone with money, or who could be paid off, got the benefits. So, that meant the famous well-to-do lounges, hotels, or businesses got first choice of everything. Chicago was hit particularly hard during the Great Depression because most of the economy relied on manufacturing. Then in 1928, a reassessment took place and forced state taxes to skyrocket, and it caused a tax strike that forbid Chicago from collecting sales tax. In 1932, the city's emergency funds dried up and normal sources of help were bankrupt. The politics went crazy, and at that point, Anne and I gave up even trying to keep up. We moved forward and prepared for war against Germany and Japan.

    In the meantime, I wanted to be among the elite crowds and the only way to mingle was to get a job at one of the local night clubs. Down the street from my apartment was the Olympic Lounge in the basement of an apartment building. It was only checking hats for a few hours at night, but it got me out among the upper class of Chicago.

It was November 1933, a particularly cold winter, but I was determined to become part of the nightlife in Chicago. I had a few extra dollars and hit the local  thrift store to shop for a new dress and coat. After almost giving up, on one of the back racks hung a red frilly dress. It was perfect; not too revealing, but alluring, at least I thought so. My total purchase for the day came to five dollars. The dress was three dollars and the coat two dollars. I probably needed a warmer coat, but I was willing to take the risk. Then, after polishing my shoes, I was ready for the nightlife.

My shift started at six o'clock and lasted until nine, and after that I was free to do as I wished. Some friends were coming to meet up with me around nine. We grabbed a table order and a glass of whiskey for the group. The band played and we were having a good time, and little did I know at the time, it was a night that would change my life forever.

I looked across the room and saw a man dressed in a fancy suit with eyes of incredible magnetism. A few minutes later he came over to our table. He knew one of my friends, and she said, "Billie, this is Jack Harris."

He looked down at me, "Hey, baby… where have you been all my life?"

I will never forget how there was something in those eyes. They were piercing and electric, yet there was an amused carefree twinkle in them too.

They met my eyes and held me hypnotized for an instant.

He asked me to dance, "Do you come here often?" I asked.

"Not until tonight, but I will more often now that you are here." His words made me feel special, something I had never felt in my life.

"Where are you from, Billie Frechette?"

Billie & John

"Around," I told him.

He smiled. "Where is around?"

"Wisconsin…"

"Chicago is a long way; how did you get here? Your name is French?"

"Yes, my father was a Frenchmen." I stopped there.

"And your mother?" he asked. I paused, and he looked perplexed. "You do have a mother, don't you?"

"Yes, she was Menominee Indian. Most men don't like that part about me."

"I am not most men," he said with so much pizzazz, it caught me off guard.

"Would you like to get out of here?" he asked. I agreed.

We headed out to the lobby and grabbed our coats; he actually held my coat. I was shocked. "Where are we going?"

"Does it matter?" he asked. I shook my head.

We headed down the street to a local restaurant, or rather a fine dining establishment. I had never been inside a place like that, so needless to say, it made me uncomfortable.

"Are you sure we should be here?" I asked.

"Of course, I can afford to pay the bill. Don't worry, you are with me."

"They're looking at me."

"So what? You are beautiful."

"They are staring at me because they're not used to having a girl in their restaurant in a three-dollar dress."

"Listen, doll, it is because they're all about your background. It does not matter where you come from, it's all about where you are going."

"Where are you going, Jack?" He smiled.

His next words were… well, he might have just told me his name upfront. I didn't know any different and never read the newspapers. To me that night, he was just Jack Harris. I had no idea he was the John Dillinger that everyone was gunning to find. He was a good-looking fellow who stood looking down at me with a smile that told all his secrets about what feelings he had for me right from the start.

He replied, "Anywhere I want." The sentiment sounded like a grand idea.

It was the most exciting night of my life, and looking back on the incident now, it happened just like you see it in the movies or a *Cinderella* storybook. I was twenty-five and like any other girl my age, I just wanted to be loved. I started a new life from that day forward. The biggest thrill to me was that Johnnie was kind. He treated me with respect and did not care about my Native American heritage.

One of our first-day shopping sprees was to buy myself a new winter coat. I remember him spending $125. That was more money than I could make in months. I quickly found out what it was like to be in love with John Dillinger. Yes, the perks were grand; however, it came with a downside: we got shot at.

Chapter Five:

Life with Johnnie

My time with Johnnie only lasted less than a year. But it was the most brilliant, exciting portion of my life. I don't believe there are words to express our feelings for each other. I remember reading an interview about him many years after his death that gave me a sense of closure. Since I was serving time in prison when he was killed, we never got to say goodbye. However, the article stated, "Evelyn was nothing of the 'gun moll', she possessed an air of singularity devoid of vulgarity. In view of the slight advantages afforded her by ancestry, education, and environment, these facts are noteworthy, because Dillinger claimed she was the best bed partner anyone could ever have. The account stated, he was the lucky one to have met Evelyn." [3]

---

[3] G. Russell Giradin, W. J. (1994). Dillinger the Untold Stories . Indian Unversity Press.

The words gave me peace, I always knew deep down how Johnnie felt, but our lives were filled with dangerous excitement that most people could not even imagine at that time. We ran hard and fast, loving every minute chance provided.

Until I met Johnnie, life was unimaginable. The economy was horrible, especially for Native Americans. The stock market crash only affected the rich; it had zero influence on the lower-class population, except to destroy employment. My job as a hat checker meant decadent wages for someone of my culture, but the disparity weighs you down. We survived on the kindness of young men looking for beautiful women. The one-nighters always slipped me some cash to function one more day. It even allowed us a ride in some fancy Hudson or Ford once in a while. Although age slowly snuck in and took over my youth; nonetheless, it granted me the freedom to be wild. As with many people, they were tied down with a home, regular job, and in most cases, children. Since I had none of those things, the allure of an incredible man who truly loved me took precedence over my life. I'd spent years just surviving, trying to keep my head down, and avoiding any confrontations, so it was time to stretch my wings and live.

In the summer of 1933, I met some people who filled my longing for prosperity. During Prohibition, racial prejudice against the Native American prevented our entrance to the speakeasies. But since I was an employee of the club, it gave me the right to drink without harassment. However, one prejudice gets exchanged for another. In my determination to expand my horizons, I met a woman named Mary Kinder. At first, we had to overcome the issue of race, as it was with many people back then. Mary was, however, fond of drinking; in hindsight, she was an alcoholic. But, with some coaxing, she overcame

her trepidations and learned to drink with an 'Indian', so to speak. We had a great time.

Johnnie, however, was highly intrigued by my culture. Not only being Native American, but my Roman Catholic religious background. He found his own upbringing in the Protestant church ambivalent, and always said he found my confidence soothing. I never considered myself to be self-assured. Johnnie filled the void.

Our evenings were spent drinking with most everyone regaling their campfire stories; although, none were more titillating than Johnnie's. I could sit and listen to his voice for hours. As my trust grew in the incredible man that embraced life, I wanted to take him home to Neopit. He kept saying the only way he could truly get to know me was if I took him to the reservation where I grew up. It was one aspect of life that most White people never experienced. Their impressions were based on the horrific accounts of people's experiences with 'savage Indians'. We were profiled as wicked, uncivilized, and not worthy as a human being. This was a sentiment I lived with every day, and maybe my desire to take Johnnie to my childhood home was to prove the rumors wrong. It was a way for me to get my retribution against the negative racial dogmas.

With his normal enthusiasm, we set a date. On the following Sunday morning, we took off together through Chicago on our way down the winding roads to Wisconsin. Johnnie had never seen primal farmland, as it spreads throughout the Menominee Reservation. Once you hit the north side of Neopit, the Shawano forest bordered an old tin building of the BIA (Bureau of Indian Affairs). Then passing back into the large fields of open range, beside the road just beyond the bureau office is an old cemetery. Johnnie was fascinated by the image and pulled over on the side of the road so we could get out and walk through the cemetery. He looked like a kid at Christmas, "Come on… tell me about this place."

"Are you sure? It's kind of morbid. And I have not been back here since I left for the boarding school in South Dakota."

"Yes, I want to hear all about your life, how you grew up, what you did for fun, where did you go to school? It's a beautiful day, and we have nowhere to go." His exuberance made me smile.

"Okay." We grabbed the old blanket out of the car and laid it down on the ground. I had made sandwiches from home for lunch, so we just had a makeshift picnic. "Where do you want me to start?"

He smiled. "From the beginning…." I nodded.

"Okay, I will start when my father died, before that nothing memorable happened. I was very close to my father, well, both of my parents. It was a shock to everyone when Daddy got sick, the Midewiwin priest said he most likely had pneumonia. It had come on several weeks before his death. We did not have doctors, nor money to take him anywhere. Besides, my father was a strong, virile man and would never have asked for help.

"I admit the night before he died, I had a restless feeling. Almost a premonition of something coming; I was very young. My sister and I slept on the floor with mats filled with corn husks from the previous harvest season. We went to sleep that night not knowing about the horrific event about to take place the next day, something that changed our lives forever.

"I stood in the middle of our one-room shack looking up at my mother, listening to her solemn words conveying the cold reality of life and death. As her words expressed sorrow about my daddy, my thoughts were drowning in agony over the loss. It was one of the most distressing moments of an eight-year old's life. One second, we were learning to walk, then run, followed by going to school, and the next, someone we loved died in the blink of an eye.

"My mother continued attempting to console me, but as a child, death was an unknown event, to which I had no idea of the real meaning. The only thing I knew for sure was my daddy would never again be an active member of my life. I remember rushing away from her when someone knocked on the door. I ran to the corner of the room, holding my ears to muffle the sounds of everyone else crying." Johnnie was mesmerized.

His eagerness to hear my story made me love him even more. "As my sobbing continued, I remembered Daddy giving me a handkerchief the prior day before we left for school. It was mid-fall and the early morning crispness of the air made my nose run. A simple piece of cloth gave me some solace. The fragrant aroma of the hankie brought a fleeting memory of Daddy's sweet kisses, whisking me off to the makeshift bed on the floor closest to the wood stove in the center of the room. In the chaos, I watched my siblings ramble about the room, lost in the reality of living without Daddy.

"My mother continued her conversation with the Midewiwin priest. I knew what happened next, it was a ritual I'd seen many times in my short life. Mama would direct each one of us with a job. My brothers would be told to gather enough water to bathe my father, while she braided his hair. Then, my sisters and I would leave to gather items to prepare Daddy for the afterlife.

"As expected, Mama summoned me directly: 'Evelyn… please go with your sisters to gather the vermillion flowers and brown fungus.' Of course, I had no choice but do as she say. At least it gave me something to do, even if only for a short time.

"We headed to the pond on the west side of town. It was the closest place to find the brown fungus. The vermillion flowers grew in abundance throughout the pasture around our home.

"'Evie,' as my sister called me, 'What do you think will happen to us now?'

"The answer was a mystery since I was only eight, how could I know what would happen? 'I don't know, Anna, but I am sure everything will be fine.' I hoped my response would give her some comfort.

"We gathered the items Mother wanted and headed for home. It was almost dark, and once the sun set it was pitch black, especially in the wooded areas. Not to mention, the cold of fall was settling in fast and winters in Wisconsin could be brutal.

"It was a solemn walk; I did not know what to say. My sister was older, and her wisdom could mentor me during these times. I only knew the death ceremony by watching others in my tribe that had passed away, but Daddy was the first person I'd ever seen die. Unfortunately, it would not be the last." He urged me to continue.

I responded, "When we arrived back at the shack, most of the town had arrived to pay their respects. Daddy was a beloved member of the community. He carried a stable job at the sawmill. Our life was difficult. We struggled to survive, but endured, nonetheless.

"My mother caught us rambling down Main Street and gestured to us to hurry along. It meant my nightmare was a waking reality: Daddy really had died. There was no more avoiding the situation. My mother was left to raise us alone.

"As I reached the shack, a chill ran up my spine when the smell of death lofted through the air. The only blessing was the cold of fall nestled in quietly as we prepped for the ceremony. It kept the odor at a tolerable level. My mother shuffled me inside past the crowd gathered around the doorway. I knew my job in the process was to grind the flower stems into a fine red powder. Mother sat me at the small table she used to prepare our meals with a pestle and bowl." I was surprised Jonnie knew what a pestle and bowl was.

"I had seen death many times as we walked home from school every day through the cemetery. But seeing bodies in a burial ground is not the same as losing a loved one. It is a heart-wrenching affair that affects you for the rest of your life. Once the mourning settles into your soul, it becomes an everlasting recollection that burns the images into your memory forever.

"The burial ground is in a large section of pasture outside the town reserved for the bodies of our loved ones. The grave was prepped by digging a four-foot-deep rectangle. It was interred with a cover for the person,  then filled with more dirt and bark, which was pinned down with heavy stones to protect the body from animals. The grave itself was always oriented along the east-west axis. Then, we covered the grave with a low wooden house that had an opening for the soul to escape. Under the hole was a shelf for food that was needed by the soul on their journey. Our Midewiwin priest would carve a grave marker with the clan totem of the deceased. It had an animal, bird, or fish carved upside down to denote death.

"Are you sure you want me to continue? I haven't shared this with anyone but my family."

Johnnie was so sweet; he touched my cheek with a gleam in his eye. "I worked diligently for almost an hour on grinding the flower petals into a fine red powder. It would eventually be used to mark my father's face. Two brown spots were made on each cheek with a red line connecting them. It was a tradition dating back centuries.

"'Come now, Evelyn.' My mother rushed me over to my father's bedside. I remember the hesitation about seeing him without his life spirit. As the fear enveloped me, I wanted to run and keep running to a time when my father was still alive.

"'Mama,' I squirmed. 'Please....' She shushed me. Daddy lay static on the mat; his lifeless skin had turned colorless.

"My mother instructed, 'Evelyn, use your fingers to place two small spots on his cheek, then make a straight line between them.' I looked at her with panicked apprehension.

"'Mama why can't Frances do this, she is the oldest?'

"'Do not argue, Evelyn!' she exclaimed.

"It took a few moments to gather my strength. The death of any soul brings fear rushing to the surface. All cognizant thought stops for a short time while our mind struggles to comprehend what has happened. The finality of loss is a reminder of our mortality that causes such terror. All I remember is that it was the last place on Earth I wanted to be.

"My mother continued to nudge, and finally, I gave in to her suggestion and dipped my finger in the bowl. The fungus felt sticky on my fingertip. It collected in a gooey round ball that made a perfect circle on my father's cheek. His skin felt cold, unprotected by life. Until that day, the thought of death was only something I'd seen among the other families. Today, it became a reality in my own existence.

"The red dye from the vermillion flower stained my finger for almost a week; a friendly reminder of my own mortality. Death has a way of changing the future.

"Our guests filtered in and out most of the night to pay their respects. Anna and I huddled in the corner, surveying the happenings throughout the horrific event. As the early morning hours waned, my mother collapsed on the bed next to Daddy. It was the last time she'd ever sleep next to her husband.

"I heard the roosters crowing precisely at dawn. It woke me from a restless slumber. The visions of my father's face tormented my thoughts. Anna had fallen asleep on my shoulder. She looked calm, absent of the emotional distress that plagued me. I struggled to get my arm out from under her shoulder, but nature called. It had fallen asleep and my fingers tingled until the blood started to flow once again. I crept outside to the outhouse. The fresh, chilled air smelled good, absent of death.

"Mother was awake when I returned to the house, she was making breakfast. I realized her responsibilities never stopped. She normally woke before dawn and went to bed well after dark every day of the year. Now, she faced the cold hard world alone with five children.

"Our breakfast consisted of fresh fruit and a slice of flatbread she made several days ago. My brothers stayed quiet, which seemed odd since they were usually rambling about some nonsense. We hurried to eat before the town elders arrived to help return Daddy to nature. His body was placed in a small casket for carrying and then removed through the large window on the west side of the shack. A body was never taken out the doorway because the soul was still hovering nearby and might carry someone else away in death. Once they reached the cemetery, the body was removed from the casket and placed in the grave."

I could not believe Johnnie's attention remained constant, he never faltered. "We had one more ritual before Daddy left our home forever. A small locket of his hair was cut and wrapped in birch bark. It would become the center of the spiritual bundle. Upon our return home that evening, we would sit around the fire and talk to the spirit bundle. It was said to help release Daddy from his Earthly existence.

"I watched the men place Daddy in the coffin and carry him out the window, still in shock over the incident. The last day was nothing more than a blur, like seeing yourself from afar, witnessing something through a piece of glass.

"We walked in solitude down main street to the burial grounds. Daddy was in front carried by several of the larger men in town, while Mama and my siblings followed close behind. A biting cold whistled through the trees, and Anna and I huddled together for warmth. She whispered, 'I love you... Evie,' then kissed my cheek. I found her heart-warming connotation settling. Mother heard Anna's words and clutched my hand.

"In the seconds following Daddy being returned to nature, a soothing feeling enveloped my soul. The sensation was unexpected, as my fear of death had consumed me over the last few days, and suddenly everything became clear. It is but an alteration of life, we simply take on another form. The enlightenment taught me death is a state of mind, something we must endure to gain our freedom from repression in society. I never again looked upon death in the same fashion.

"Daddy had taught me many things in my short life, and he continued to instruct me in the afterlife. I would call on his assistance for many years to come.

"Mama prepared us a special fire that night, one made with the love we shared for my father. We sat together and revealed our deepest desires for the future, releasing Daddy's spirit on his journey.

"My father died on October 15, 1915; it was the beginning of fall. The leaves started to turn colors and the ground hardened from the below freezing temperatures. It was a difficult time for many Native Americans. Our living conditions were horrendous, to say the least."

My story paused while Johnnie leaned in to kiss my lips. He was sensational in his actions, so brilliant and full of life. Then he urged me to continue.

"None of our houses had running water, bathrooms, or insulation from the cold. We worked for many months gathering food to sustain us during the season. I can remember the woodpiles piled as high as the roof on our shack. We would use the excess tree bark for insulation against the icy winds. It would be nailed or glued on the inside over the gaping holes. Many young children were suffocated during the harsh season. Their parents would let them sleep in their beds, and during the night the infant would get trapped under the father and die. A vision no human wants to think possible. The cemetery is filled with young children covered by miniature domes concealing the body. We were reminded of this tragedy each time our walks carried us through the burial grounds. However, there were some good times during the winter solstice. Most Native Indians did not celebrate Christmas as many Americans did in that era, but we rejoiced with traditional storytelling. It was like receiving a gift. Since much of the fall was spent hunting and gathering, we saved the winter for other activities." He smiled.

"As I was taught, it was a time to celebrate the Earth and all its precious creatures. An interval of rejuvenation for the animals, plant life, and humans.

During the winter moon, families would gather together around a warm fire and listen to the stories of our ancestors. We cherished the event immensely.

"At night, my mother would sit by the woodstove and sew while we slept. Each one of us was given new moccasins, a dress for the girls, and pants and shirts for the boys. Then before school started in the spring, we had a new outfit to wear. Our old clothes were kept for work and play. If we had any holes or damage, it would be mended. It was hard being one of the youngest because we always got the hand-me-downs. The older kids got the newest stuff; however, most of the clothes were passed around town. When someone passed away, or a child outgrew their clothing, it was given to another person. I never knew what it was like to buy clothes or shoes in a store. So, even though the winter regaled us with blinding snowstorms, my mother worked tirelessly mending, cooking, and cleaning to prepare for the summer months."

He interrupted, "You mean all your clothes are hand-me-down?"

"Yes, usually from Goodwill. I cannot afford new clothes."

He grimaced. "Well, that stops now. You will have anything you want from now on."

"Johnnie, the only thing I want is your love. If you have not learned by now, those things are just things, they don't bring happiness." He smiled and kissed me again.

"Should I continue?" He nodded. "On clear days, when the snow was not so deep, we could play outside, but when a blizzard came through the children had to spend their days indoors. It was the one time being a girl was more fun, we at least had dolls. Although, my mother used them to teach us about raising children and being a woman. The boys played with many different games, but all were to teach us life skills. One winter was so bad we were housebound for almost a month. The snow piled so high over the plains, we had to force our way out the rooftop and my brothers had to shovel the snow away from the front door. At first sight, it was a wonderful vision. The only thing you could see were the tops of the shacks and the last several feet of the treetops. Nonetheless, it gets stressful being cooped up inside with your four siblings for months on end. I can only imagine what my mother must have been feeling; trapped with children and no adult companionship. She was a saint, and I miss her dearly."

It was difficult to tell my story. I had not thought of these things for years. I teared up many times. "One late afternoon in March, the year after Daddy died, my mother sent us to gather water from the nearby stream. It was starting to thaw in the midday sun so we could fill the buckets and carry them back home. My brothers took one side of the bucket, we held the other. Charles, my older brother, bent over the bank to break the ice with a large stick and the icy crust broke and he fell in the creek. The undercurrent rushed swiftly as the ice melted. It carried him downstream almost a mile before we could catch up and lay tree branch across the stream for him to grab.

"By the time we pulled him out, his lips and fingers were turning blue from the bitter cold. He shivered uncontrollably as we helped carry him home. My mother tended to his every need through the night, as we hoped and prayed for his survival. Everyone in the house remembered Daddy lying in the same bed shivering and sweating from pneumonia.

"Anna and I huddled on the floor next to the fireplace watching Mama kneel in prayer for her son's life, just as she did every night while Daddy was sick. It took several days, but Charles pulled through. He lost a few of his fingers; nevertheless, he was no worse for wear. It was a joyous occasion for the family. Mama made a wonderful dessert to celebrate. It was during that time in my life things started to change for me. I wanted more than just to survive. I watched my parents live in squalor during my adolescence and knew there had to be a better way.

"The days and months passed, and our hearts mended from the pain, yet it's amazing how life never slows down, not even for a fleeting moment. We just go from one minute to the next not knowing what lies ahead and are completely ignorant of lurking dangers." I paused to look at Johnnie. He was the most handsome man I had ever seen.

When I met Welton, he was handsome in a dark way, but something deep down kept me at a distance. Then the second I laid eyes on Johnnie; my whole world changed. We fell madly in love, and no one will ever replace what we shared. I believe everyone has a soul mate, and sometimes we get lucky enough to find them. There is an unexplainable connection; you finish each other sentences and thoughts. The idea of an argument seems pointless because your brains are connected on a spiritual level. Even when you are apart from that person, an emotional sensation fills your body. You share the same thoughts. We finished our sandwiches and made love on the side of a vacant road in the middle of the Menominee reservation.

By the time we finished it was getting late afternoon and time for some refreshments. The general store was alongside the Bureau of Indian Affairs building. We grabbed some Camels, a few bottles of soda pop, and snacks. I sauntered through the store, looking at some very familiar faces. Inside, I knew none of them approved of my actions. But I was tired of being judged and ready to live with the man l loved and who loved me. In hindsight, I would have done the same thing over again, no matter how much pain was involved.

Chapter Six:

The Big Escape

My trip to the reservation with Johnnie was exciting; however, it was the last time I'd see my homeland for some time. It seemed my choice of men left a bad taste with many of my tribe members. At the time, I was ignorant of the gossip. However, their chatter was unimportant. I met a man who loved me, and I loved him. Until that point, my experience with men left a lot to be desired.

As a Native American, we have completely different views than that of the average Christian, or Western culture. Our beliefs

40,000 buffalo hides displayed at a buffalo hide yard. Dodge City, 1878

coincide with the Earth – Mother Nature. We cherish life in general.

Our culture learned to live as one with the Earth; only kill for food, shelter, or clothing. And use every ounce of the animal for survival. We do not hunt as a show of force, or as a way to control the human race. By no means do we create life from the destruction of others. In hindsight, I truly believe that was something that Johnnie found most appealing. Our lifestyle in the short time we spent together was reckless, and over the top on certain occasions. Yes, I did turn a blind eye to the chaos. It was something that was of no concern to me. All we cared about was being at each other's side.

At the very moment I laid eyes on Johnnie, he stole my heart forever. It was the one thing he never kept to himself. Anytime he introduced me to anyone, it came from love and respect. I don't believe that he wanted me to have any part in his illegal lifestyle. Our relationship was an escape from the world, a society that had destroyed his self-worth, as it did mine. In many ways, we were misfits, like putting a square peg in a round hole. So, regarding any of the internal dealings of his bank robberies, he kept me in the dark. Much of what I knew was from reading the newspaper, or gossip.

Johnnie's story started when he was in his twenties. He grew up in Mooresville, Indiana, a small farming community. A short time later, after being arrested, he confessed to robbing a local grocer. The Great Depression was in full force, and Johnnie had a large impact on public opinion. I remember the reporters calling him a modern-day Robin Hood. His actions stemmed from stealing food for his family. His accomplice pled not guilty and got two years. Johnnie, on the other hand, was sentenced to ten to twenty years, after which his wife divorced him. Granted he only served eight and a half years, but the time embittered him. In his mind, it was retribution for the way he had been treated. Not unlike the actions toward the Native Americans. In many ways, I found his attitude refreshing.

On our first big escapade, Johnnie went to the barber because of scalp itch. We thought it was dandruff; however, the issue continued to get worse. So, he talked with a friend who could find a doctor. Arthur McGinnis was supposedly a close companion, but in reality, he had been a police informant. He agreed to call a trusted doctor, and the first appointment was scheduled. Dr. Eye, a dermatologist, treated Johnnie and made a second appointment several weeks later as a follow-up.

Johnnie introduced me to a brand new '33 Essex with a Terraplane V8 under the hood. I had never seen anything that fancy. His doctor's appointment was on the SE corner of Irving Park Blvd and Keeler Ave.
Since Johnnie needed to stay out of the public eye, we were supposed to meet with Dr. Eye at nine o'clock p.m. I could see the thrill of adventure in his eyes when we left.

As we pulled up to the doctor's office, he said, "Evelyn, please wait. This won't take long." He smiled and kissed me. "Oh, keep the engine running." I agreed.

The appointment only took about ten minutes; he emerged on the sidewalk. He paused to look at the cars parked along the street. Several of them appeared to be parked facing the wrong direction. In most cases, at that time of night, the street was normally very quiet with little traffic. I noticed Johnnie looking down the street at one particular vehicle; it was about two car lengths away facing the Essex. Across Keller Ave was another car parked fifty or so yards back, pointing in the same direction as us. At the time, I had no idea what that meant, but Johnnie did. He sauntered down the sidewalk at a calm but hurried pace.

He jumped in the driver's seat and told me, "Hang on," and smiled.

I found out later, long after his death, that the detectives wanted him dead that night, and were ordered to shoot to kill. Johnnie caught them all off guard when he slammed the car in reverse, and we flew backward into oncoming traffic on Irving Park

Blvd. I admit the chaos had my stomach churning; it was an experience far beyond my purview. Another detective parked across the street hollered to ram our car as we passed, but it stalled before he had the chance. Otherwise, I may not be alive to tell this story. threw it in first and sped off, just barely missing oncoming traffic. Only one car gave chase as we drove out of town. Most police cars could not keep up with a Terraplane V8.

I noticed the car chasing us, Johnnie was concentrating on the road. A few seconds later he pulled up next to the driver's door. He yelled, "Get down!" My heart pounded when I saw the barrel of a .38 directed at the window.

The detective just kept shooting; I thought his gun would never run out of bullets. Then, after he emptied the pistol, he opened fire with his shotgun. We screeched a hard right on Elston Ave. The encounter seemed to last forever, but in reality, maybe only a mile.

The chase kept rolling along, while Keller worked to empty his guns. At one point, I remember him leaning out the car window; thank God neither one of us was hit by the flying bullets. I admit it was not the most solid decision I ever made to be in that car with Jonnie. But love makes you do funny things. As a matter of fact, watching him drive that car so expertly was alluring. We continued to speed down the road with the police car right next to us until Johnnie took a hard right on to Elston, where we ended up on a dead-end street. I thought that was it. We were either dead or going to jail. Somehow, Johnnie averted Detective Artery's car as he raced past the street. We rocketed backward out into oncoming traffic again and headed in the opposite direction, and there was our escape.

Johnnie shouted, "We did it, baby... come on over here and cuddle up!" I smiled. It was the time of my life. We drove up to the North Side and ditched the car and took a cab.

Our next destination was the apartment on Russell Clark. A party was in the planning with music and dancing. Johnnie's gang had been staying there. It was a surprise. Mary Kinder answered the door, and we stumbled inside. I went to the bedroom to freshen up, while the gang caught up on the happenings. I guess Johnnie thought it was a syndicate hit, but it turned out to be a police sting.

The morning papers were plastered with stories of the Dillinger shootout. Articles related Johnnie and his gang to the James Boys and Harvey Bailey. But this is kind of where some of the detective's hatred for Johnnie came to light when they professed he was shooting back. Only he was too busy driving to shoot at anyone. I witnessed the whole event. Most of the gang involved had no idea who betrayed him, but Johnnie who knew it was McGinnis.

Once Johnnie cleared the air with the other gang members, he came back to me. I loved that about him, he made time for me. We had some drinks, listened to music, and danced. However, my favorite part of the night was making love when the party died down. Johnnie was so passionate, he made me feel like a queen. It was never rushed, we made love over and over until we both passed out from exhaustion.

The next morning, well early afternoon, we made haste and moved out of our apartment on Clarendon Ave and went across the street to Russell Clark's. We did not know until the next day that the apartment was raided shortly after we left. Harry Copland, one of Johnnie's partners, was a heavy drinker and spilled his guts to the wrong woman. However, none of the police chases or investigations slowed down our plans. Johnnie had told me a few weeks prior that he wanted to take a trip to Florida. They had to do a few more jobs, and the trip was scheduled.

Johnnie was brimming with excitement about learning to fly an airplane, driving to Florida, and spending some time on the beach in the hot sunshine with me. He kept teasing me about seeing me in a bathing suit with red sunglasses on the beach.

Chapter Seven:

Our Florida Vacation

I was slowly growing accustomed to this lifestyle, but there were unexpected twists that kept everything in a constant state of turmoil. There was a continuous state of rotation of women, and men for that matter, in and out of our lives. Just as I tried to become  friends, something would happen and they either disappeared (not because they died) or went off somewhere else, due to the barrage of police, FBI and detectives chasing us. By being a part of John Dillinger's life, you learned to be unencumbered by anything tangible. We stayed on the run every minute of every day.

After the murder of Sergeant Shanley, the hunt for Johnnie and his gang went on high priority. The newspapers started calling them 'Public Enemies' who must be stopped immediately. So, the gang felt that under the circumstances a rest period was in order. We abandoned the apartment on 1850 Humboldt Park Boulevard and headed for Florida. Our group consisted of Johnnie and me, Pierpont, and Mary Kinder. While the police set out to find Hamilton, we headed for some sunshine.

I remember our first night out, Johnnie stopped at a local grocery store for some smokes and snacks, but he came back with several shopping bags filled with stuff. He had that typical slanted grin and hopped in the driver's seat and said: "Hang on baby...."

I paid no attention to his comedy as it was normal. It was December 19, 1934, a cold winter in Chicago, so the change of scenery was wonderful.

Many of the local papers reported Johnnie and his comrades robbed the bank and got off with 10,000 dollars. But we were not even in Florida at the time. At that point, people wanted to be famous and started claiming John Dillinger was robbing banks everywhere.

We found a small side road motel to stay for the night. I always loved the nights with Johnnie. It was just him and I; his attention never strayed when we were alone. However, we learned that at a moment's notice the police could come knocking and it would be time to flee for safety. Anyway, after we checked in, Johnnie grabbed one of the bags and hit the bathroom. I admit his actions caught me off guard, so I just unpacked and changed my clothes to stay in for the evening. About a half an hour later, he came out with red hair. I laughed until my sides ached.

"Jonnie, what did you do?" I asked. He grinned.

"Well, baby, one has to keep up with appearances. Since we are supposed to be incognito, I thought a change was in order. Plus, I thought growing a moustache might be appropriate. What do you think?"

I grinned, "I think you would look handsome no matter what." My statement got his attention.

"What do you say, when we get to Florida, we go on a shopping spree? I think you need some new dresses...."

"I love it, what more could a girl ask for than looking good for her man?"

I was never afraid of Johnnie; however, many people were terrified. When you lived as my people did at that time, diplomacy was the best way to fight battles. I just learned how to read him, he loved me, and I loved him. We had a rapport that no one understood. Johnnie was an incredibly handsome man that I found insatiable. We could not get enough of each other, both sexually and in companionship.

We headed out the next morning after breakfast in our fleet of four cars. The day went as planned. We drove most of the day, except when we stopped just outside of Nashville, Tennessee. Harry and Mary found a local jewelry store. Mary talked about Harry proposing a few days prior but wanted to wait until we got to Florida. The subject was still a bit touchy with us since my marriage with Welton had never been annulled. Johnnie had asked me to marry him right after we met, but we could not, due to me still being married. I thought it best most of the time to avoid the subject. In hindsight, my reason for not marrying Johnnie is still a mystery. Nonetheless, at the time, we were in love and swept up by hormones, maybe. I guess a small part of me kept its distance for fear of getting too close. Since my last marriage failed miserably, I did not want to jinx this one as well. Besides, it gave us time to fool around in the car while we waited. Johnnie found an old abandoned barn that we hid the car inside and made love in the backseat. We were giggly young kids, times that changed my life forever. Sometimes, I can still feel his lips on my neck as if it were yesterday.

Jonnie told Harry he had an hour, and to meet us back on the road by 2:00 p.m. Mary came back with a huge rock on her finger, smiling from ear to ear. They looked so in love. I admit the sight filled my heart with sorrow, seeing that ring on her hand.

Once we got back in the car, Johnnie looked at me and said, "That could be us, you know. My offer still stands as long as I am alive." I acknowledged his offer with a smile.

"I know… thank you." He nodded and pulled me over next to him in the car.

It took us four days to arrive in Florida. We stayed in Daytona in a seventeen-room house with a front porch facing the beach. I had never seen such a house. I walked in the front door and just stood looking around, "Wow! Johnnie this is incredible." I kissed him and ran to the front porch. "Take me to the beach please?" I begged. He grinned.

"Let's get our stuff unpacked and we will go." I agreed.

Johnnie helped Harry carry in the guns, which were kept in a locked trunk. It was usual to keep them hidden in a closet out of sight from any stranger entering the residence. It took them almost an hour to haul in all the luggage, so Mary and I got changed for the beach and traded stories.

I can remember my first time seeing the ocean, it was an incredible sight. The cool breeze rolling off the coast was light and airy. I could have stayed in Florida forever. Yes, I grew up in Wisconsin with the lakes, but nothing compares to the real ocean. Johnnie heard us girls laughing and talking in the bedroom while the men worked. He came in grinning. "You two are just having too much fun in here, while we are slaving away."

"Oh, Johnnie…. I love it here. Can we stay forever?" I thought it was worth a try.

"Maybe, baby, you never know."

"Are you ready? Can we go to the beach now?"

"Yes, get ready. I will change."

"We are ready, just waiting on you slowpokes." I smiled.

"Well, go in the other room, I will be out in a minute."

Mary and I headed for the living room. Harry was seated on the couch with a drink in his hand. "Oh, my… there are two of the most beautiful women I have ever seen."

Mary giggled. "Thank you, Harry. You are both lucky to have us." Harry and I flirted innocently it was all harmless fun.

When Johnnie came out of the bedroom, I had never seen him look so contented. He was wearing a white silk shirt and beige casual dress slacks. My heart melted all over again. "Wow, Johnnie, you look so handsome." He smiled.

"Are you ready?"

"Yes, let's go." We grabbed the picnic basket and headed to the beach.

I felt like the family pet, hanging my head out the window. Even on the warmest day in Chicago, it could never feel this good. We found a nice secluded section of the beach and made ourselves at home. Mary and I grabbed hands and headed for the water. The sand warmed my feet, it tickled my toes with a soft delicate touch. I just stood in one place for what felt like forever. Mary headed out to the water. She kept turning around and looking for me to follow.

The whole sensation left me dumbfounded. I was a young Native American who went from squalor to living life like the rich. If you had asked me a few years ago if I could imagine myself being here like this, it was not even a distant thought. People had been telling me for years that I was trash, not worth human skin. After a while, it tends to work on your soul. I remember lying on the ground naked while those men raped me, completely exposed to the world, wondering if I would even be alive the next day. It scarred my soul permanently, but it made me strong. I lost my fear of dying that day. Little did I know, it was preparing me for what is to come.

"Evelyn, are you coming sometime?" Mary yelled.

I smiled. "Yes, on my way." She took my hand and we ran along the beach, letting the sand squish between our toes. When I turned to look for Johnnie, he was sitting in his chair under the umbrella with a huge grin.

"Come on, Evelyn, let them be sticks in the mud. We can have fun without them." I agreed.

For the next several hours, we played in the water like school children. At that point, it was the most fun I'd ever had outside making love to Johnnie. By the end of the day, we looked like lobsters.

"Hey, you two…?" Johnnie called out. He had walked down to the water in his bare feet.

I obliged. "Yes?"

"Come on, let's go get something to eat… let's say we have a nice meal."

"Sure, that would be great!" I announced.

"Evelyn, you look like a lobster." We giggled.

The day was right out of a fairy tale. I became Cinderella pledged to a king.

We went back to our temporary home and got dressed for dinner. "Evelyn, wear that red dress I got for you in Chicago," Johnnie told me. I agreed. "Oh, baby, you look ravishing, good enough to eat."

"Stop it, Johnnie."

"Shall we go?" He held out his arm and we went on our way.

We found a nice, out of the way lounge with dancing and a live band. Our days at the time were long and the nights longer. Johnnie had a rule about drinking in public, so we kept it low key and just ate and talked. It was nice to see Johnnie relaxed. I mean, he was always on guard, but he seemed almost normal that trip.

The band started and we made our way to the dance floor. "Evelyn you look so beautiful. I can see myself with you until the day I die. Please, tell me you won't ever leave me?"

"I won't ever leave you, promise."

At that time, I wanted to grow old with Dillinger as well. He had captured my heart; I really did not care about the money and gifts. Yes, it was every girl's dream, but Johnnie was good to me and treated me like a queen.

The next morning, we woke at about noon. So, you could say the next afternoon. Johnnie was up raring to go as always. We made love in the shower and headed out for some shopping. Christmas was the next week and he wanted it to be a holiday I never forgot.

We found the nearest tree lot and bought a tree and all the trimmings. It looked like the Beverly Hillbillies with our tree tied to the top of the car and the backseat full of gifts. Johnnie was all about his looks. He spent hours in the bathroom shaving and keeping his hair just perfect, not to mention his clothes. One man should have so many clothes, except he never wore them more than a few times, and then it was off to the get new suits tailored. He had some casual clothes, but they were dress slacks and collared shirts, always silk, and most of the time, bright white. I can remember the women fawning over him whenever we were in public. At times it made me uncomfortable, but he never paid much attention, except he loved the interest. You could see his eyes light up from the girls gawking at him.

I can say that was the first-time going Christmas shopping for me; until then we just did something special with loved ones because money was scarce and buying presents was impossible. However, Johnnie refused to let me buy him anything. So, we agreed that I could trade out my gift. He bought me a real intimate undergarment. The gift was well-received.

Our shopping spree must have hit every shop from one end of Daytona to the other. While we were out, Johnnie picked up a newspaper to keep up with the latest affairs. One of the Chicago papers said the Dillinger Gang was being anxiously pursued. Plus, on our way back to the house, a news report claimed Johnnie had hit and killed a dog in Chicago. Apparently, he had been previously identified. We both giggled at the false report.

After we got home, he told Mary and Harry, "Guess what? I apparently hit and killed a dog in Chicago two days ago, Hell… that's gone too far. How can I hit a dog in Chicago and be in Florida at the same time?"

"Seems our fame is spreading," Harry commented.

"I guess you're right," he replied.

Their business talk stopped quickly. I think Johnnie wanted a break from all the attention. Don't get me wrong, deep down I believe he loved it; however, it got overwhelming. It was nice to live like a normal person for short bursts.

Most of the gang had joined us by then, so to pass the time they played poker and drank. Sometimes I played but did not find it appealing. So instead, I decided to decorate the tree. Mary joined me later when she and Harry finished in the bedroom. It was fun popping popcorn and stringing garland. Mary and I shared several bottles of wine, laughing and talking on the couch. Johnnie stayed sober, as with most nights. Our night ended as the sun was rising.

Johnnie and Harry left for a few hours the next afternoon, so Mary and I took a walk to check out the neighborhood. All the houses on the block were incredibly large and decked out with Christmas decorations. I felt incredibly comfortable in Florida; not one single person made me feel like a second-rate citizen. Florida was intermixed with many cultures, so they were used to seeing people of all races.

The boys were back when we got home with a brilliant surprise. While we were in Daytona that year, the county fair was in town. They bought us four tickets, and needless to say, the trip just got better.

I exclaimed, "Johnnie, you are too much. When are we going?"

"Right now, why not?" The group agreed.

We piled in the car and headed for the fairgrounds. "How about the Ferris wheel first? Please?" I pleaded.

"Alright, I'll try anything once," Johnnie stated.

"Oh, come on, a big tough guy like you is afraid of a little height?" He scoffed.

We waited for our turn and climbed in the chair. I can say that Johnnie's knuckles were white. I knew at that moment he loved me if he was willing to make that kind of sacrifice. The view from up there was incredible. You could actually see the curve of the earth against the horizon. Now, at that time, it meant nothing to me being so young, but I have played those days over and over in my head for decades. It's funny how you can see some things like

they were yesterday but cannot remember what happened yesterday.

The big day finally arrived: Christmas, I had never been so excited. Only my expectations would be blown out of the water. Johnnie woke me up about eleven with a blindfold and said he had a gift but did not want me to see it yet. I put on the blindfold and he led me outside, and parked in the driveway was a 1933 Essex, just like the one that got shot full of bullet holes in Chicago.

I screamed, "Johnnie is this for me?"

"Of course, it's all yours. I will transfer the title the first business day after Christmas."

"Oh, you are too much. Can we go for a drive?"

"Yes, but first you have to have this."

Johnnie pulled a small jewelry box out of his pocket and handed it to me. "What is this?"

"Open it…."

I lifted the lid and saw a wedding ring, a diamond wedding ring. "Are you officially asking me to marry you?" He nodded his head.

"Yes, yes… but what about— I am still married to Welton."

"I know…. we are going to remedy that. Stay with me until New Years and then you head to Wisconsin and get that annulled."

"Wait… are you not coming with me?"

"No, I have other business; you will be alright." I never gave it another thought.

We all stayed inside that day, mingling among ourselves. By night-time, we gathered around the tree and exchanged gifts. Mary bought me some silk undergarments and gave Johnnie a nice pen and pencil set. Not that those things made any sense to me, but he took them in stride and was thankful. Johnnie had pizza delivered and we partied the rest of the night. Of course, my new lingerie came in quite handy that night.

But even in paradise, discord can happen. On Christmas morning I got up before Johnnie, and Harry was in the kitchen making coffee. We chatted some at the table completely innocent; although, I believe Harry had a secret crush on me. Mary and I were very different personalities. Anyway, Johnnie came into the kitchen and got very upset. He thought I was paying too much attention to Harry in a flirtatious way.

We argued. "Please get dressed; we need to take a drive."

I obliged. His voice sounded serious, but I had no reason to think anything negative.

Johnnie grabbed the car keys and walked me outside to the car. He did not say a word as he opened my door and walked around to the other side. We took a drive along a deserted road next to the Florida sands.

He suddenly stopped the car, and turned to face me, "Get out!" I started to ask why when his look stopped me. We stepped out. Johnnie walked to the front of the car and waited for me. "You have been playing around with Harry too much." I noticed the anger in his voice, he had never spoken that way to me before. "What do you have to say for yourself?"

I admit he caught me off guard, but I never showed any fear. "You know that is not true, I am faithful to you. But I am not afraid to die, not anymore. And I don't want to live anyway if you believe a thing like that about me."

Johnnie looked puzzled at my reply, and there was a long pause. I did not know if he was going to pull a gun and shoot me in the head or kiss me. Finally, he said, "Alright, baby… let's go and forget this ever happened."

I knew deep down he was really bothered by what he thought happened in the kitchen. Nonetheless, we never spoke of the incident again. A few days later, he sent me off to Wisconsin to see my mother. It was New Year's Day, and I had several thousand dollars for traveling, and for buying Christmas gifts for Johnnie's family in Indiana. We said our goodbyes and I headed off to Wisconsin in the dead of winter alone, with no idea of where I was going.

Chapter Eight:

Alone on the Road

As age has caught up with me, I realize the concept of driving alone in the dead of winter across the country was not the best idea. I had only driven a car a few times, so in essence, I learned as the drive went along. Nonetheless, hitchhiking alone from North Dakota definitely took a much greater toll on my life than driving across the country. Only this time, I at least had money and maturity.

Our parting had me shook up inside; however, it was the last piece of information that I would have passed along to anyone. Johnnie and I spent a lot of time together and to see him react towards me in that way was highly upsetting. He never knew, but I left Florida with tears in my eyes wondering if his love for me was lost forever. I watched Johnnie fade out of sight in my rear-view mirror.

My first stop was the local convenience store for snacks, drinks, and a US map. If you learn anything from living off the land as we did, it's best to have extra clothing, food, and water. We traveled lightly with all of our belongings in one knapsack.

Most of the driving was on Route 41, it went from Florida to upper Michigan. So, all I had was a jog across Illinois then up to home.

Actually, my priority was to not get caught without a driver's license. To this day, I can't believe the trip went off without a hitch. Don't get me wrong, I had a few close calls, but escaped unharmed.

The weather held until I hit Kentucky. Then the snow hit; if I remember right, it started just outside of Nashville and did not stop all the way home. So, I enjoyed the warmth through Tennessee. It took me four days since the last thing I wanted was to drive at night. Once the sun started to set, I found a small, out of the way hotel to stop.

Car radios at the time were spotty at best and got only three channels. One was all news and the rest played mostly music. Needless to say, there was a lot of silence. I tried my best to keep my mind focused on positive things, but it kept turning to Johnnie and our disagreement.

The anger in his eyes that day was incredible. I told him I was not scared to die and that part was true; however, the last person I wanted to kill me was the man I loved. The incident in the kitchen that morning kept playing over and over in my head before it dawned on me the issue had been building for some time. I guess it is just my nature to be nice, and that meant to everyone in Johnnie's gang. Harry was a bit of a flirt to most of the girls, but the only one that mattered was me in Johnnie's mind. A few weeks prior, we were holed up in the apartment building partying as usual, and most of the time, we all got pretty drunk. Harry caught me in the kitchen and made some comment about me ditching Johnnie and coming to bed with him. I had no idea anyone heard the remark, except there were no secrets among that crew. I should have known; only there was no chance in hell I would have ever taken that course of action.

Plus, that was not the only incident with Harry. I guess it just came to a head that night. Johnnie was never good at settling down. He had to be on the go all the time. His restless streak would kick in and off we went. If he was not robbing banks or shopping, we were making love or taking trips. I had the time of my life, there was no doubt. It was an experience not many Native Americans had the privilege of having.

My first night stop was in a small town just south of the Florida-Georgia border. The owners were a local couple in their mid-forties and very kind. They gave me the room right next to the office in case of any trouble; but shortly before dinner, I stepped out for a bite to eat at the restaurant down the street when I saw a young couple check-in next to me with a baby. The sight almost made me collapse; it was the first time I had thought about Billie in years. I guess the talk of Johnnie and I getting married brought up feelings of having a family. One of my jobs on this trip was finding an attorney and to get my marriage to Welton annulled. Once Johnnie had finished in Florida, we were to meet back in St. Louis. The rest of the gang headed to Tucson, Arizona—it was meant to be the cooling-off period.

I stood there watching the couple holding their little girl for what felt like an eternity. They looked so happy. It made me envious in many ways. As with most young girls, they want the white picket fence life, a husband to take care of them, and to grow old together. All of this was fading fast in my mind at the time; needless to say, when you are young the idea of your future is non-existent. You live in the moment, as we did.

My mind ran wild with images of little Billie playing in the backyard of a nice house, watching me and Johnnie rocking on the swing. I can still hear him giggling with the dog as they ran around in the grass playing. I knew from the moment Johnnie and I met our love was a fleeting miracle that was never meant to last. So, we enjoyed every nuance of life while it lasted. After I regained my strength, it was getting dark and time to get some dinner. That was the first time I had been alone since Johnnie and I had met, and admittedly it bothered me greatly. We had become inseparable. The remainder of my evening went slowly; I thought the night would never end. I left the next morning right before dawn, it was time to be on my way.

When I hit the border between Florida and Georgia my nerves were on fire. I had heard horror stories of Native Americans being brutalized throughout the state. Here I was, a young Native woman traveling alone in an expensive car across country. Several times I thought about jumping on another road through Alabama but figured it might be just as bad. After some deliberation, I figured it best to just stay on course and stop only when necessary. There was plenty of food in the backseat and I could run into a gas station quickly.

The weather did hold out gratefully until I hit Tennessee, and then the rain turned to ice. At one point, traffic was down to fifteen miles per hour up the highway. There were abandoned cars everywhere. The owners had left them to find shelter. I was lucky enough to catch a blue ford going the same direction, so we traveled together for the next several hundred miles. I made it through Tennessee in one day, thank goodness. It was just a short span across Kentucky, and I was back in Illinois. My last night on the road, I was getting ready to find a hotel when a police car came speeding up behind me. He slowed and followed me for a long time. I kept waiting to see his lights flash. Then out of the blue, he hit his lights again and flew past me. Boy, that was a relief. A few miles ahead, I saw a Burma shave sign altering me to a gas station and hotel. It was well after dark, and the road conditions were getting bad. The day had exhausted my energy, so I skipped dinner and went straight to bed. I was so happy to be almost home; one more day and I'd be back in Chicago. I planned on staying with my sister and then heading to see my mother the next day after a good night's sleep.

When I got up the next morning, the car windshield was frozen solid with about a foot of snow on the ground. The snowploughs had worked most of the night clearing the roads but the roads were horrible at best. A month later was the Blizzard  of 1934 that dumped fifteen feet of snow in a matter of a few hours. The temperature dropped to fifteen degrees below zero. It was the coldest on record. I decided to wait a few hours and let it warm a few degrees before I left. My idea was sound; nevertheless, it was dangerous. A part of me was angry with Johnnie for leaving me to drive alone back home, and yet at the same time, I could never stay mad at him.

The weather broke somewhat about 10:00 a.m., so I decided to take a chance and make it back home later that day. Believe me when I say it was freezing; I bundled up covered from head to toe. The only part of me you could see was my eyes and nose.

There were no heaters in the cars at that time, so driving in winter was miserable. It got so bad that I had to stop every few hours and thaw out with a hot cup of coffee and heat. But I finally made it just after dark, and gratefully my sister was still in the same apartment. I have never been so happy to get out of that car and just get warm. It took hours before I could feel my fingers and toes. We huddled by the steam heater most of the night.

I had not seen my sister for several months and it was great to be with family. They have a way of making you see different outlooks. "Evelyn...." she screeched. "Where is Johnnie?"

"I am alone, he is not with me."

"What do you mean he is not with you? How did you get here?"

"I drove from Florida."

"Florida... you drove alone from Florida?"

"Yes, alone... the last two days were miserable."

"I don't understand, what in the world happened that he let you drive all that way alone? You don't even have a driver's license."

"I know…. But no matter, I am here safe."

"That is not the point, you don't let someone you love drive in weather like this. Especially a woman."

"Sis… I know, but it is what it is. Can we just sit down and get some coffee? I will explain everything."

"Sure, come on, let's get these clothes off. Go into my room, you can wear anything in the closet." She nodded. "I will get the coffee started."

I went into the bedroom and dug through Anna's closet for the warmest night clothes I could find. It did not take long before I missed the warm beaches in Florida. "Oh, there you are. Come on, get your coffee."

"Thank you… I feel much better. It's cold outside."

"Yes, the weatherman on the radio said it was in the negatives. I cannot believe you made that drive alone. Please now, tell me what happened."

"Not long after Johnnie found out one of the gang members ratted him out, he decided to take a break and head to Florida. A cooling-off period he said, so we went where it was warm sun and beaches for Christmas."

"So, all of you were really in Florida?"

"Yes, we arrived first with Harry and his girlfriend. The rest of the gang joined us a few days later. We hit every road that traveled the coastline in Florida, then we went shopping. It was great fun sunbathing on the beach, eating out at fancy restaurants. Plus, Johnnie was relaxed and at ease down there. I thought everything was fine. We were having a wonderful time, then Christmas morning he took me outside and presented my gift, the Essex. He promised to teach me how to drive and help me get my license after we got back to Chicago."

"Wait, he bought you a car?"

"Yes, a car, the one I was driving. We went before I left and put the title in my name."

"Wow... go on?"

"So New Year's Eve we had a grand celebration. The party was alive all night. We went out and shot off the Tommy guns, and cheered in the new year. Johnnie and I made love, and he asked me to marry him. Then—" Anna interrupted.

"John Dillinger asked you to marry him?" I nodded.

"Yes, look... he gave me a ring."

"Oh my God, that this is huge. It must have cost a fortune."

"Indeed... anyway, I got up the next morning and Johnnie was still sleeping. When I went into the kitchen Harry was making coffee and breakfast. He offered me coffee and I agreed. We sat at the table talking when Johnnie walked into the kitchen. He never said anything, just turned around and walked out of the room. I got up and followed him back to our room. He questioned me for almost an hour, then told me we needed to go for a drive. He made me get dressed and come with him. We headed out to a deserted road, alongside the ocean and he suddenly stopped the car and forced me to get out—" I paused to regain my composure. Anna waited patiently. "I—got out and stood in front of him, then as plain as day he wanted to know what I had to say for myself. I asked what he meant, and that is when he got mad. I had never seen him angry with me. He replied, what is happening with Harry? I told him nothing was happening, and I was not afraid to die, but if he truly believed I would do such a thing, then please just kill me."

"What did he say?" Anna blurted out.

"He calmly said, 'Okay, baby, then we won't speak of this again.' I did not know how to react. I thought he was going to shoot me in the head and leave. But at that point, showing fear would not have gotten me anywhere. The next day, New Year's Day, he asked me to leave with the premise I was to go visit Mom and buy Christmas gifts for his family.

Then while in Wisconsin get my marriage annulled with Welton."

"Evie… I don't know what to say. Are you okay?"

"I am not sure how I feel. He was so mad…."

"You know, maybe that was a show—"

"A show, what do you mean?"

"He has to show strength with his men, or they won't trust him. The only way for him to save face was to force you to leave. Make them all think he remained in control."

"Are you sure… do you believe that is what happened?"

"Yes, I do. Evelyn, I have seen the way he looks at you. That man is in love with you, head over heels. I bet something was going down and he wanted you out of harm's way."

"I hope you are right, Anna."

"I am. Did he arrange to see you again?"

"Yes, of course, in St. Louis. He is supposed to get word to me."

"See, then there you have it. This is all a show of force, but I will warn you about one thing, he is dangerously jealous. Be careful from now on, especially with any one of his gang members."

"Agreed, I guess you are right. I can see that now."

"Believe me… I guarantee you John was pacing the floor worrying about you driving alone. It must have torn him up inside. He could not handle you getting hurt because of something he did. Just look at that car. It's one of the most expensive cars on the market. I bet it set him back about nine hundred dollars."

"Oh, that is nothing…" I got up to fetch my pocketbook. "Look at this."

"What? There must be more than a thousand dollars there."

"Yes, several thousand. Here, take this and pay your rent for the next several months. I worry about you. Johnnie won't care. But you have to come shopping with me tomorrow."

"Agreed. Are you sure about giving me this money? Does he expect you to return what you don't spend?"

"No, he would never do that. Johnnie does not care about money; to him, it's a tool."

"Okay then, thank you. It will help a lot. You are going to stay with me for a while, right?"

"Of course, if you will have me…?" She giggled.

Anna helped me find peace with the situation. Her advice that night was much appreciated. We spent the next two days of shopping. The idea of going into a store and buying whatever we wanted was an experience neither one of us had ever enjoyed. She had always been kind to Jonnie anytime we met with her, even the times we stayed in her apartment. I did finally come to terms with what happened and realized Anna was right. The next week I took off to visit my mother and hire an attorney to annul my marriage before Johnnie and I met up in St. Louis in a few weeks.

Chapter Nine:

No Contact

Over the next few weeks, I had a chance to mull over the incident in Florida and come to the conclusion that Anna was correct. I felt the love of Johnnie through my soul and he would never intentionally do anything to put my life in danger. Nonetheless, it left a mark on my soul from that day forward. We never spoke of the situation again. It was as though nothing ever happened. Johnnie was funny that way. It was like the past did not exist. He only lived for the future.

After returning from Neopit, it surprised me that I had not heard from Johnnie. It was unlike him to be forgetful when it came to the knowledge of my whereabouts. However, knowing the gang, I knew where to begin. My first phone call was Mae Clark. If she knew how to find Opal Long the problem was handled. I got through to Pat Carrington who disguised herself as Ann Jackson. Her telegraph stated, "Where can I call you at 6:00 pm? Important." At the time her message was confusing, so I replied: "I don't understand."

Ann replied, "Seventy-five East Windemere Street, High Park, Michigan."

I replied, "Cannot meet there but come to me on 901 Addison Street." It was our new apartment in Chicago that Anna had rented.

I immediately packed my bags and headed for Chicago. It was thrilling to drive such a fancy car. I learned very quickly to love the speed; however, my haste left me in a minor traffic accident that damaged the Terraplane. So, in my fugitive state, I employed a car dealer who worked for cash to keep his mouth shut. We agreed on a new car with $175 credit. I gave up the old car that was damaged and paid $250 for a new one. It was a 1932 Terraplane that carried more than a thousand miles before we exchanged it for a new car.

I should have taken the accident as a bad omen that 1934 would be an unhappy year. My new apartment was two blocks from Wrigley Field, a nice neighborhood. Nonetheless, all of us had to be very careful about traveling anywhere in Chicago. Our faces were known to everyone. It was a wonderful feeling to dress with class. I had the engagement ring that Johnnie gave me on Christmas Eve, a platinum wristwatch studded with diamonds, plus my fitted leather jacket and a brand-new red dress I bought while shopping in Florida. It was so cold that the only way to keep warm was to bundle up with a wool overcoat trailing to my ankles, and a hat. The clothing alone kept me in disguise. I had made arrangements to meet up with Johnnie the next day on January 15, 1934.

Johnnie and I met just outside the city limits. It was the first time since we met that I saw him agitated, almost angry. At the time, I had no idea that they had just come

from the bank robbery in Indiana where Officer O'Malley had been killed. They had driven all night to make the meeting with Red Hamilton. I never asked him about their escapades, just assumed if he wanted to share anything, he would have told me. The news later blamed Johnnie; however, eyewitnesses said it was Red Hamilton.

Our conversation drifted to my divorcing Welton, which was to no avail. Since he was in prison these things took more time than we expected. So, Johnnie told me he knew of someone in St. Louis who could help push it through. We rode back to St. Louis in silence. He just pulled me over next to him and drove. As I look back, his decision to send me away left him anxious. He seemed to be much more relaxed when I was with him all the time and in hindsight, so was I. We complemented each other.

It was dawn by the time we arrived in St. Louis and I could tell Johnnie was exhausted, sleep-deprived, and had not showered in days. It was completely unlike him to have not been fully dressed, shaved, and showered. I knew deep down whatever happened during their robbery upset him greatly. We stopped at a local gas station, grabbed some coffee and snacks, then headed for the closest oil service station. We asked the mechanic for directions to the car dealer. It happened to be the Hudson-Frampton Company. We posed as Mr. and Mrs. Sullivan. I remember the salesman vividly; he had a strange demeanor. Nonetheless, he was attentive and made sure Johnnie got what he wanted.

The guy walked up and introduced himself, "Hello, I am JC Jones."

Johnnie nodded. "Hello, give me a black Hudson with a long wheelbase." The salesman looked astonished.

"Mr. Sullivan, we don't have a black Hudson, but I can offer you a bison brown?"

Johnnie smirked. "I need to ask my wife first." At the time, anything like that was unheard of. The salesman looked irked.

"Do you trust her to drive the car as well?" Johnnie laughed.

JC nudged him with his elbow in jest and I could tell he knew immediately that Johnnie was carrying a shoulder holster. Suddenly, things got more serious. I approved of the 1934 Hudson Club Sedan; it was $1,229. We used the Terraplane as a trade-in which brought the price down to $954. Johnnie paid cash of course. When the salesman returned and told us the car would not be ready until the morning, I could see the anger on his face. We planned to be in Phoenix by the twenty-fifth. As the dealership wanted our business, they agreed to put us up for the night at the Roosevelt Hotel. We agreed to the deal.

JC grabbed our luggage and placed it in the backseat. He was then forced to sit with us in the front seat between Johnnie and me, plus my bulldog puppy. I admit in the cold confined car with Johnnie's several days old body odor, the puppy smell, and my perfume, it was cramped.

We pulled up to the hotel entrance and JC jumped out and pulled our bags from the backseat.

He commented: "My it feels like you are carrying around an anvil."

I smiled. "A lady has to have considerable baggage when traveling." It seemed to appease him.

It ended up taking more than two days to get our new car, and Johnnie was anxious. It took some real zest to keep him placated. It was around the time when the Lindbergh baby disappeared, and everyone was suspicious of people. In our case, Mr. Davis, the manager of the car dealership, was concerned about our presence. Most people traveling want to visit the sights; however, we had no interest in any of them, plus our luggage and the heavy bags. I admit now we looked highly conspicuous. Our car arrived on the morning of the twenty-first. We grabbed our baggage and quietly left the hotel under a cloak of darkness. Years later, I read how the employees of the hotel learned that the discreet well-dressed clean-shaven man was indeed John Dillinger.

In Johnnie's haste to get to Phoenix, I could not help the notion that it was a bad idea. My gut was telling me, "Don't go to Tucson."

Then the closer we got the more frustrated I got, although my objections fell on deaf ears with Johnnie. Our conversations were basically on the fact that my marriage was not annulled from  Welton. He could not understand my reasoning for marrying such a man. It was during a dark time for me; the grief over losing my son lay heavy on my soul. Welton was my first love, exciting and dangerous at the same time. We were looking for someone to take care of us. In a moment of passion, it seemed like the right thing to do and gave me an income. Most of the people in Chicago were starving, and money was almost non-existent. If you were able to find a job, it was usually part-time and minimum wage. Or they were short-term temp jobs. Just like me working at the hotel checking in hats. Johnnie did not fully understand what life was like being a Native American woman in the '30s. Well, not just then; I guess our plight started long before I was ever born and continued for many years later. The discussion on several occasions during our drive got heated about why I married Welton and did not divorce him sooner.

I truly believe the police were getting close, and Johnnie had become public enemy number one. The pressure was getting to the whole gang, hence the reason for running to other states. It's just something about the timing that felt wrong. Several of the gang members had left for  Tucson several weeks before us: Charles Makley, Russell Clark, and Opal Long. They had rented separate rooms on the top floor of the Congress Hotel. And Johnnie found himself anxious, he wanted back in the game. They all thrived on the adrenaline rush. At first the danger scared me, but even I got used to the thrill of being chased. But Johnnie kept me hidden from the internal dealings of the gang's plans. However, spend enough time with anyone and you will pick up their lifestyle habits.

When we arrived in Tucson, we rented rooms at the Arizona Tourist Court some distance from everyone else. But Johnnie never wanted us too close. We had separate rooms as well from Harry Pierpont and Mary Kinder. After settling into our rooms, we hooked up with the rest of the gang. Most of the others had been mingling around town at all the tourist traps, bars, and dance halls. I have to admit the environment was unlike anything we had ever seen. There was barely a blade of grass or flower; only dirt, cactus and rocks as far as the eye could see. However, in January compared to Chicago, it was heavenly. I knew deep down Johnnie and the gang had big plans for Tucson; nonetheless, the best-laid plans often go awry.

The following morning, after we got up and ate, Opal rang saying their hotel was on fire and they had to get out, but their luggage was still inside. As I found out later when the firemen arrived, two men had attempted to put a ladder against the burning building and were climbing up to retrieve their luggage. When the fireman caught them, they agreed to get the luggage and the guys tipped them twenty dollars, which seemed very suspicious. What the firemen did not know was that the bags held their Tommy guns and ammo. Johnnie was not too happy when we got the news. The firemen recognized the men as part of the Dillinger Gang and called the police. The hotel and house were immediately staked out and everyone but Jonnie was arrested. The trip to Tucson started a downhill spiral in our relationship and the Dillinger Gang.

We were unaware at the time the police had arrested Russell and Opal at the house on East Second, and Johnnie and I showed up later that evening just before dark. I  waited in the car while Johnnie got out and started to walk up to the house. My instincts were right, the pit in my stomach grew stronger every day. As I sat in the car the scene unfolded right before my eyes. Just as Johnnie reached the steps in front of the house, he looked down and realized there were bloodstains on the cement and started to turn around, but Detective Herron snuck out from behind a bush, meeting Johnnie square in the face. They were about five feet apart, and I thought for sure it was going to be an old west shootout.

I heard the detective say, "Put your hands up!"

Johnnie had a look on his face of utter surprise. I knew we were not getting out of this one. He shouted again, "Up or I'll bore you."

Johnnie raised his hands slowly. "What's this all about?"

A few seconds later, two other officers walked up from behind the house across the deck. Herron hollered, "Cover the car!"

They both nodded, "Yes, boss."

I watched the officers approach the car as Herron grabbed Johnnie by his shirt collar and pushed him toward the police car. When Johnnie was safely in the car, they came and got me. It was not the first time I went to jail and hoped it might be my last.

We spent the night in the Pima County Jail, until our arraignment the next morning. Of course, the arrests were front-page news. The next morning, we were taken in shackles to the court for a bail hearing.

I was sitting in the front of the courthouse behind the defendant's table when they walked Johnnie past. I smiled, and he paused to bend down and kiss me. They did let Johnnie and I sit next to each other, which gave me some stability.

It was hard to keep my face away from all the photographers. My time to face the judge was dead last, and I sat through all the hearings before they got to me. Essentially there was no evidence, so Ann

Martin (Me) had to be released. Mary was taken to jail, but Opal and I were freed.

It took us days of fighting to get some of our personal belongings back; however, we ended up with the clothes on our backs. We were left penniless in Tucson. Our attorney tried to demand they give us back the money in our wallets; however, it was held pending  investigation. I did at least get my dog back. We were finally done with the Pima jail on January 30, 1934. In my time with Johnnie, I learned a few things. Opal and I devised a plan to try and get the utility money on the house back. It was only twenty dollars, but that seemed like a million that day. We headed for the utility company and met a man named Paul Hardwicke.

We entered, poised for the upcoming events. "Hello, our husbands rented a home on 927 East Second Street, and we would like to get the security deposit back." I smiled.

"Certainly, we will refund your money. Do you have a receipt?" My heart sank.

"The men have gone, and we are left here alone with no money. We ma—" I started to cry. "May never see them again…."

Opal jumped in, "Please, can you make an exception just this one time? We are 2000 miles from home with nothing. Not even a place to sleep."

Paul smiled. "Alright, this one time. Please sign this card and I will advance sixteen dollars." I knew from the look on his face he had read the papers, so he knew who we were. But, gratefully, he still took pity on us.

Our only option left was buying train tickets to Detroit. Opal had relatives in Kansas City, Missouri. Once we got there, I could get some money to go home. My sister was still living in Chicago, so I could stay with her. Besides, at the time the only thing I cared about was Johnnie.

The whole incident in Tucson left me extremely somber, as I did not understand why

Johnnie was being so anxious. It was completely unlike him to be reckless. When I finally got back to Chicago, Opal stayed in Detroit with her relatives for a stint.

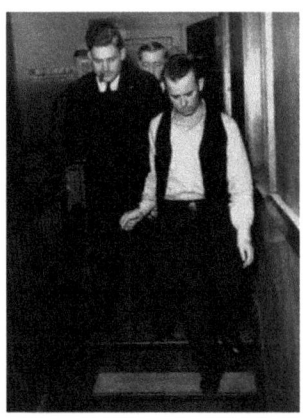

I can still remember the cold when I stepped out of the train station, it chilled me to the bone. My first stop was finding Anne, and as usual, she took me in. It felt like déjà vu after leaving the boarding school; penniless and broken. The love of my life was in jail. I had no home nor a future without Johnnie.

Chapter Ten:

Charged with Murder

I can honestly say the next few months of my life were excruciating. Johnnie was in jail being charged with murder, which left me alone once again. The gang scrambled around trying to piece the plan together to try to get him out of jail before the trial on March 13, 1934. After the arraignment in the Pima County Courthouse, several states were in an extradition war on who got precedence of the trial. Needless to say, Indiana won the battle. I can remember the fear that ran through my body like it was yesterday, sitting in that courtroom with Johnnie. He was so calm, patient even. He just leaned over and kissed me. "Keep hold of yourself, honey. They've got nothing on you." It helped somewhat, but inside I was terrified.

The decision to send him to Indiana came from the charges for killing patrolman William O'Malley. At the time, it took five transfers for them to finally land in Chicago. All total I believe thirty-two officers escorted him to Lake County Jail, which is where he met Sheriff Lillian Holly.

I had a deep respect for her as she was a woman holding a man's job in the '30s. She was a single parent, whose husband died and left her to raise children alone. The Lake Country Jail residence sat above the jail, and the cells were below the main building. As I  understood, she was upstairs baking cookies when Johnnie and his group were escaping below. The whole incident ruined her law enforcement career, and she never spoke of the details until the day she died.

Many years later, one of the photos that appeared across the media said that Johnnie was posing as Robert Estill signaled for the gang to smuggle him in a gun. Robert's career was ruined as well after posing with public enemy number one.

 Johnnie immediately hired Louis Piquett. At the time, he was a nobody in defense litigation; however, that would soon change forever. Once things settled down a bit, I made it to Indiana and Louis got me in to see Johnnie. Let me say, Sheriff Holley took her job seriously. The only way I was able to see him was by claiming to be his wife, but then was strip-searched. Being Piquett was an attorney, he was exempt from the search. I had a message from Red Hamilton and money to pass off to Johnnie. So, Louis distracted the guard while I gave him the  note and ten dollars. Red was not in favor of blowing up the jail to get Johnnie out. But that was not going to stop him, believe me.

We exchanged our affections, and they rushed me out quickly. All Johnnie told me was be ready, as more information would be passed along very soon. As a woman in her twenties, the chaos was exciting in many ways. We were in love. There are times, thinking back, I would have done almost anything for Johnnie.

After some serious bribery, Johnnie was able to get a gun; however, it's not what you are thinking. It turned out to be carved of wood, probably the most  iconic item associated with Dillinger. The gun was supposed to replicate a Colt .38; if you saw the real item in person it was very impressive. Crudely carved on the right side is "Colt .38", and on the left, which kept in tune with Johnnie's humor, is "Pat Mar 3, 1934," the day he escaped. One inmate took off with him: Herbert Youngblood.

During the escape, he was able to snag a Tommy gun. They made their way out of the jail kitchen and out the side door of the alley into the parking garage where Sheriff Holly's car was parked. The two stole the car and headed for Chicago. I was given word to purchase a car, of course, a 33 Essex Terraplane V8, as it  was one of the fastest cars on the road at the time. Our agreed meeting place was on Ardmore and Kenmore Avenues. Until that day, the FBI had no jurisdiction over Johnnie, but once he stole the Sheriff's car and crossed state lines, they got involved. It became a nationwide search to find him.

  I was sitting in Piquett's office when a call came through that Johnnie had escaped the jail and was on his way to Chicago to pick me up and wanted money. When he got off the phone, my only thoughts were that the police would shoot him on sight.

  Piquett shouted, "Quit your squawking, they'll probably never see his face again."

I never truly liked that man. He had issues with women in general, especially Native American women. But we needed confirmation, so Piquett called the Crown Point Jail. They told us what we already knew, and that no one was killed or harmed, and they stole the Sheriff's car. Nevertheless, the police were multiplying outside quickly. A few minutes later, Louis ordered me to leave the office out the back door and head to his secretary's apartment on Wellington Avenue. Piquett and his thugs followed shortly in a taxi. O'Leary stayed in his office waiting for the call from Dillinger; per a later conversation, it was at about three. He only asked, "Where will I go?"

Outside the apartment building, Piquett leaned against the wall wearing a hat and full coat. He saw the car pull up and he moved to the curb. Herbert was lying on the floor in the backseat holding two Tommy guns.

"Where do we stay, is this the place?" Johnnie asked.

"No…. We need to talk first, then I will take you. Park the car and come inside the lobby."

Johnnie parked the car curb side and walked in behind Louis. He was the most beautiful sight I have ever seen. I leaped into his arms and kissed his sensuous lips. Piquett led them upstairs where his secretary lived, but she refused to let them stay. So, we decided to go stay with my sister in the meantime.

Piquett came downstairs to meet us a few minutes later and asked him for money. "Come over about seven tonight and bring money." We left with a roll of cash totaling three hundred. Johnnie thanked him and we headed out to the car.

By the time we got to my sister's place, it was getting hot in the car. We almost stopped several times to make love, but in light of the manhunt, it was best we waited. I could tell Johnnie missed me. He had not been that passionate with me before that night. The thrill of being chased drove our ambitions wild. My sister left for work right after we showed up, so the whole place was ours for hours. We stopped and I made some dinner about six and Piquett showed up right at seven.

Johnnie regaled us with the story of what happened in the jail. His intelligence never surprised me; he was so far ahead of most everyone. By the time they figured out what was going on, Johnnie was already gone.

Afterward, Piquett asked, "Hey, am I ever going to see any money from you?"

Johnnie burst out, "What? My father hired that other lawyer, did he not pay you anything? He took my dad's money and pocketed it, then. You tell him to cough up the five Gs or I am coming after him." Piquett nodded.

He left a short time later, and we made love again and again for most of the night. It was almost noon when we got up. Johnnie spent the afternoon talking with his new gang members. John Hamilton arranged everything with the Nelson Gang.

We took off right after dark, out a side entrance of the apartment building and headed for

Minnesota. It had been just thirty-six hours after the escape. When you're young, smart decisions don't always take precedence over life. By this time, I knew what was going on and looked the other way. I was in love! Life was exciting, and Johnnie made me a part of his life without strings attached.

Nelson's gang arranged for a place at the Santa Monica Apartments on South Girard Avenue in Minneapolis. Our cover names were "Mr. and Mrs. Olson." I went inside first and gave the janitor fifty dollars and we prepped the place. I distinctly remember Johnnie wiring the drapes closed. He did not want anyone seeing the weapons thrown on the living room floor. Gratefully, all the places we stayed in were furnished.

Johnnie and the Nelson Gang seemed to have an immediate rapport with each other as if they'd known one another for years. But, at the time we were not aware that Baby Face Nelson was highly unstable. I remember reading a newspaper article on him the day before we arrived, where he and one of his sidekicks got in a heated chase with a salesman heading home to his family. Needless to say, Nelson shot and killed him right in front of his home. I worried about him every second after reading that. I think, to Nelson, it gave him the prestige to work with Johnnie.

The bank robbery at Security National Bank and Trust Company went badly, not what Johnnie and his gang were used to handling. I know Nelson lost it when one of the tellers hit the button and it went off in the lobby. But for the first time since meeting Johnnie, he needed the money. Nelson clearly had different philosophies in life. The haul got them a total of eight thousand per man, but my life of being in the shadows was about to fade.

After my admittance to the Crown Point Jail, Sheriff Holly was able to track down my true identity. A special agent, Melvin Purvis, interrogated an informant by the name of Ed Shouse, during which time he gave up Dewey and Pearl Elliot. At the same time, they told him Johnnie someone might contact me (Ann Martin), his wife. The conversation got heated and Shouse told Melvin that I was known to the gang as Billie. From there, they tracked me to the reservation in Wisconsin. Of course, here is where my failures as a young woman proved reality. Since I never annulled my marriage with Welton, it gave me a record on file with the FBI. They immediately contacted Leavenworth and confirmed my connection to Welton. They found my real name on Welton's approved mailing list as Evelyn Frechette. Although, it was spelled wrong. My fingerprints were sent to the agent in charge. An apprehension order was issued, and two thousand copies filtered their way to law enforcement over the next two weeks.

Over the last several months, Johnnie's frame of mind had changed, especially after the Tucson affair. I was worried. His calm, casual demeanor vanished and things became erratic; almost out of control at times. I admit, my stress outlet was drinking; it made me feel as though I fit in with the gang. But, after my alias was exposed, life with Johnnie changed for me. I could not go home to Wisconsin because of the fear and damage it might cause to my family. Not to mention, my reputation on the reservation had been badly tarnished. A wave of depression overtook my soul, unlike anything I had ever experienced. Suddenly, I found myself on the run and among total strangers. Johnnie was running around the country with the Nelson Gang trying to get money for all his expenses, and the only time we spent together was a few hours here and thereafter one robbery in transit to another. We'd make love and enjoy our bodies for a short time, but that feeling faded quickly after he left.

Johnnie quickly came to my rescue when he got word of my alias being exposed, so he moved me to Detroit with Opal Long, Russel Clark's mother. Since his affiliation with the Nelson Gang was fading fast, he needed to find other underground contacts he could trust. So, he raced off to St. Paul and met up with Homer Van Meter and John Hamilton.

Since John's original gang members had been killed or captured in the Tucson catastrophe, he had to find new men, and that meant we moved around a lot. I suddenly felt completely lost and out of place.

The new members and their girlfriends did not like me much. So, at the time I clung to the one person with who I connected: Opal Long. We became very close. You would think after all I'd been through with the Indian Boarding School and being raped, then having a child who was mentally and physically disabled, the chaotic lifestyle would be familiar to me. Unfortunately, it was having the opposite effect. I found myself in a house full of people, children, animals, strange men and their girlfriends in and out constantly. I shared a room with Opal when Johnnie was not at the house, and believe me he was seldom around. If he showed up, it was to get clothes, eat, or shower. Our communication had dwindled to making love. Don't get me wrong, I enjoyed every minute, but the environment forced a major depression to envelop my body.

In the time I spent in St. Paul, the only time we left the house was to make phone calls, and that was only in pairs of two. We dressed in overcoats and hats to hide our faces. The police had the house under constant surveillance. In my depressive state, I turned to alcohol. It seemed to be the only thing that took the pain away. Since I was young and had been raised a Native American, I loved my heritage. It helped me feel a connection to my home and family; granted my young home life was not grand and we had been dirt poor, but it was a stable environment. But now, with the FBI on to me and knowing my real name, it sent me into a tailspin. I found out from my sister that a family relative had died, and she wanted to tell me about the funeral service; nonetheless, it was something I could never attend under the circumstances.

    I cannot begin to tell you how much of a strain the situation I was in put on my mental state. All of a sudden, I lost all attachment to my family. The option to go home vanished, as well as talking to or seeing my sisters. It was not until sometime later that the news of my relationship with Johnnie got around the reservation and basically blackballed me, as if I was taking sides with the Western culture. It could not have been further from the truth, but I learned the true meaning of what prejudice meant.

Yes, that sounds like an oxymoron, but this time it was against me by my own people. I had become the outsider and it left me terrified. Suddenly the one place I felt comfortable and loved was gone. Now, I was stuck in the Western culture without a safety net.

The year 1934 as I remember was the worst of the Great Depression. Homelessness was rampant, and unemployment had increased, despite what the records were saying. There was fighting in the streets, and unsettled tension with everyone around the country no matter where you went. Just the fact we were living in the city made matters horribly worse. Not to mention, America was about to enter the war; tension had been building in Germany with Hitler. Their government was planning the same eradication of the Jewish people as America had done with the Native Americans. This would lead to the  death of millions of Jewish citizens and others deemed "undesirable" during the Holocaust. I knew of their plight first-hand, which was why the issue had such an effect on my soul. So, my outlet became drinking.

One day, Johnnie got up early and told me he had some things to do but to be ready as we were leaving the house and going to a new place. It was a heartfelt goodbye with Opal, she had been my rock. I can remember leaving the house wondering if I'd ever see her again. She agreed to take my bulldog, and Johnnie and I headed off to a new apartment. We registered under "Mr. and Mrs. Stevens". The place was situated around the corner from Eddie Green, one of Johnnie's new gang members. Needless to say, however, we were again unwelcome. It seemed that no matter where I went during that part of my life, no one wanted me around. The only person who truly loved me was Johnnie. Green and his partner had been living a solid life in his underground world and were not eager to accept outsiders, especially Dillinger. Although, begrudgingly, they took him into their affiliation. I knew from the moment of our meeting, their detest for us showed brightly.

My days turned from horrible to almost unbearable. I tried to advocate for my man, but even that was difficult, since Bess hated him. She thought he was an arrogant asshole. Luckily, our affiliation was limited. She gave me lip service while we visited, but drew the line at entertaining Johnnie. Anytime we came over she scurried to the kitchen and stayed there during our visit.

A short time later, we arranged for another party. It was exciting, since Opal, her sister, and Pat would be coming. It felt good to be among family again. The next morning, as always, everyone left at different times. Hamilton took off first, followed by Pat and Opal, who went to the store. Shortly after they left, a couple in the apartment called the police and two FBI agents showed up at the door.

"Hello, can I help you?" I asked.

"We are looking for Carl, does he live here?"

In my flustered state of mind, and all the commotion, I said, "I don't know any Carl."

"Are you sure?" he replied.

After thinking for a few minutes, I responded, "Oh, yes I remember he does. But is out right now." The men insisted on coming inside to wait, and at the time, what choice did I have? So, I made the excuse that I was not dressed, and they would have to wait in the hall for a few minutes while I got dressed.

I ran in the bedroom to wake Johnnie, "What? What did you tell them?"

"I told them, I have to get dressed and would be back in a few minutes. What happens now…. are we trapped?"

"Don't worry, we have been in worse spots. Just get your things while I get dressed. Just stay quiet."

I held back the tears and struggled to quickly pack my bags. But while we were rushing, there were gunshots in the hallway.

We looked at each other. "Stay here—" Johnnie grabbed a pistol and headed for the door. A few seconds later, he yelled, "Evelyn…. It's clear! Go to the garage, I'll be right behind you."

I took off down the hallway and ran for the garage. Johnnie was right behind me, shooting back to keep the feds away from us. Then right in the alley he got hit with one of the bullets. It knocked him to his knees and the luggage went flying.

"Get the bags if you can… go get to the car." I nodded and grabbed several bags.

The bullets were flying down the alley as we ran for the Essex. "You drive, go to Eddie Green's apartment."

"Me…?"

"I can't drive, I've been shot." I reluctantly agreed. We headed for the Greens' as he knew they would not snitch us out.

When we arrived, Johnnie stayed in the car, and I ran upstairs to get Eddie. He took us to a medical facility, Doctor May. After looking at Johnnie's leg, the doc wanted us to stay in a private place for a night or two with a nurse. Luckily, the bullet had gone straight through, so there was no real damage. By Saturday he was up and walking around.

I found out later that our stop for help with the Greens had tipped off the FBI. After they left, us Eddie, and Beth moved out of the apartment and had arranged to have our things sent to an undisclosed location. As Eddie arrived at the old apartment, the maid threw everything out in the hallway and told him to get lost. It was a signal, and he knew something was wrong. He ran to the parking garage and found himself in an all-out gunfight. As Eddie was exiting the building, the agent covered his car with bullets from a machine gun. Beth heard the gunfire and ran downstairs, but by the time she arrived, it was too late. They had shot Eddie and she was arrested. He died from his injuries shortly after. Once the news of his death hit us, we moved out under the cover of darkness for Mooresville, Indiana. It would be my first time at Johnnie's family farm.

Chapter Eleven:

A Back-Country Road

We hit the dirt running as we high tailed it out of town. Since the news of Ed Greene hit us, the reality of the situation smacked us both in the face. The feds and police were closing in fast, and my gut wrenched in pain with concern over our well-being. But Johnnie always stayed positive no matter what happened, at least with me anyway.

The trip out to Mooresville was actually fun. We took every back-countryside road available. Johnnie knew the roads well, I admit. It took us three days, but it gave us a break from all the chaos. We  laughed, talked, and just relaxed, like a special honeymoon, the kind I always dreamed of having with Dillinger. We even talked about getting my marriage annulled and retiring in Mexico. Johnnie told me he had been stashing money aside in a secret place just for our future. At the time, I desperately wanted to believe him, but no matter what he said, I could not shake the horrible feeling nagging my soul. Nonetheless, I think we both just wanted to forget everything and just be a young couple in love for the next few days. In hindsight, I honestly believe Johnnie wanted a chance to say goodbye to his father.

We pulled in on April 7, in the early morning. The house was dark and still, so we huddled up in the backseat of the car and made love before dawn. When the sun rose just after six, we headed inside. His dad was already up and moving around.

I'll never forget his face when he saw his son. "Johnnie…." He choked back the tears. "I did not know you were coming. You should have called—" Johnnie smiled.

"I wanted to surprise you, Pops."

"Oh, I don't care. Sit and have some coffee. Where is Evelyn?"

"She went to the restroom."

"I'm glad you two came to see us."

I walked in a few minutes later; he jumped up and wrapped his arm around my neck. "Evelyn, come here girl."

"It's so nice to see you, John," I replied.

"What's this John? Call me Dad."

I smiled. "Alright."

"Would you like some coffee?"

"Yes, please," I replied.

"Oh, you both must be starved. Audrey will be up soon, and we can make breakfast for everyone."

"Okay, Dad. Sounds good," Johnnie replied.

I watched him talk to his dad with such love. The joy oozed from his face. It was a side I rarely saw and loved with all my heart.

We sat in the kitchen for almost an hour and drank coffee. I got to hear about all the silly stuff Johnnie did as a kid. As with most parents, they liked to regale guests with stories from the past. Audrey got up a short time later, and I helped her make breakfast for everyone. I can remember Francis, his little sister, she was a doll, and Hubert, a handsome lad just like his brother and father. He had bought a new car and asked Johnnie to help with work on the engine in the garage. They spent most the afternoon fixing things, as the  men said. While they were busy, us girls cooked and cleaned. Audrey made coconut cream pie, as she said it was Johnnie's favorite. Then later, John Sr. came in and helped Francis wash and dry dishes, while we took pictures.

Johnnie and his brother came in later. "Hey, we got the car running and are going to take it for a drive."

"Okay," I replied, "have fun."

The two were headed into Indianapolis for parts, but I think they just wanted to get drinks at the bar. On the way home, Hubert fell asleep at the wheel and crashed the car. I guess they had to limp it home a few miles, but by the time they arrived, both of them were laughing like a pair of hyenas. We settled in for a night of just fun and laughing with everyone. They made me feel at home, as with my own.

Johnnie and I snuggled in just after one. It was the first night of sleep in a long time that I'd felt safe. We woke up just before dawn, as the family was going to church on Sunday morning. Under the circumstances, we thought it best for us to stay hidden at the house. We had no complaints, as it gave us more alone time. I loved having Johnnie to myself for a few days. Usually, other gang members or women and children were running around everywhere. Most of which, I had no use for, nor did they for me. It was funny back then, the entire time we stayed at the Dillinger farm I never had one drink; the time was a sobering experience.

After the family came home from services, John and the boys went out and gathered up two fresh chickens for dinner. It had been years since I had chicken fresh off the farm. It took me back to helping my mother catch and clean the chickens when I was a kid. A job I hated; cutting off their heads and bleeding them out, then having to boil them to get all the pin feathers out. *Oh, I don't miss that for anything.* Johnnie and I relaxed on the sofa; it had a perfect view of the driveway. Reality was creeping its way back into our lives.

Our evening conversation centered around the toy gun Johnnie used to break out of jail; however, I really don't think he liked the topic of conversation, as he kept changing the tone. But he pacified the family. According to John Sr., a carload of state troopers and policemen had come to the house many times searching the place for any sign of John.

At one point during dinner, John Sr. asked point-blank, "Johnnie, have you killed anyone in all your business dealings, especially in Chicago? I want to pray for your soul if you had."

John looked very solemn. "I was in Florida at the time Dad, and no I have never killed anyone and don't intend to."

"I am glad to hear that, son."

"But Dad, if it comes down to going back to prison and being caught, I will shoot my way out." His dad shook his head.

The room got quiet for the next several minutes until Audrey spoke up. "Anyone for pie?" She smiled.

"I will, it sounds yummy," I spoke up.

Johnnie grinned. "Me too, Audrey. Thank you."

"You better since I made it especially for you." Everyone laughed.

I went to help in the kitchen and deliver the servings, and while out of earshot, Audrey said, "Please, Evelyn, take care of him. It will break my father's heart when he gets killed."

Her statement caught me off guard. "I will, promise." I knew it was a false commitment because she was right. It was not if, it was when. "Well, let's just enjoy the night. Leave all the mess alone for now." She agreed.

"Alright everyone, who wants pie?" I asked while sauntering into the living room.

We ate until our stomachs ached. Most of the time, we got junk food from a convenience store somewhere on the fly. But that night we were special; it was a night that would live in my heart forever.

The next morning, I woke up late and Johnnie was already up and moving. He knew we had stayed too long, and it was time to leave. I could see the stress slowly creeping over his face again. I wanted to cry and just stay there forever; I didn't care about the money. The only thing I wanted was to live married to the man I loved. We gathered our things and stayed for lunch, then about four we headed out. But before we left, Audrey wanted pictures. So, Johnnie grabbed one of the toy wooden pistols and posed. We laughed until we cried. Then, his dad begged for one of us together.

Years later, I read a newspaper interview with his father. "I had been living the life of a parent who had been informed their child had terminal cancer. I knew that there could only be one ending, death." The words broke my heart because I could feel his pain.

We drove straight through to Chicago that night; the last place I wanted to be. Opal Long contacted Johnnie and assured him that Larry Streng could put us in a hideout. He had dated Opal for many years, and Johnnie trusted him. However, three days prior, Larry ran his mouth to the wrong person. It happened to be an informant; he told them of the exact meeting time and place. It was scheduled at the U Tavern in Chicago.

On April 9, we arrived in town and met with Arthur O'Leary. Johnnie asked him about Piquette, I guess he was in Washington at the time. While meeting with O'Leary, he made a confession that almost knocked me to my knees: "I want him to refer me to a plastic surgeon who can change my face. I am tired of running."

After we left O'Leary, I asked, "Is that true? You want to leave this life?"

"I do, Evelyn. After spending time with my family, it reminded me of the good life. This running is getting old. I love you and want to grow old together. We can get your marriage annulled and leave town." Those were the best words I had ever heard.

By the time our conversation was over, we had arrived at the bar to meet with Larry. "Okay, you know the drill, right?" John asked.

"Yes.... I love you, be right back." I gave him a long, passionate kiss, and he smiled. It took everything I had to leave the car that day. I wanted him to just drive away.

My job was to go inside and then step back out so John would know the coast was clear. As I got out of the car, a sickening feeling came over my soul. But it was too late to turn back. I walked into the bar, and before anything else could happen, two officers grabbed me.

The agents tried for several minutes to get Johnnie's whereabouts but nothing was going to make me squeal. I mocked them for some time. "He was sitting in the back of the bar. You idiots walked right past him."

"We have been here for hours; now, where is he?" one of them demanded. My lips were sealed.

"Fine, then you're going to jail—" I shrugged while cringing inside. I knew that my tactics had stalled them long enough for Johnnie to getaway.

I was taken to the federal offices in the banker's building for the night. No one wanted the public to know of my arrest. If they kept it quiet, the gang would not have time to escape. The next morning, April 10, two agents showed up to question me. One was Harold Reinecke and the second was

Murry Faulkner. Over the next two days, they took turns questioning me. Needless to say, their tactics were less than humane.

On May 15, my trial started and some startling discoveries were exposed about my arrest and holding before arraignment. As I said, the hatred for the Native Americans was still alive and well. The agent's words exactly were, "You are a dirty Indian." It felt like déjà vu. I had been portaled back to the boarding school where they had scrubbed out my private parts with lye. We were kicked in the stomach, dragged around by our hair, and slapped or punched in the face repeatedly.

I admit the idea of dying over the few days was very real. They left me locked in an interrogation room with no food, drink, or sleep for two days. Of course, during the trial, a whole different story evolved.

Louis Piquett questioned each agent, Reinecke went first: "Isn't it true, Mr. Reinecke, that you slapped the girl in the face?"

"I did not slap the girl at any time," he replied.

"Isn't it a fact that you continually went like this repeatedly?" He mimed slapping.

"Oh. I believe that can be explained."

"Yes, please, by all means, go ahead."

"Miss Frechette had a manner of not looking at me while talking, making it impossible to hear what she was saying. So, I would take my two fingers and place them under her chin, forcing her head back in my direction, saying, 'Please, Evelyn, look at me when you are talking or answering questions'."

"Miss Frechette tells a completely different story, care to explain that?" Then, Louis looked at me. "By the way, did you hear Agent Reinecke say those words on several occasions? And ask you to look at him during questioning?"

I replied, "Yes, I did hear him say that."

"And did you oblige?" Piquett asked me.

"Well, he did not say 'lift your chin', nor did he say please."

"But he did have his hand under your chin?"

"Yes, he did have his hand on my chin, but to hit it up, instead of lifting it."

"And were you or were you not faced with a lot of lights in that room?" Louis asked me.

"When I arrived the first night, Monday night, I was. I remember one man asking me if the light was too bright. Then he intentionally shone it in my face."

"And can you please tell us what happened then?"

"I was questioned, intensively, without being given food, water, or sleep for the next two days. The only time I was allowed to sleep was in the hallway before court. As a matter of fact, these are the same clothes they arrested me in."

"So, you mean to tell me and the court that you have not been able to change your clothes since the arrest?"

"No sir, nor have I been able to eat much or brush my teeth."

Piquett desperately wanted to secure my release. He understood what would happen if Johnnie broke me out of jail. I would end up dead or on the run the rest of my life. Therefore, the best option for my life was overcoming the charges.

After court that night, they locked me back in the same room, where they allowed me to sleep for a few hours. In the middle of the night, I was awakened by 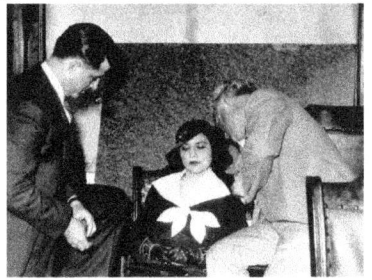 three agents who took me to an apartment at 1036 N Dearborn Street. We stayed there until the warrant was obtained for my transfer to St. Paul.

My official bail was set at $60,000, which Louis fought like hell to get reduced. It was an amount that none of us had to spend. I knew deep down Johnnie would do everything in his power to get me freed, but neither Piquett or O'Leary wanted to pursue that option, since it would have been a blood bath and would destroy their careers.

Johnnie had kept to his word at this point and sought out a plastic surgeon, but the cost was extensive. The only way for his plan to work was to continue the robberies. Since it was too  hot in St. Paul, the gang searched for an out-of-the-way place. On a lake near Mercer, Wisconsin was Little Bohemia Lodge. Johnnie and his buddies met at the lodge to arrange their future operations. Shortly after their arrival, a raid took place, led by Melvin Purvis. A gunfight broke out and one agent was killed, and two others wounded. Johnnie escaped out a second story bedroom window. At that point, he got desperate and made some rash decisions.

The jury deliberated for several weeks but finally came back with guilty. All of the previous efforts failed. I was fined a thousand dollars and sentenced to two years in federal prison in Milan, Michigan. Johnnie did come through and paid my fine, routed through my sister, Patsy. Piquett pledged to file an appeal, but it never showed up in the court records. I cannot say for sure either way, except it was apparent that he wanted to be done with defending the Dillinger Gang members.

Piquett came to visit me on a few occasions after the sentencing, and I gave him messages for Johnnie, asking him to break me out; nonetheless, it would have been suicide. Fate had spoken, and I had to accept the decision. It was only two years, and I suppose the time away from all the chaos did me good. However, those feelings come from hindsight. At the time, my emotions ran wild with distress, frustration, and agony.

Chapter Twelve:

Sentenced to Prison

The whole concept of going to prison was no different than any other Native American experience in the US at the time. We had spent more than 100 years fighting for our very survival. The Western culture wanted us dead and stopped at nothing to succeed. So, my going to prison taught me another valuable life lesson. The only difference this time was, it was my choice to be with John Dillinger. Other than love, that is my only explanation. When you grow up in poverty the way we did, you find yourself seeking affection from anyone willing to pay you some attention. Our situation happened to be compounded by the  Great Depression and the Dust Bowl, then pile on World War II and you get a recipe for disaster.

As we drove around the countryside running from the police, the US was under an incredible drought, the likes no one had ever seen. It started in late 1933 when strong winds from Canada hit the farmlands of South Dakota. It stripped the topsoil from the ground, then continued with one storm after another. It was followed by one of the driest winters in history with no rain through the spring, so we went into summer in a bad way. On May 9, 1934, a two-day strong wind hit the Great Plains, removing what was left of the topsoil and blew 12 million pounds of dust across the country to New York City. After this, the drought continued into the next year. Another storm hit on April 14, 1935; we called it "Black Sunday." When twenty black blizzards spread over the Great Plains, the dust was so bad you could not see five feet in front of you. It turned the daylight to darkness for several days. I remember reading the following clipping in the newspaper. The incident called Black Sunday became known as dust storms.

"Spearman and Hansford County have been in a cloud of dust for the past week. Ever since

Friday of last week, there hasn't been a day pass but what the county was besieged [sic] with a blast of wind and dirt. On rare occasions when the wind did subside for a period of hours, the air has been so filled with dust that the town appeared to be overhung by a fog cloud. Because of this long siege of dust and every building being filled with it, the air has become stifling to breathe and many people have developed sore throats and dust colds as a result." — Spearman Reporter, March 21, 1935

    People were dying from dust pneumonia caused by the dirty air. I knew people in Kansas that were dying from high fevers, chest pain, and breathing problems due to the dust. The Red Cross even traveled around distributing dust masks. Many musicians started singing songs about the Great Dust Bowl. The effects were devastating, to say the least; driving around the Great Plains you could see machinery buried in dunes. It started looking like the great plains of the Serengeti. Newspapers reported that 3.5 million people moved out of the Plains states and headed to the West Coast, like California,

Arizona, New Mexico, etc. As the devastation spread, it affected everyone, not just farmers. People needed to feed their families, so teachers, lawyers, and small businessmen became farmers to support the population. A common saying was "Broke, baby's sick, and now car trouble."

Shortly after my release from prison, President Roosevelt developed a project to create windbreaks in the Great Plains. It was part of the Soil Erosion Project. By the end of 1942 over 220 million trees had been planted. The trees started from the Canadian border and stretched to the Brazos River. Later that year, another program began to help put people to work and conserve our natural resources. It was called the Civilian Conservation Corps. Needless to say, the program was a huge hit, since it supplied families with shelter, clothing, and food. Plus, they got thirty dollars a month. Many Native Americans participated in the program since our lands had been stripped of life-sustaining resources as well.

The CCC created an Indian division that was separate from the federally recognized tribes, *The Indian Emergency Conservation Work.* Of course, it was another way for Western culture to force segregation. Native men worked on building roads, bridges, clinics, and shelters along with other public works near their reservations. We were acknowledged as camps, but no permanent shelters were ever built. Native Americans had to move their families from one project to the next; however, they did receive a rental allowance in their pay. The next year after its installation, Congress passed the Indian Reorganization Act of 1934. It ended allotments and helped preserve tribal lands. My people were encouraged to re-establish self-government. Of the eighty-five thousand involved in the program, forty thousand left the work and returned to the reservation for city jobs supporting the war effort.

One more action by the government that disgusted most Native Americans was the drought relief service starting in June 1934. I was still in prison at that time. The DRS came and bought cattle for the farmers who were devastated from the Dust Bowl. In the beginning, the prices ranged from fourteen to twenty a head. The part that sickened me had to do with families starving, because even if they had the money for food, it did not mean it could be used to buy livestock. The program eventually bought almost 8.3 million head of livestock, yet fifty percent of those were killed, or worse, driven over cliffs. Instead of packaging these animals for meat to feed the population, they were killed. Another atrocity by Western culture; my people kill for the most part to survive and feed our families, not for money or power.

I admit, however, being in prison kept a constant roof over my head, clothes on my back, and most of the time, food to eat. The prison was opened on April 6, 1933, but only held female inmates. Then in 1939, it transferred to a male correctional facility. Their programs had a familiar ring, recidivism to bring reconciliation to the victims of the community, and inmate personal transformation using the participant's commitment to faith. It seemed that I went from one government program to change my culture to another. My love for Johnnie went deep, and he looked beyond the color of my skin or heritage, unlike most of society at the time. Our time was spent learning how to cook and clean; basically, to become compliant citizens once released.

As I watched from the side-lines, my heart went out to Johnnie. He was not the same after my verdict. In many ways, I was his foundation. It was like sending a kid into the soda shop with five dollars to spend as they please. We had spent those few days with his family and Johnnie wanted out of the game. He planned to have plastic surgery done and run away with me. Then I got arrested and all our plans were void. The news left him in a lurch of what to do next. He wanted desperately to break me out of prison, and I know he even drove past the facility several times and knew the act was impossible. I wrote letters and sent them to Pat Carrington, Hamilton's girlfriend, pleading with him to let it go, he would be killed. I found out years later, he sat and cried like a baby at the idea of leaving me in prison. Johnnie felt guilty deep down, because of my verdict.

After the Little Bohemia incident, it changed the face of Dillinger's gang forever. Once they were free Johnnie, Hamilton and Van Meter were on the run toward St. Paul. But just south of town they encountered a roadblock; they changed direction and headed to Chicago. The battle report was not good, as the media proclaimed the city was on high alert. Amid the chase, a truck emerged from the side road and the three of them barely escaped. As they raced on, they had been running on no sleep, and Johnnie was falling asleep at the wheel. So, on an old country dirt road, he pulled the car over and they rested their eyes. About an hour later, the distant sound of gunfire alerted them to the oncoming police cars.

Johnnie started the car and hit the gas, but as they raced off, Hamilton grabbed his hand, "I'm hit!"

"What do you mean you are hit?" Johnnie shouted. "Van Meter take over. See how bad."

"Yes, boss." Van Meter jumped in the back seat, and Hamilton soon followed.

Johnnie glanced at the seat next to him and saw it covered in blood, and it looked bad. He admitted later if they had a rifle in the car, none of the cops would have been able to pursue them. A rifle bullet had punched through the trunk into the backseat and hit Hamilton in the back, exploding his spleen. A few miles ahead on the road, Dillinger saw a couple heading toward them, and slid his car sideways in the road and demanded the couple get out. They moved Hamilton into the new car and sped off. Just outside of Jenkinsville, Wisconsin they found an old shack to get out of sight. Red (Hamilton) was in bad shape, and most likely going to die. But Johnnie did not give up on his friend, so they left him in the shack and headed for town. It happened to be Dubuque, Iowa, a few miles from Piquett's home. Anyways, they purchased medical supplies and newspapers. On the way back, they asked an old farmer for some milk, eggs, and clothing. The old man was so distraught over helping them and being discovered he committed suicide. By the time they got back to Hamilton, he was in terrible pain. Dillinger and Van Meter stayed with him for another three days, and he died on April 27, 1934. But the shooting hit Johnnie hard; they had a connection, as with most of the boys in his gang. Pat Carrington, his girlfriend at the time, received a large sum of money shortly after his death. It made her whole and settled any debts.

The heat was on the last of his gang members, and Johnnie vanished from the public eye. There were rumors he shipped off to Europe, but in reality, it was Piquett making up stories to the press and taking the pressure off Johnnie.  They carried all their stuff around with them, stopping only when they had to eat or sleep.

Johnnie had engaged the services of Arthur O'Leary as an errand boy, so to speak. When Red died on April 30, the boys did not reappear until May 1. When Johnnie called O'Leary and told him to meet them in a designated location, he apprised him of the details on Hamilton's death and instructions on supplies they'd need. But then, for the next eighteen days, O'Leary did not hear anything and feared the worst. When he finally met up with him again, Johnnie was very ill. His temperature was almost 104 and he was weak, so Arthur headed for town to get cough syrup and a pint of whiskey. They met again about midnight and exchanged the medicine. However, much of the conversation revolved around me and if O'Leary had any updates on my trial. He explained Piquett was doing a good job, but there was no verdict as of yet. Johnnie gave him a note to pass along to me.

I nearly collapsed, reading his words: "Evelyn, my dearest.

I miss you terribly and hope you are doing well under the circumstances. Piquett assures me he feels confident about getting you acquitted. However, in the event you are sentenced, I will break you out. The only thing I want more than anything in life is to die in your arms. Please… be safe, I love you.

Yours truly, Johnnie."

My heart sank and the tears rolled down my face. His words were more than I could stand. The last thing I wanted was him to be killed trying to break me out. As O'Leary waited, I jotted down a message.

"My dearest Johnnie.

I love you with all my heart. Please don't try and rescue me from jail. In the event I am convicted, I will gladly do the time, and know you are safe. Then we can run off away from this madness and love each other forever. Be safe. I love you, Billie."

O'Leary met with Johnnie one more time and gave him my note. All he wanted was to make sure their arrangements with the plastic surgeon were set up. Johnnie met up with O'Leary at Jimmie Probasco's house awaiting the surgery.

My trial was in the courthouse, and of course it was a circus with all the press and bystanders. I remember one of the defendants disappeared and the judge nearly threw the case out of court. For a few minutes, I thought the mess was over. But then he ordered everyone to lunch and reconvene in two hours. As the jurors and spectators left, I simply got up and walked out with them. I had almost made it until one of the bailiffs noticed me, with a small fib they ignored the incident and let me go. The rest of the day was spent listening to the prosecutor ramble about all his evidence.

The following day, as court convened, Piquett moved along with the crowd outside when someone softly called his name, "Counsel?"

Piquett turned to find Johnnie. "What the hell are you doing here?"

"I just wanted to know how Billie's trial is going." He chuckled.

"You're hotter than a Tommy gun right in this town!" Johnnie shrugged.

"Can you get her off or not?"

"I can't tell yet. But we will do our best."

"Do everything you can for her. I'll get all of you paid. See you in Chicago."

I admit Piquett did an admirable job in my defence. Maybe he was afraid of Johnnie, I am not sure, but I was grateful for his efforts.

Anyway, he told the jury, "Miss Frechette was willing to go all the way with Public Enemy No 1 out of love. She was not privy to his happenings and should not be punished for one man's mistakes." It only took them one night to deliberate and they found me guilty.

I never lost hope that Johnnie would be waiting for me when I was released. We continued to communicate through O'Leary most of the time, as Piquett stayed clear due to his connection with Dillinger. The idea of spending the rest of my life with Johnnie kept me sane during my incarceration.

Chapter Thirteen:

Life in Prison

Life in prison remained the same day in and day out. The guards woke us at the same time, we went to the showers, got dressed, ate breakfast, and then we were sent to what they called trade schooling. The government thought at the time, women who have tradecraft after being released from jail will most likely pursue a more civilized lifestyle.  Yes, where have we heard that from before? The Western culture had developed a scheme that every human on the planet must live under a specific set of principles to be civilized.

After I was shipped off to Michigan, my communication with Johnnie dropped nearly to nothing. It was almost impossible for him to get messages sent in and stay in hiding. So, what I heard were stories from the local newspapers. And we all know what that entailed. I hated the fact that we were apart, but the only solace was knowing Johnnie was making arrangements after my release.

Johnnie was born on June 22, 1903. He told me once that he was born in a bungalow at 2053 Cooper Street in Indianapolis, Indiana. There are many rumors of different dates; however, his family agrees that it was indeed June 22. His family moved shortly thereafter to a small farming community outside Indianapolis. 'Honest Dillinger', the townsfolk called his father, who married a lady named Mary Ellen Lancaster. Their first child was a small, red-haired beauty named Audrey. It would not be until another fourteen years that Johnnie was born. At some point, when Johnnie was about three, his mother died. Her death kind of destroyed his life.

We spent many hours talking and I remember him telling me of a story during his mother's funeral, that the family found him dragging a chair over to the coffin. Then he stood on the chair and shook his mother to wake her. It was apparent that her maternal duties had been successful.

In the short span, I knew Johnnie he was full of life. He had his problems but always had a good heart. His father later married again, and she loved the children as her own. The old man owned a grocery store in the small town, so everyone knew the Dillinger family very well. Audrey, the oldest daughter, took over as mother to little Johnnie.

Audrey soon thereafter married Emmet Hancock and they had boys. Johnnie spent much of his time with her and their boys. His teachers said he was a bright, cheerful child who was very intelligent with high energy. Along with an invariably neat, clean appearance. I guess his one flaw was math, but he loved to read. When Johnnie started school, his father got married to Elizabeth Fields, his second wife. She had two of her own children and then had two more with Johnnie's father. But other than normal mischievous things, Johnnie was a good person. He dropped out of school in the eighth grade and got a job at the Veneer Mill. He worked hard and was usually unmatched by anyone else. I know for a fact that he gave much of his money away to his fellow colleagues for clothing and such. In his off time, he enjoyed hunting and fishing; he loved his guns. Johnnie was a master marksman and prided himself on his ability to hit the target.

As a youth Johnnie was on the shy side, believe it or not. But maturity replaced puberty, and the woman swooned over him and he eye balled them. During which time, he found his second love, baseball, and joined the Mooresville baseball league. He started out playing shortstop and then moved on to pitcher; however, this is when his intelligence kicked into high gear. The routine of everyday life got boring and he discovered the exciting times of nightlife in the city. Johnnie fell in love for the first time, with a woman named Frances Thornton.

As he tells me they were inseparable, only her father did not approve. After their engagement, her father forbade them to see each other and he took the break up hard. When he told me about her, I could see the pain in his eyes. Thereafter, he joined the Navy, not a good decision. On July 23, 1923, he enlisted, but a short five months later he deserted. The service never pressed charges or looked for him, but then after his first arrest, they charged him with a dishonorable discharge.

The choice landed him back in Mooresville doing odd jobs to make ends meet when he met Beryl Hovious. I think it was a rebound relationship to help him get over Frances. When Johnnie chose to do something, he went all-in with both feet, including love.

Johnnie's decisions from this point pointed his life in only one direction: bad to worse. He met a man named Edgar Singleton who was a career criminal. Many of the young impressionable men about town found him to be exciting, including Johnnie.

One night on September 6, 1924, the men were drinking, and they got the idea to rid poor Frank Morgan of his hard-earned money. Both Johnnie and Singleton were beyond drunk from the moonshine and waited in the alley for the man to come by with his grocery money sales. They tackled him and started beating him with an iron bar wrapped in cloth. Morgan was able to grab his revolver and pulled the trigger. Apparently, he was a member of the Ku Klux Klan. When his buddies arrived, the assailants took off. Singleton grabbed a car and Dillinger escaped on foot. When Johnnie realized what he had done while drunk, he stumbled back into town asking questions, which of course, drew attention to him. The police came to arrest him on Monday, but he denied any involvement and they let him go. But later on, Singleton was caught and proceeded to blame Johnnie.

His father was so upset by the incident that he later convinced his son to plead guilty and take the lighter sentence. But since the evidence was shaky at best, it most likely would have been dropped. Since

Dillinger's father did not have enough money to hire a lawyer, and neither one of them knew how the law worked, he took the plea. Judge Joseph Williams sentenced him to the maximum sentence, ten to twenty years for assault with the intent to rob, concurrently two to fourteen years for conspiracy to commit a felony. Way overboard. Ed, the hardened criminal, hired an attorney. He pled not guilty and went to trial; he got two to fourteen years and was out in less than two.

The injustice grew like a cancer in Johnnie. Since Johnnie was just twenty-one and had never been convicted of a crime, he was taken to Indiana State Reformatory at Pendleton. In his three years there, he reportedly tried to escape once and had several disorderly conduct issues but was never considered dangerous. I know he wrote his wife many heartfelt letters, filled with a loving sentiment. He was unaware at the time that his wife had filed for divorce. She had already waited four years, and still had no idea how much longer the incarceration might last.

He later explained his feelings about her decision: "I began to know how you feel when your heart is breaking. For four years I had looked forward to going home, and now there was nothing to go home to."

A month later, the parole board denied his request. Shortly after he asked to be sent to Indiana State Prison in Michigan City. Some say this was to be closer to his baseball team, but I think he wanted to catch up with his friends, Harry Pierpoint and Homer Van Meter. It did allow him to play baseball and be with what would become the Dillinger Gang.

It took many more years before the Judge conceded that he overstepped the judgment. On May 22, 1933, he was finally released from prison. His father, Hubert and Norman Hancock were waiting at the gate. On their way home to Mooresville, Hubert explained that his 'mom' had been making a homecoming cake and had a stroke and died. That was the last time Johnnie cried until he got the news of my sentencing.

Johnnie suddenly found himself in a place that once saw him as family, and now looked upon him with disgust. The first steps into his father's home brought memories flooding back of his biological mother dying and now his second mother's funeral. One small town country judge robbed him of a life filled with joy and love. So, he sought the next best thing, life with his prison buddies. July 16, 1933, was the beginning of the Public Enemies.

Their first robbery included Harry Copeland and Hilton O. Crouch. I had never met these men, so all I knew was from what Johnnie had told me. The next afternoon, they held up the Commercial Bank of Daleville. They yielded $3,500; there were no policemen in town. At that point, the gang was hooked, so to speak.

Johnnie later told a robber friend, William Show, "Never trust a woman or an automatic pistol."

In the end, it was the 'woman in red' that sold him out. Ann Sage, the harlot who took my Johnnie. Ann Sage, born Cumpanas, was from Romania. In 1914, she moved to the United States and settled in

East Chicago, Indiana. She married Michael Chiolak, who was only seventeen. A year later they had a son named Steven. Now, remember, finding work in the US at the time was nearly impossible, so many women turned to the age-old profession of prostitution. Ann went to work for 'Big Bill' Subotich's place on Guthrie Street in East Chicago. While working there she met the infamous Martin Markovich. Apparently, her husband did not tolerate the acquaintance or her chosen career and ended their marriage. Then in 1923, after her employer passed away, she took over the establishment. The business grew dramatically, and she opened another house in Gary, Indiana.

In a short time, her reputation grew wildly, and the place was soon known as 'Katie of the Kostur Hotel' and the seedy underworld found the accommodations delightful. The basement of this brothel was another story; it earned the nickname 'Bucket of Blood', due to the stabbings and murders that took place there regularly.

As rumors go, Ann played the role of Judas in the death of Johnnie. However, the glorious details will remain forever a secret since most of the people involved needed to stay silent for self-preservation. It was even thought that the FBI, in their inept attempt to catch Dillinger, staged the whole scene using an innocent person to die in his place. The choice to believe the rumors are up to the reader.

When the heat in East Chicago and Gary Street hit, Ann moved to Chicago. Then, except for her connection with Officer Zarkovich, she disavowed everyone else. In 1927, Ann found her new home appealing and opened several more houses; however, even with her law enforcement connections, she dealt with her fair share of raids over the years. In 1930, she was fined sixty dollars and while criminal records were taken against her, she was never disposed. Somehow in the following years she received two pardons from Governor Harry G. Leslie. But while in court, FBI agents raided her houses, and began proceedings to have her deported back to Romania as a low-ranking immoral character. Go figure….

It was a well-known fact that she and Zarkovich were lovers and had been for years. They claimed it was mutually advantageous. The third member of this trio was Polly Hamilton, a twenty-six-year-old waitress and a previous tenant of Ann Sage's brothel. According to some of the narratives, none of them had ever laid eyes on Johnnie until a few days before the shooting. Now, this is where all the myths come into play, explaining the wild accusations of the days before Dillinger's death. Ann Sage professed many times that she had never seen or heard of Johnnie until he was brought into her house by Polly. As she stated, once she found out about his true identity, she feared for her life and had to contact the police. To this day, the story is a fairy tale. Johnnie had been to see a surgeon for plastic surgery, he wanted out. So, why would he tell anyone his real name, especially someone he did not know and trust? We spent far too much time together for him to have done such a stupid thing. I know for a fact Johnnie had good connections with many of the underground in East Chicago, like Hymie Cohen and Jimmie Regan, and none of them would have sold him out. Zarkovich and O'Neil were dirty and trying to cover their tracks for the murders of two other officers.

Johnnie was a meticulous planner and would have sought out a hiding place before he left Probasco's place. To my knowledge, Johnnie never spoke of Ann Sage or knew her personally. So, he would never have introduced himself as John Dillinger. At that time, I believe he used the name Jimmy Lawrence, a stockbroker's clerk. It fit his attire. Piquett attests, however, that his cover was blown when he left Probasco's hideout because he was using the name Roy Keele, Polly's former husband, a police officer. In light of this information, the three had a past connection that remained unknown to the public.

On July 6, 1934, Johnnie moved his things, including the arsenal, with Ann Sage. On the same day, Polly called her boss and claimed she had been in an accident and could not come to work anymore.

She was rarely seen after that day. It seems Polly, Ann, and her son Steven were living in the same house.

I guess when Van Meter heard of the situation, he went crazy, saying, "I have no use for that bunch in East Chicago, what is going on with you? You are going to get yourself killed."

Zarkovich had to have known Dillinger was staying with Ann because they both had a lot to gain by his capture or death. The FBI had already started proceedings to have the harlot deported, and Internal Affairs were investigating Zarkovich for underhanded dealings. Not to mention, the reward placed on Johnnie's head of fifteen thousand. Over the next few days, they began planning Johnnies capture, or death in this case. Zarkovich brought Tim O'Neil in on the plan, and Polly would serve as the innocent victim.

About the middle of July, Zarkovich vetted Melvin Purvis to recite the well-scripted lie told by Ann Sage. Naturally, it excited all the right people who wanted Johnnie dead. The appointment was made on the nineteenth with the FBI. Zarkovich drove with Sage to meet the detectives and spun the concocted tale. Of course, Zarkovich and Purvis split the reward and Sage was promised to have the deportation removed. And the FBI was finally close to getting rid of Public Enemy No 1.

    They all seemed to have his fate in the palm of their hands, while I was sitting in a prison cell completely useless. It was to the point that nothing made sense anymore. The only thing that had kept me going was hope for our life together after my release. Johnnie had followed through with everything he promised up until now, and I had no reason not to believe him. But the corruption in the police department and federal government at the time was incredible. This was mostly due to, I believe, the fate of society. The Great Depression was waning but far from over, and people would do almost anything to survive.

    We had one hour every evening after dinner to walk around the yard or sit in the common area to read or watch the news. On most days, I usually went outside, but for some reason that night I stayed inside. I sat down in one of the chairs and noticed a book on the table. I recognized the title as one of the books Johnnie loved to read and my mind started to wander. Suddenly, we were in Florida on our vacation down at the beach. Johnnie was sitting in a chair under a huge umbrella wearing his usual white silk shirt and tan trousers reading a book. He looked so happy and peaceful that day. I just watched him for some time until he noticed and shooed me away. We exchanged glances and he just smiled back at me.

Then during my reflection, a news broadcast grabbed my attention. I nearly vomited; the story brought my heart to a complete stop. It seemed the Brooks Farm in Michigan run by Rev. Edward L. Brooks was under investigation. Investigators (FBI) were looking into more than twenty-five infant deaths over many years. I know one of the victims was wrapped in newspaper with a fractured skull. In this situation, there are no words to express my emotions.

I begged one of the guards to let me call the Brooks Farm in Michigan, but they would not tell me anything about Billy. Some of the parents were contacted about claiming the remains of their children. I prayed many nights to be one of the parents; however, it never happened.

Over the next several weeks, I stayed in a deep sorrow-filled anxiety. My heart ached, and I prayed for his precious little soul. There was good reason to believe that some of these little victims came to their deaths by means of poison, violence, or consequences of some criminal act.

The precious little boy I held in my arms that day died a horrible death. It is something that plagued my soul until the day I died. We don't ever get over the loss of a child, we just learn to live with the pain.

Chapter Fourteen:

The Fatal Shooting

Sunday, July 22, 1934, was a day that would haunt me for the rest of my life. I sat behind bars completely helpless to what was going on in the world. I knew Johnnie was in trouble but had no way to warn him of the impending doom. Needless to say, my life had gone from bad to worse with the news of my Billy and my concern over Johnnie's well-being.

After Dillinger moved in with Ann, Polly, and Steven, all went quiet for the next few weeks. He was trying to settle into the new surroundings and healing from his surgery, while staying abreast of any updates with the people left alive in his gang. Van Meter was furious with him for residing with anyone from East Chicago and wanted him to leave, but Johnnie had convinced himself it was safe. Since my arrest and conviction, Johnnie was not in a good place. We wanted to leave this life and go away together. Now, we were apart and helpless to change the situation. I pushed the news about Billy to the back of my mind for the meantime, but the pain was overwhelming.

As I was informed shortly before dinner, Johnnie told Ann and Polly he wanted to go see a picture show; another gangster film was playing he wanted to see. Now, that was just like Johnnie; he loved trying to life the 'normal life' even though that was far from the truth. The date was made for eight o'clock. When Ann heard the news, she immediately phoned Purvis and told him of the plan.

She said, "If we are going to attend the Biograph Theater, I will be bareheaded, but if we go to the Marbro across town, I'll be wearing a hat." She wanted to be sure that were no mistakes this time, so her attire consisted of a white blouse and orange skirt.

The Biograph Theater sat in one of the oldest parts of Chicago, 2433 Lincoln Avenue. It just happened to be around the corner from Ann's apartment. Since it was the middle of summer in Chicago, the heat could be unbearable, so Dillinger wore a white shirt, grey trousers, white shoes, and a straw hat. Polly had worked at the sandwich shop that day for a colleague and met them at the theater. The plan was in full force.

    They arrived at about eight-fifteen, bought their tickets and entered. Outside sat more than twenty federal agents, commanded by Purvis and Cowley. They all found a comfortable spot to wait out the movie. One of the theater managers got concerned about all the men gathering outside and called the Chicago Metro police. When the police arrived, agents told them a federal stakeout was ongoing and they would have to leave. Supposedly, they left the scene.

    Purvis and two other men entered the theater and tried to locate Johnnie, but in the dark the only one they recognized was Ann. I cannot imagine anyone sitting next to someone like that knowing you would be responsible for their death in the next few hours. She had to have known that a stray bullet might hit and kill her at the same time.

As the movie ended and the crowds emerged from the entrance, Johnnie, Ann and Polly exited at 10:35 p.m. Both women walked on either side of him. Purvis hid in the shadows, struggling to light his cigar as that was the signal. When he finally, got it lit, the agents and police rushed the scene.

According to Purvis, he made no account of calling out Johnnie. Yet bystanders recall someone saying, "Stick 'em up, Johnnie."

Then someone pushed Ann aside and the bullet zipped past, hitting Dillinger in the neck first. It came out just under his right eye. The second one entered his left side. They said he took three steps and fell face first into the concrete. One of the agents claimed to take a pistol from his

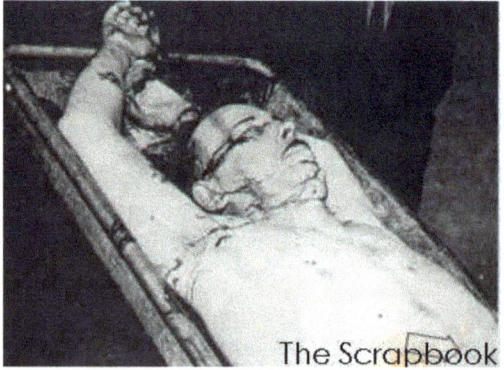

The Scrapbook

hand in self-defense, while others said he did not have one. They placed him on a stretcher in the back of a police wagon, and he died about five minutes later, with Purvis overseeing everything.

Ann claimed at first, he had a gun, but later stated she was wrong and he did not have a pistol. The police claimed to see a .38 caliber in his belongings, but one was never officially entered into evidence. Law enforcement fought over who made the fatal shot; nonetheless, no one cared to investigate any further. In my mind, the Chicago police were to blame for the death, as they needed to hide their illegal actions and Dillinger could have talked. The main agenda was to make him out as the most dangerous criminal of all time.

Then adding to the lies, the police claim Johnnie was only carrying seven dollars in his pocket. Please… I knew him much better than that, he always carried serval hundred to thousands at any time. Then there was the issue of his watch. Polly claimed the photo inside it was of her, but I can tell you for a fact the photo was of me. Of course, no one ever saw the watch after that day. The police escort drove him to Alexian Brothers Hospital where the medical staff examined him inside the wagon, pronouncing him dead. Then they took his body to the morgue.

Polly ran off during the shooting and got on a train; she was conveniently forgotten in all the chaos. Once Ann was freed, she took off home to her apartment and changed into dark clothing and went back to the theater to oversee her damage. When the officers stripped Johnnie of his belongings, two keys were found: one for Ann Sage's apartment and the second opened the locked door of her closet. Then later that night, after everything died down, Ann went and gathered up Johnnie's guns and dropped them off below the Diversey Bridge. Imagine that, she somehow miraculously got the key to the closet.

I remember Piquett smiling when he was first told about his death because reporters were always claiming Dillinger was dead. So, when Piquett got home and called, and gave them the riot act: "Where is Dillinger's body?"

"The morgue...." Piquett had to see the evidence for himself.

New heights hit the city upon news of his death, thousands upon thousands showed up for his funeral and seeing whatever they could at the morgue. The city obliged, displaying Johnnie on a cold cement slab for anyone who wanted to pass by and see Public Enemy No 1 dead. It made me sick to my stomach.

The news spread like wildfire, hitting Mooresville in the middle of the night. They opened the central store as a meeting hall. The town gathered until way after dawn. A grim procession made it out to the old farm to inform Johnnie's father, the poor man. He 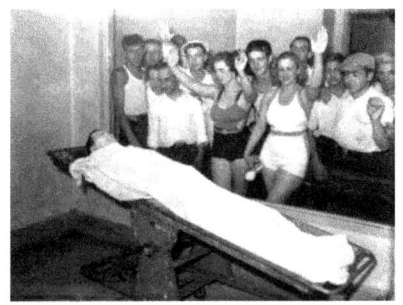 answered the door in overalls and a plain stained cotton shirt.

He dropped to his knees, exclaiming, "I knew this day would come. I've been expecting it." After several minutes, the looky-loos stared waiting for some reply. "Are you sure it's true this time? I have heard this before." He turned and walked into the living room, flopped into a chair, and sobbed. Audrey showed up shortly thereafter, cradling her father as he let out his sorrow.

At that time, families sometimes brought their hearse to bury a loved one. So, his father gathered the undertaker and they set out for Chicago to collect Johnnie's body. While at the station to sign paperwork, his dad broke down, yelling, "I wouldn't want a dog to be slain that way. You never gave him a chance, just shot him in the back dead."

Johnnie was buried with a Christian service as his mother would have requested. Thousands of people lined the streets as the hearse left the city headed for Mooresville. More than fifteen thousand onlookers were preparing to see his funeral. So, the family decided to have a private service. Johnnie is buried at Hillside Christian Cemetery.

The next morning, every newspaper across America headlined, Public Enemy No 1 shot dead. The indecency of law enforcement trying to prove a point was portrayed by the newspapers, printing photos of his body stripped of clothing and bloodied skin. I cannot begin to tell you the pain I felt, seeing those images of the man I loved.

Ann Sage was promised the reward money, but the FBI changed their minds and she was never given the reward. Several days after Johnnie's death, agents raided Probasco's hideout; however, during the interrogation, he somehow jumped out the window and fell to his death. His wife wrote a letter to the Attorney General claiming agents hung her husband out the window from his feet and when he refused to confess, they dropped him. Polly's involvement with Dillinger was never revealed in the newspaper, and she eventually left Chicago and went back home to Fargo, North Dakota. I admit, though, when the FBI reneged on their deal to allow Ann a renewed visa, it made my heart glad; she was sent home.

Van Meter fell into a trap with Baby Face Nelson. He was, as Johnnie said many times, a crazed sociopath and never to be trusted. So, when he found out that Van Meter was in St. Paul and planned a meeting with another underworld colleague, instead of confronting his enemy, Nelson called the police. On August 23, when officers commanded him to surrender, Van Meter opened fire and ran down a nearby alley. Machine gun bullets riddled the alley, knocking him into the mud face first. He died almost instantly.

Inside jail, Pierpoint, Makley, and Clark waited their fate with Johnnie dead, so they decided to attempt a similar escape with guns made out of soap. Only they got caught when the newly fabricated steel doors would not unlock. Pierpont was shot in the back leaving him paralyzed, so he met a quick end when they carried him to the electric chair. After being sentenced to death for the killing of Sheriff Sarber, Makely was shot and died within a few minutes.

A few months later, in the aftermath of Dillinger's death, a case reappeared with Ann Sage. Apparently, she was upset about being called the 'woman in red' and demanded the record be set straight, since her shirt was indeed orange. Following her outlandish behavior, federal agents gathered them up into protective custody. Two weeks later, Ann got on a bus to California. Cowley visited her and offered five thousand dollars for a sample of Johnnie's blood. When the settlement did not satisfy her anger, she threatened to talk, and they took steps to have her deported.

Of course, I could go on and on about the aftermath of Public Enemy No 1, but nothing was going to take away the anger and heartbreak of being stuck in prison, helpless to do anything. I still remember listening to Johnnie and Van Meter, especially laughing at the daily reports about their escapades. One of their favorite, "Well, I see I made the headlines again today. Hey, Van, let's see if we can find a little something about you…" he'd giggle.

"No, they never mention me by name," Van Meter replied.

One certain fact, there will never be another John Dillinger. He was truly one of a kind, a throwback, so to speak, of someone who can thrive in society under unsettled times. As a matter of fact, the common phrase among the police was 'Dillinger Luck'.

He once told me, "I would give anything for a second chance to start my life over again."

We got caught up in the thrill of adventure. All I saw was destruction. The Great Depression was more than just the stock market crash; it entailed racism of the worst kind, food shortages, and corrupt federal government agencies. Just plain lawlessness. It was a period of ethnocide, which means 'forced assimilation', and we had no civil rights. Despite constitutional law, the Native Americans were exempt from the protection.

Between 1887 and 1933, over half of the tribal land base was lost to land thieves, tax sales, and governmental sales of "surplus lands." These policies created a cycle of poverty that continued throughout my life. Thus, lack of education and ill health became hallmarks of tribal societies in the U.S. But these racist missionaries and civilizing policies failed miserably. Instead, many Native peoples strengthened their resolve to nurture and cling to their old traditional ways. Although many Native Americans had become U. S. citizens through treaties, they were wary of being declared citizens through "competency" since it often meant that their federal land allotments and treaty rights no longer protected them from confiscation or sale. A significant amount of the tribal estate was taken from Native Americans through fraud and state tax sales. In fact, thousands of newly created Native American citizens saw their lands removed from federal protection and sold out from under them through the 1930s.

It meant increased poverty and homelessness among my people. I remember the Dawes Act being an unmitigated disaster for tribal units. In 1900, land held by Native American tribes was half of that in 1880. Our land holdings continued to dwindle in the early twentieth century. When the Dawes Act was repealed in 1934, alcoholism, poverty, illiteracy, and suicide rates were higher for Native Americans than any other ethnic group in the United States. Our identity was dwindling at the hands of Western culture. It always amazed me how Western culture considered us hostiles, yet we were the first Americans. Our pride was challenged by a nation of new immigrants determined to treat us as some sort of ratified exotic race, not worthy of living among Western culture.

Since Western culture came to the Americas, various policies from federal and state governments mounted an attack on Indian cultural identity in an attempt to force assimilation. These policies started with banning traditional religious ceremonies, and forcing our culture of hunting and gathering to begin farming; often we were given land that was unsuitable for producing food. Then we were forced to cut our hair in a way to pressure us to adopt Christianity. Indian parents, including mine, had to send their children to boarding schools where the use of our Native languages was not permitted. Plus, our freedom of speech was revoked, or restricted. We were not even permitted to travel between reservations. Many Native Americans struggled with their identity, including me for several years. I suppose that explains my draw to Johnnie; he saw me for who I am. No matter what people thought of him, he always treated me with respect. Only one thing that never happened in my life. Otherwise, nothing much occurred before that fateful night in the cabaret when I laid eyes on Johnnie for the first time. We fell in love…. Falling in love with Johnnie was something that took care of itself.

Chapter Fifteen:

Agonizing Pain

F ollowing Johnnie's death, shock kept the pain at bay for a few weeks. It felt like being in a whirlpool of despair; my whole world ended. Suddenly, again, I had found myself stuck alone in a world that hated my people. The one man who loved me for who I am was dead, lying in the ground, unable to protect me from the troubles I faced. However, under the circumstances, being in prison with the state of society still had its  benefits. At least we were given everything necessary to survive, which was more than most of the people in America.

The next year and a half were excruciating, to say the least. I spent weeks crying myself to sleep. By the time I woke, my eyes were almost swollen shut, red, and burning. Nonetheless, I did not care for a long time. Then one night, while lying in my cell staring at the ceiling, Johnnie appeared to me in the dark. He looked handsome, dressed in his usual white silk shirt, tan trousers, and wing-tipped shoes. It took me a few moments to figure out if I had died as well.

He smiled. "Hiya, doll," he said.

"Johnnie!" I yelled. My heart leaped with joy. "I miss you. We are going to miss out on our life together now."

"Only for a short time…. Someday we can love each other with no pain, fear, or timeframe."

"But…. I am alone now—I don't know how to live without you anymore."

"Sure, you do… did you not learn anything from me? Life is an adventure. Just do me a favor: once in a while, watch a baseball game for me, okay?"

"Okay, I can do that."

"I have to go now, doll, but just know I will always love you, forever...."

"Please... don't goooo—"

In that second his image was gone, but I knew deep down he would always be with me in this life or another. I don't know to this day why he came to me that night, or if it was just a dream and I imagined the whole thing. But needless to say, it did not matter; his words made life in prison bearable.

I can say that the correctional prison system at the time did a fairly good job preparing us for life after our release. Nevertheless, as reality smacked me in the face once again, finding employment on the outside after my connection with Johnnie was next to impossible. The FBI made their feelings on crime very well-known.

In 1907, Teddy Roosevelt founded the Department of Investigation (BOI) to investigate government corruption. Then in 1924, J. Edgar Hoover took over as director, but their only job at the time was to investigate crime. Agents had no power to arrest or carry weapons, they just had to report findings to state law enforcement officials. In the 1920s, Americans were afraid of the national police force who'd become secret police

Teddy Roosevelt

working behind closed doors. So, Hoover created this campaign to humanize the organization. By 1925, Ford Motor Company had produced over ten million Model T cars, so crime was not just centered in states alone, now criminals could easily cross the borders into other states. The action of crossing state lines made it a federal crime, which was essentially Johnnie's downfall. Since the whole scheme of the BOI was still new to the public, crossing the border with a stolen car brought in federal agents. After the jailbreak from Lake County Jail, it wasn't the fake gun or weapons he stole that caused the issue, it was crossing state lines with a stolen sheriff's police car.

Of course, with any federal government agency at the time, racism fell into play. The only members allowed to apply for the BOI were white men; all women and minorities were excluded. Not surprising, as that was standard practice during those times. The first official crime lab was started on November 24, 1932. By 1936, they had six million fingerprints of criminals on file. Special Agent Melvin Purvis took over the Chicago office in 1932 as well. I believe Purvis was an honorable man, for the most part; he was a well-educated attorney and retired from the military. During WWII, he had served as an intelligence officer with the ranking of colonel. After he was promoted to head of the Chicago office, he launched a manhunt for Baby Face Nelson, Pretty Boy Floyd, and John Dillinger. Hoover thought Purvis had become media hungry and demoted him, putting Samuel Cowley in his place. A short time later, Cowley would be shot by Baby Face Nelson and die in the hospital. Purvis got the praise after his death; however, he later stated that Hoover was jealous over the attention he gained for killing Dillinger. Although, he was not without suspicion himself. One account states Purvis and his agents killed Dillinger without any assistance from the local police. Chester Smith, a local police officer, stated he shot Floyd first, and Purvis never had a chance to shoot. Many years later, FBI Agent Hopton wrote in a letter that agents were not even present at the time of the shooting. Neither account has ever been truly proven, except that Hoover was on a mission to prove the BOI was above corruption, and Americans could trust them.

In the beginnings of the FBI, agents were just paper pushers, they investigated crimes only. But Hoover expected military discipline, after the situation at Little Bohemia where agents killed an innocent man and wounded two others. In his memoirs, Purvis gave a detailed account of the incident, blaming the urgency of the situation for the lack of preparation.

He wrote, "It is true that during the last several years the Federal Bureau of Investigation has been organized on an emergency basis...." Purvis also blamed understaffing. In the spring of 1934, the BOI only had about 400 special agents.

Then on May 18, 1934, Roosevelt signed a bill giving the federal government more power to fight crime. At the ceremony he said, "I stand squarely behind the efforts of the Department of Justice to bring to book every lawbreaker, big and little." The bill lifted restrictions preventing federal agents from making arrests and carrying arms. Hence, the manhunt was brought to another level in dealing with the Dillinger Gang. By making the country safe from public enemies, they represented faith and the federal government's restoration of a nation that had been on the brink of collapse.

Hoover's response was simple; however, he was very jealous of Purvis's popularity, which briefly surpassed his own. "No one employee of this division can be responsible for the successful termination of any one case.... Through cooperative efforts, a case is broken."

Shortly after Dillinger's death, society returned to normal and he became just a memory. Hoover assigned Purvis to bad cases and subjected him to extreme scrutiny, and he resigned a year later. Although he had many job offers, Hoover sabotaged his attempts to find work in law enforcement or a related field. Purvis was forced to earn money by making commercial endorsements, which he found humiliating. It was later reported in 1960 that he committed suicide in his home at the age of fifty-six.

In 1935, Max Stein wrote a book called *Bring Em Back*, a scientific detection of public enemies. He reported that Dillinger's robberies totaled over a million dollars from twelve banks. After Johnnie's death, government agents continued to round up the last members of his gang, starting with Homer Van Meter, which I discussed earlier. But then they arrested Charles Mackley, a college man who escaped from Michigan City where he was serving ten years for robbery. He was held for execution and died shortly thereafter. Harry Pierpont, the trigger man as they called him, was also executed on

October 17, 1934. Then there was Baby Face Nelson; I was not sad to be away from him. He was shot down on November 17, 1934, during which agent Cowley and Hollis were killed.

The next, and most likely Johnnie's favorite, was John Hamilton. His body was finally recovered on August 28, 1935. They found him in a quarry near Oswego, IL. It appeared he had died many months before Dillinger's death, as per Johnnie's statement. Hamilton was born in Canada and held a dual-citizenship, and was reported to have above-average intelligence. His father died when he was young, after which he ran wild. Like Johnnie, they both loved to fish, hunt, and crack a shot. Jack had lost two fingers in a sledding accident. He dropped out of school in the tenth grade and moved to Great Lakes, Michigan. In 1921, he married Mary Stevenson and they had two boys. However, Mary had expensive tastes, and to keep her happy he began his life of crime. Hamilton was arrested in 1924 and Mary left him, taking their children. She died of cancer in 1930. While in prison, he underwent surgery for an appendicitis attack, and a telegram came explaining his wife had died. Johnnie, Pierpont, and Van Meter met in prison, where they quickly became friends. Hamilton later stated he liked Johnnie because of his charismatic personality, a likable fellow.

One rumor that is still in existence is that John survived his bullet wounds. He supposedly escaped back to Canada where he lived until the 70s. The story is supported by his great-nephew, Bruce Hamilton of Shiprock, New Mexico.

Tommy Carroll joined Johnnie after they escaped from Crown Point, Indiana. He delivered the cash payment after helping him escape. Three days later, they robbed a bank with Nelson and Carroll shot a motorcycle officer while leaving. Carroll was replaced as the wheel driver. The next week they made their biggest heist, First National Bank, totaling $52,344. Johnnie and Hamilton were both shot, but Carroll drove them away safe. They headed to Little Bohemia and the rest is history. Carroll was shot and killed by a Waterloo detective in Iowa.

At that point, Johnnie was not the leader of their gang, but he had leadership qualities. He could instill trust, loyalty, and confidence among the members. Most importantly, he could regain their composure when they got hostile. It was especially important with Hamilton, since he could be impulsive and daring.

In May of 1934, when Johnnie underwent his plastic surgery, they removed his fingerprints with boric acid at that same time. Dr. Cassidy later committed suicide. Supposedly, when Johnnie had his bandages removed, he wanted to try out his new face, so they attended the Barrel of Fun Club and he met Polly Hamilton. The FBI sent him a birthday present that year at his celebration dinner, of calling him Public Enemy No 1, the first person placed on the FBI's most-wanted list. Just a few weeks before Johnnie's death, Pat Cherrington and Opal Long were sentenced to two years for harboring charges, like me. They were placed in Milan Correctional Facility.

After Hoover turned his sights on capturing the public enemies, it kept him from focusing on the real problem: millions of dollars had disappeared in the government due to corruption, a convenient choice since he was powerless against stopping organized crime. Hence, the urgency to put an end to the Dillinger escapades. Once the case had concluded with killing Johnnie and capturing many others associated with his gang, it was considered as the beginning of the end to the gangster era and the evolution of the FBI.

On April 6, 1934, I was fingerprinted and assigned a number, #2376. I am in Federal Prison. In other words, a convict. I'm not Billy Frechette anymore; I'm a number, like Machine Gun Kelly's wife, who is here too, and like the rest of the girls on the farm.

I guess this is where they all end up. Maybe I've got it coming to me. I don't know. But I keep telling myself that I'm different. I'm in here because I fell in love with the wrong man— not wrong for me, you understand, but wrong if I wanted to keep it in the clear.

The next phase of my life was about to begin without the man I loved. Many people had their doubts about whether or not Johnnie truly loved me since he was seen with other women after my sentencing, except they were not privy to the intimate details of our relationship. We had packed the day we arrived back in Chicago and I was arrested; he wanted out and was going to do whatever it took to make that happen. Johnnie was always faithful to his commitment where I was concerned. Although, I have learned over the years, fate has its own plan, and all we can do is follow along, willingly or under duress, the choice is up to you.

Evelyn Frechette – Life with Johnnie

1101 North Clark St, Chicago IL

901 W Addison St Chicago, IL

Evenly Frechette & John Dillinger 1930s

John Dillinger 1930s

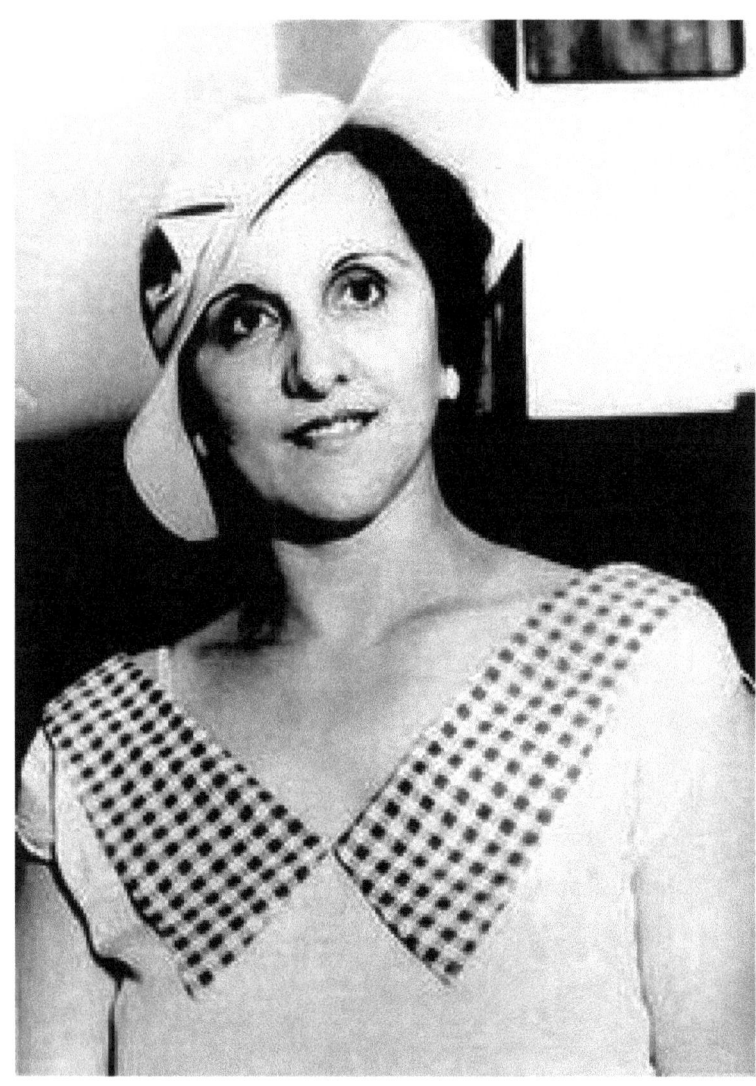

1933 Essex Terraplane bullet holes

Crownpoint Prison escape

Crownpoint Prison

Crownpoint Jail kitchen

Dillinger on the run meet 1934

Sherriff Holly's Essex stolen

John Dillinger capture attempt

WATCH YOUR CREDIT / INTERNATIONAL CHICAGO
9838   4-5-34

SCENE OF DILLINGER CAPTURE ATTEMPT

ST. PAUL, MINN.- THE HOUSE ON RONDO, STREET, ST. PAUL, WHERE FEDERAL OPERATIVES AND POLICE STAGED THE SECOND SHOOTING IN AN ATTEMPT TO CAPTURE JOHN DILLINGER. EDWARD GREEN, A DILLINGER GANGSTER, WAS SERIOUSLY WOUNDED BY GUNFIRE AND A RED-HEADED WOMAN WHO WAS WITH HIM WAS CAPTURED HERE WHEN THEY DROVE UP TO THE HOUSE IN AN AUTOMOBILE. SENT HEARST PAPERS AND FAST MAIL CLEVELAND TO WEST COAST. (INTER) GREEN FELL AT SPOT MARKED "X". OFFICERS SHOT FROM CIRCLED WINDOWS.

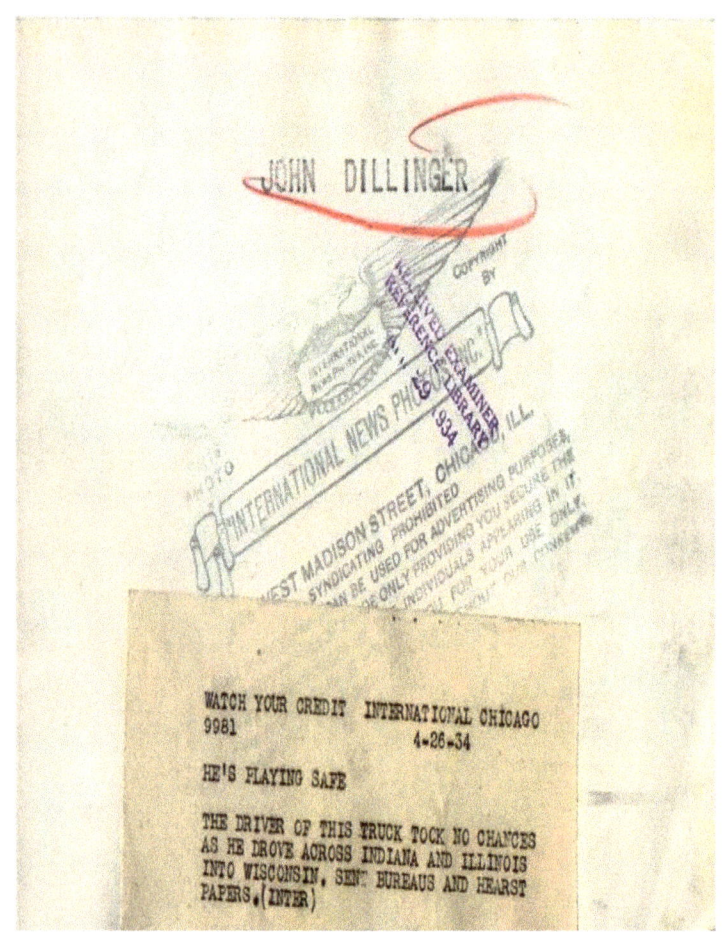

Dillinger in court

Weapons from Dillinger robbery

Dillinger with Tommy Gun

Melvin Purvis & General Homer Cummings

Little Bohemia

1933 Essex after gun fight

Little Bohemia after gun fight

Dillinger hideout

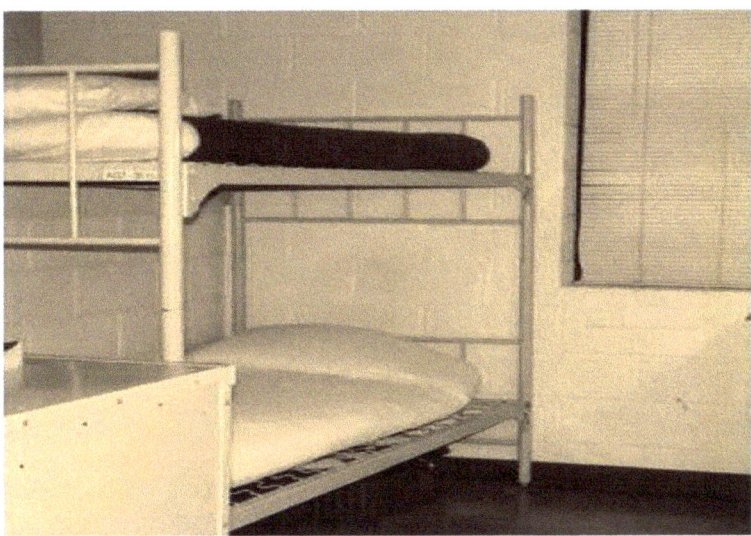
Dillinger jail cell

Motel in Arizona

Rental house in Tuscan

927 North Second St, Tucson, Arizona

Crown Point escape

Evelyn court hearing

John Dillinger

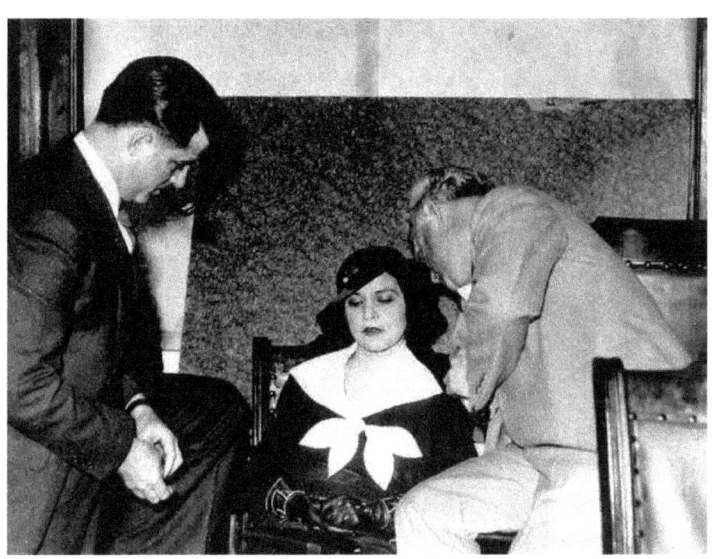

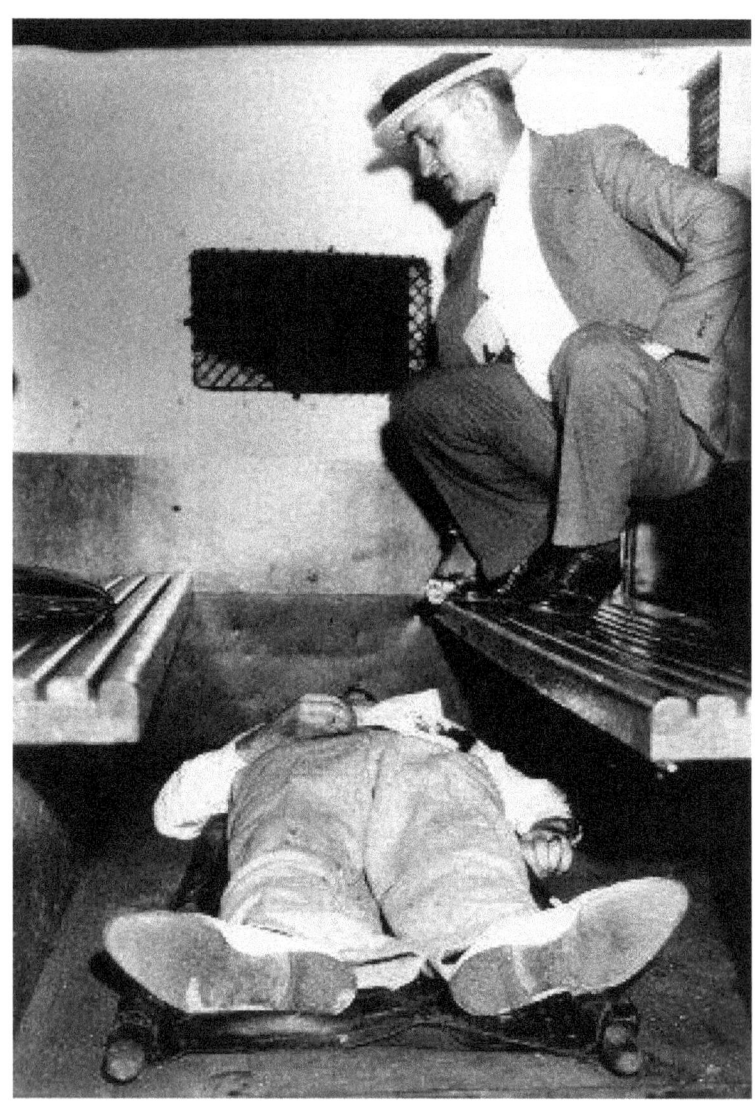

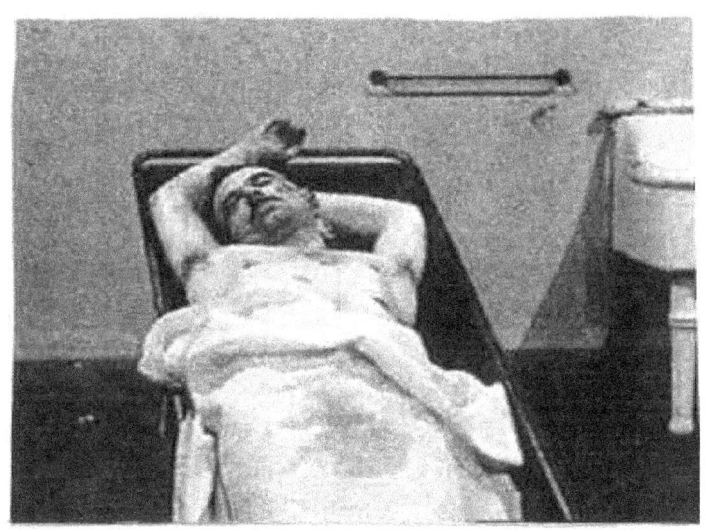

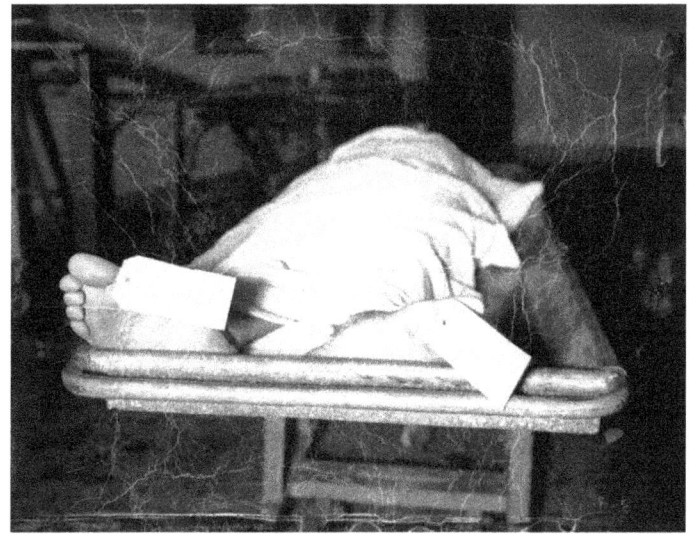

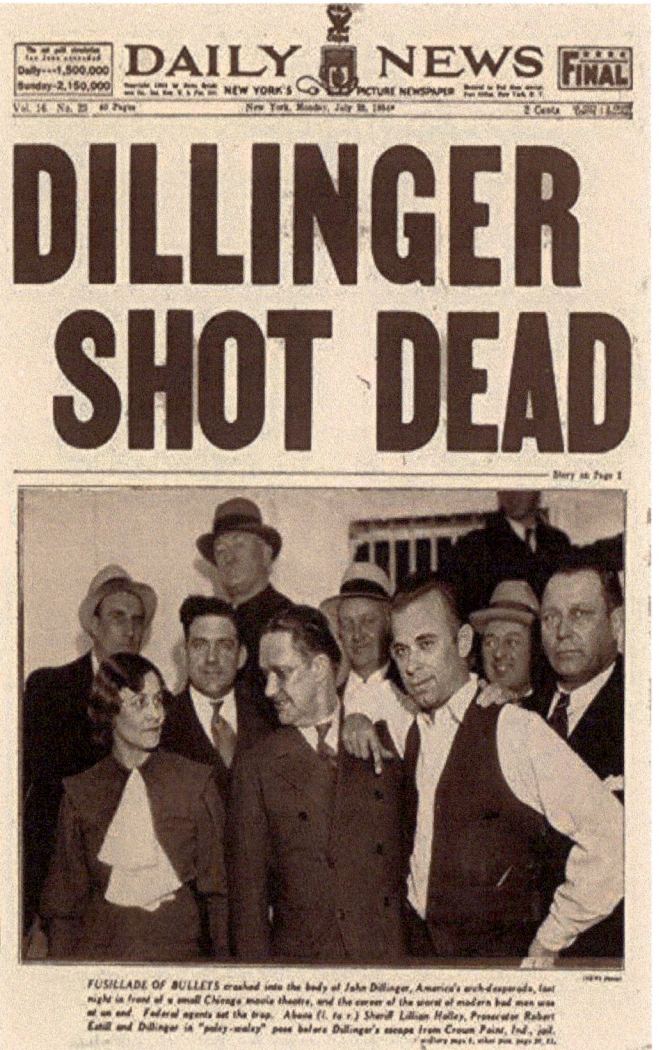

Dillinger shot dead

Chapter Sixteen:

I'm Free

I was finally released from prison on January 30, 1936, a few months short of my two-year sentence. A North American cold wave struck the northern states and more than one hundred people died on the highways, and temperatures averaged -85°F. I had spent many years in North Dakota and Wisconsin, but it was nothing compared to that year. Since the weather made driving miserable, I did not want my sister coming to get me from Milan. So, I had kept some money from Johnnie before he died and used it to get a  train ticket to Chicago. It was the only place I had known for some time. At that time, I was not ready to go home just yet. The best thing for me was to get back on my feet as best as possible and heal. I needed time to grieve the loss....

As my release grew close, I started receiving letters and messages about the FBI and how they were watching everyone involved with Dillinger very closely. It was not enough they gunned him down in the middle of the street, we had to be followed and surveilled as well. I may not have been intimate with his business dealings, but I had friends who kept me apprised of the happenings, including some of the wives and girlfriends of our gang members who were serving time in the same prison; word gets around quickly.

A short time before my release, I was contacted by several publications and the radio/carnival roadshow called, *Crime Does Not Pay*. I figured it was the best way to prove my innocence. Since G-men would be following me, I might as well give them what they

wanted. Not to mention the fact that it was an income. It was not something I enjoyed, but we were able to educate future generations on the negative effects of a criminal career. The one positive aspect was being able to travel with Johnnie's family. We lived in seedy motels and ate at some horrible places, but I did love spending time with them. It gave me a sense of closure, which was exactly what I needed to heal.

The producers encouraged me to write a short booklet about some of my experiences with Dillinger and how committing crime does not pay. When I appeared on the show, they would sell my booklet for 25¢ each. I agree that part was thrilling.

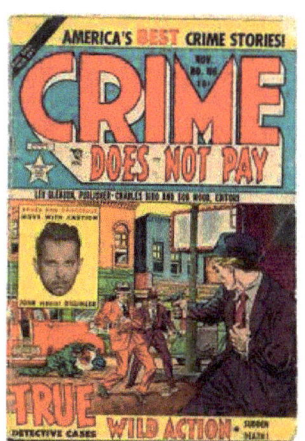

The country was on the tail end of the Great Depression and most of the farmers were beginning to repair the land after the Great Dustbowl. Plus, Roosevelt signed a bill that put many men back to work installing electric poles to the outlying rural farms. Many of them lived for years without power after the cities were electrified.

I can remember sitting by the radio on September 30, 1936, when the World Series started. It was the first World Series the Yankees played without Babe Ruth. He had been released and began playing for the Boston Braves. We listened every afternoon, rooting for the Yankees to win; it took them six games to earn their fifth championship. Johnnie would have been screaming in the stands. I felt a surge of energy each afternoon waiting for the game to start; watching sports was never my thing until that year. I started to follow it on the side, and it made me feel closer to him.

The day of my arrival in Chicago the temperature was below freezing, yet the reporters never failed to get the scoop on a hot storyline. Johnnie had been gone for almost two years and believe me; his fame soared throughout the US. A *Herald* reporter caught me getting off the train and demanded a set of interviews in five instalments.

Against my better judgment, I agreed. The first one is quoted below:

The *Chicago Herald* and *Examiner* originally published a multi-part article written by Evelyn "Billie" Frechette in August 1934. In it, Frechette told of her life with John Dillinger. Reproduced here are the first and fifth instalments of her story.

'What I Knew About John Dillinger'— By His Sweetheart.

"Evelyn Frechette, sweetheart of John Dillinger, herewith presents the first chapter of the story of her hectic life with the nation's late public enemy No. 1.

"How she fled with Dillinger after his 'toy-gun' escape from the Crown Point jail; how they strove ingeniously to dodge capture or death; how they retreated from a St. Paul machine gun— all these details figure in an amazing story, which carries the inevitable moral that the criminal cannot escape the penalty for his crime.

"Now behind prison bars, Evelyn Frechette tries to find a reason for her fate. Because she followed, unthinking, an impulse of her heart, she lost her freedom. Though the reason may escape her, it stands out unmistakably as an object lesson not only to youth but to all that attach themselves to criminal pursuits." Part One - August 27, 1934

The words in the article upset me terribly. Yes, I fell in love with a bank robber, but Johnnie was more than a common criminal. He just happened to be the one Hoover decided to hone in on instead of facing the real problem of organized crime. I had suddenly gone from hiding to avoid the public eye to being the object of every reporter's dream story. It was a long five years traveling with the Crime Does Not Pay Show, but it paid my bills and allowed me to save some money.

Crime Does Not Pay!
By Evelyn Frechette

My first show was scheduled after the winter broke and summer peeked over the horizon. After the *Tribune Post* came out, I wanted a reason to leave the city. The questions pertained to, of course, why I involved myself with Dillinger.

"Why did you involve yourself with John Dillinger, a notorious dangerous bank robber?"

"Only one big thing ever happened to me in my life. Nothing much happened before that, and I don't expect much from now on— except maybe a lot more grief. The one big thing that happened to me was that I fell in love with John Dillinger.

"I'm in prison on account of that. The government people said that I 'harbored a criminal'. The criminal was John. I lived with him for several months, if that's what they mean. I loved him. I followed him around the country— from Chicago to Florida and then to Tucson, where we were caught. And then after we got out of the jail in Crown Point with the wooden gun, he came to me again and we beat it to St. Paul, where we had the shooting scrape and nearly got killed."

"So, is it true that Dillinger was waiting as police seized you?"

"So, you see I was with John Dillinger from the time he came to Chicago after breaking out of the jail at Lima, until I got caught in Chicago last April—the time the police took me away while John was sitting in his car down the street waiting for me."

"He just let you… get arrested?"

"John was good to me. He looked after me and bought me all kinds of clothes and jewelry and cars and pets, and we went places and saw things, and he gave me everything a girl wants. He was in love with me. If that's harboring him, all right then. I harbored him."

"I'd have to say that is real commitment—"

"Have you ever been in love, I mean in love? John's dead. I'm not sorry I loved him. That part I couldn't help. I'm sorry what happened to me and what it cost me after I was caught. But if I could do it all over again, I would not think twice. That's true love."

Then two weeks after the first show, I got word that the FBI had been alerted to my whereabouts from the Chamber of Commerce in Camden, South Carolina. I believe it was April 8, 1937.

The Letter to The FBI Read:

"Dear Sir:

It has come to our attention that a promotional group is making a circuit of the smaller cities of the south with a billing of 'Evelyn Frechette' as guest.

I noted posters in the windows of the stores and shops to the effect that this Dillinger 'Moll' was to appear on the stage of the Haigler Theater here in person on Friday evening.

I may be wrong, but I have a suspicion that this is just a promotional racket being worked by some irresponsible parties who are making these smaller towns under the belief that no one would detect the fraud, if such it may be.

The writer is a former Wisconsin newspaper editor and being in touch with affairs in the middle west as I am, I was under the impression that this Frechette woman was at her home in Neopit. Can you advise me as to whether this woman who is with the theatrical group can possibly be Evelyn Frechette? If this is a fraud, which I strongly suspect it to be, I feel it my duty to inform the various chambers of commerce in the south as to that effect.

I would appreciate a reply…. Frank Health, Sec.

Initially, the letter didn't bother me, and I never expected the FBI to respond. But when they did, I was terrified they were going to arrest me again, only this time I had no one to protect me. The Chamber of Commerce received a response on May 3, 1937.

Mr. Peake, formerly employed by the *Washington Herald*, telephoned and wanted to know if the director was in the city and whether he would meet Evelyn Frechette if she called at the Bureau this afternoon.

Mr. Peake advised she was in the city playing at a carnival and had expressed a desire to meet the director and go through the Bureau. I informed him the director was absent from the city and the date of his return was uncertain and that apparently this was an attempted publicity stunt on the part of Miss

Frechette. He denied this and wanted to know who could meet her if she called at the Bureau and was informed that I knew of no one who desired to meet her.

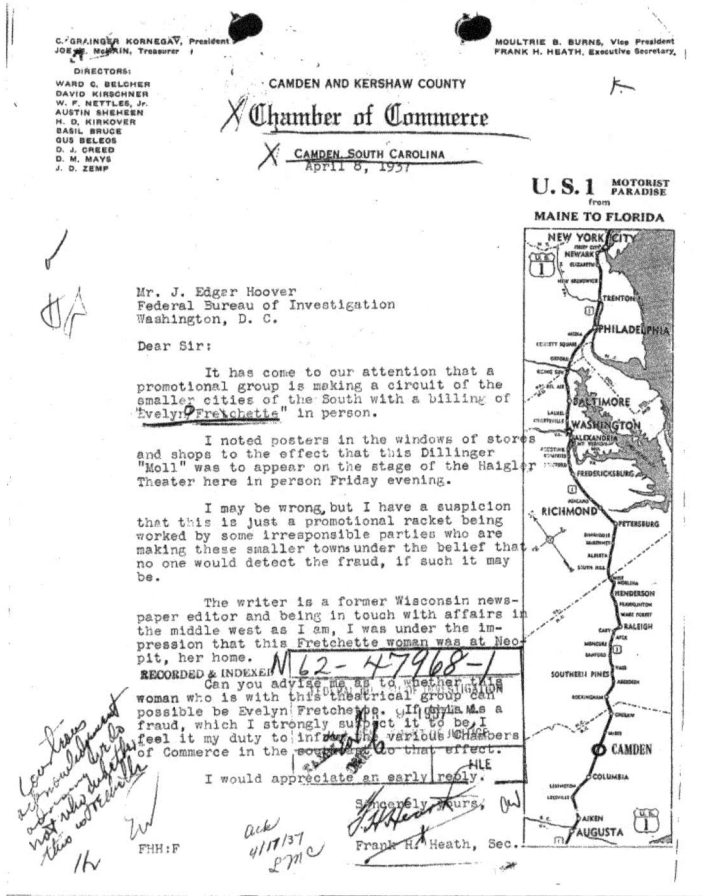

EMH:JDLF
62-47968-2

RECORDED

May 5, 1937.

Mr. J. B. Drury,
Federal Bureau of Investigation,
4244 U. S. Department of Justice Building,
Washington, D. C.

Dear Mr. Drury:

I am in receipt of the pamphlet entitled "Public Enemies - U. S. War on Crime," which you recently purchased at the Johnny J. Jones Shows in Washington.

It was thoughtful of you to submit this pamphlet and I want to thank you for this courtesy and also for your comments concerning the appearance in one of the side shows of Evelyn Frechette.

Sincerely yours,

John Edgar Hoover,
Director.

CC-Washington Field

Another letter was received on May 5, 1937 a few days later. It was signed by John Edgar Hoover.

Dear Mr. Drury:

I am in receipt of the pamphlet entitled 'Public Enemies' – US War on Crime, which you recently purchased at the Johnnie J Johns show in Washington.

It was thoughtful of you to submit this pamphlet and I want to thank you for this courtesy and also for your comments concerning the appearance in one of the side shows of Evelyn Frechette.

Sincerely yours,

John Edgar Hoover

I can say, all the media attention had me nervous. The last thing I ever wanted was to talk about our lives with a reporter or agent. But you have to understand the severity of the economy at the time. People were starving; they had lost their homes, and had no jobs. The best ones went to the elite or personal acquaintances. Then add on the fact that now I had been convicted of a crime and my chances of a steady job flew out the window. I thought being a Native American was bad; nonetheless, adding a federal crime to my record took the difficulty to another level.

Imagine most hotel rooms cost approximately eight dollars a night plus food and clothing. My wages of twenty-five dollars a show was very good money. Plus, most of the show's talent shared rooms when possible, so we could split the costs. And I got to travel again, like I did with Johnnie.

I suppose one of the most difficult shows dealt with being convicted. As a Native American, we were used to being seen as second-rate citizens, but to actually have your name removed and replaced with a number is upsetting.

Crime Does Not Pay!
By Evelyn Frechette

"So, how do you feel about being only a number now in federal prison?"

"I'm a convict. Since the third of last June, when a federal judge in St. Paul sentenced me to two years. I've been in the United States detention farm in Milan, Michigan. I'm not Billy Frechette anymore, I'm a number, like Machine Gun Kelly's wife, who is here too, and like the rest of the girls on the farm.

"I guess this is where they all end up. Maybe I've got it coming to me. I don't know. But I keep telling myself that I'm different. I'm in here because I fell in love with the wrong man—not wrong for me, you understand, but wrong if I wanted to keep it in the clear.

"Falling in love with John was something that took care of itself. There are lots of reasons why. Some of the reasons are John's and some are mine."

"What drew you to Dillinger? What was he to you?"

"I liked John's kindness. I don't mean because he was a criminal and carried guns around, and wasn't afraid of the police, or anyone. There was something else. John might have been a soldier or something else besides what he was. He wasn't, of course, because something happened along the line.

"I always figured that what he did was one thing and who he was another. I was in love with what he was. Oh, maybe I was wrong, but you can't argue yourself out of falling in love! You just can't sit down and think it out."

The interest in my shows quickly increased. And of course, the FBI were also interested. They went so far as to send someone who could identify me in the program. Another letter was sent to Washington reporting the results of their findings. This letter was dated May 29, 1937.

Federal Bureau of Investigation
United States Department of Justice
Washington, D. C.

TDQ:A Date May 3, 1937.

MEMORANDUM FOR MR. TOLSON

    Mr. Peake, formerly employed by the Washington-Herald, telephoned and wanted to know if the Director was in the city and whether he would meet Evelyn Frechette if she called at the Bureau this afternoon.

    Mr. Peake advised she was in the city playing at a carnival and had expressed a desire to meet the Director and go through the Bureau. I informed him the Director was absent from the city and the date of his return was uncertain and that apparently this was an attempted publicity stunt on the part of Miss Frechette. He denied this and wanted to know who could meet her if she called at the Bureau and was informed that I knew of no one who desired to meet her.

RECORDED & INDEXED.

62-47968-3
FEDERAL BUREAU OF INVESTIGATION
MAY 7 1937 P.M.
U. S. DEPARTMENT OF JUSTICE
FILE

Signature

Dear Sir:

In reference to the deceased John Dillinger, it has been ascertained that the Johnnie J. James Carnival and Circus, appearing in Pittsburgh, Pennsylvania, during the current week, has a sideshow attraction; a unit known or billed as "Crime does not Pay" the main feature of which is Evelyn Frechette, described as a gangster-girl and a gun-moll of John Dillinger.

Miss Frechette gives a general discourse on her association with John Dillinger and answers questions put to her by the audience. In answer to the specific questions from the audience, she stated among other things, that Dillinger had two "mobs" composed of six members each, not mentioning names; that she did not know who killed Dillinger, inasmuch as she was in a Michigan prison at the time; that she did not personally know the "lady in red" as John had "taken up with her" while she, Frechette, was in prison on charges of "harbouring John Dillinger".

This information was submitted by Anthony M Frahlich, the stenographer of this office, who attended one of the performances and who states that the girl is really Evelyn Frechette, identified from pictures in the possession of this office.

The above is furnished to the Bureau in the event that Frechette's location may be known for the purposes of the interview, or otherwise if desired.

Very truly yours,

RJ Untreiner

When I finally got them to move away from the discourse of the Dillinger Gang, we could talk more about my life as a Native American. In many of the shows, people were curious about my heritage but had been so brainwashed over the centuries they were afraid to ask. The show opened the opportunity for me to teach Western culture about my culture from a true standpoint.

"Okay, Evelyn, tell us about your home. Where are you from?"

"I come from French-Indian stock. Maybe that has something to do with it. I'm proud of my Indian blood. My tribe is a good tribe and my people are good people. Maybe I'd better tell how I was brought up.

"I was born on an Indian reservation in Neopit, Wisconsin sixty miles from Green Bay. I had two brothers and two sisters. My father died when I was eight years old. He was French and pronounced his name without the 'e,' like Freshet.

"My mother was half French and half Indian. Her tribe was Menominee. They called them the wild-rice eaters. They used to have their hunting ground around Wisconsin and Michigan a long time ago before the White man came and pushed them around."

"So, you often think of your people roaming the lands hunting?"

"I think about that sometimes when I look out through the bars of the window at the hills and the trees here in Michigan. I get to thinking that my people use to roam around over those hills — long before the White man came along with his rules about harbouring outlaws.

"And I get to thinking that maybe the Indians had rules about things like that too. Maybe if they caught a girl that was running around with an enemy chief, they'd hold her and wait for him to come for her so they could kill him. But I figure they would let her go after they killed him."

"So…. What was reservation life like?"

"Nothing happened to me when I was a child. I don't remember anything that happened to me that was unusual. We had to work around the reservation with our Indian relatives and neighbors. My mother had a hard time bringing us up after my dad died.

"I remember I had an uncle that the government people thought a lot about. They sent him to Washington to do things for the Indians and he was a big man.

"I got most of my schooling in a mission school on the reservation and then when I was thirteen, I went to a government school at Flandreau, South Dakota. I stayed there for three years and then I went to live with my sister in Milwaukee.

"I worked as a nurse—when I could get work and that wasn't very often. I wanted to come to Chicago. I hadn't been any place in my life and Chicago was a big and wonderful place for me."

"Now, I understand your sister is an actress in amateur plays?"

"I was eighteen then and worked when I could — nurse, and housework, and waitress. My sister, Frances, was there. She had a lot of Indian friends and they went around to churches and put-on Indian plays. She was a good little actress.

"They called themselves 'The Indian Players' and I remembered they put on plays called 'Little Fire Face' and 'The Elm Tree'. They got all dressed up in their feathers and beads and painted their faces and danced the way we used to on the Indian reservation.

"It was a lot of fun and I used to go around with my sister to the church socials. I wasn't a very good actress. But I helped wash the dishes, and cook parched corn, wild rice, and other Indian dishes. And when they needed somebody, I'd put on my costume and dance in the chorus."

As I did these shows talking about my childhood it made me homesick. I remembered that as a child I wanted to leave and get away from that place. However, now as I grow older, it's the one place I miss the most. We are judged by Western culture. Yes, reservation life is difficult, but it's honest, free from the nonsense of city life.

One of the following appearances included talking about my life after arriving in Chicago. I discussed one of the biggest mistakes of my life, and it was not falling in love with Johnnie.

"Evelyn, please tell us about Welton Sparks."

"It was fun, as I said, but it seems that nothing exciting ever happened to me and I was all alone, you might say. Then I met this man I married. I wasn't really in love with him, but I was lonesome. His name was Welton Sparks. Not long after we were married, he was arrested, and they sent him away to Leavenworth for fifteen years.

"I don't even know what he did. It had something to do with the government mail. He never told me what he was up to. Being married to him didn't amount to much. I lost track of him right away."

"Now... according to your words, this is when your life changed forever. Is that right? You met Dillinger in a North Side Cabaret."

"I kept on working here and there and I got some girlfriends and we would date up often and go out cabareting. I liked going out where people were laughing and having a good time and cutting up. It was in a cabaret on the North Side where I met John Dillinger.

"I'll never forget that. It happened the way things do in the movies. I was twenty-five years old and I wasn't any different from all the other girls that were twenty-five years old. Nothing that happened to me up to that time amounted to anything. Then I met John, and everything was changed. I started a new kind of life.

"It was in November, I remember. I was sitting at the table with some other girls and some fellows. We were having a good time."

"You told me once, that the attraction happened in just a few seconds?"

"I looked up and I saw a man at a table across the room looking at me. He didn't look away when I looked up, as most men did when they realized I am Native American. He just stared at me and smiled a little bit with the corner of his mouth. His eyes seemed to go all the way through me. A thing like that happens to a girl often and doesn't seem to mean anything. This was different. I looked at him and maybe I smiled. Anyway, he knew one of the girls I was with, and pretty soon, he came over to our table.

"She stood up and said, 'Billy, this is Jack Harris'."

"Jack Harris was that the name he used? Didn't you know who he was?"

"He might just as well have said his name was John Dillinger then because I didn't know any different. I didn't read the newspapers. I didn't know for a long time after that what his real name was. I didn't know he was the John Dillinger everybody under the sun was looking for.

"But to me that night, he was just Jack Harris—a good looking fellow that stood there looking down at me and smiling in a way that I could tell he liked me already more than a little bit.

He said, 'Where have you been all my life?'"

'Crime Does Not Pay' *(In the next chapter of the story of her life with John Dillinger, Evelyn ("Billy") Frechette will tell how this casual meeting grew into a love affair with the nation's No. 1 criminal— an affair that was interrupted only briefly when Dillinger and his gang were captured.)*

Part five of my appearance was more intense because they wanted to know about my life with Dillinger. It was difficult to talk about those days; the wives and girlfriends loved their men and it felt like we were being unfaithful. But again, the choice fell upon needing to make a living. I took a few months off after the last show to rest up and spend some time with my family. The time did me good, it gave me time to grow and mature, I guess. We re-engaged on August 30, 1941. The country was preparing for joining the war effort, the European Axis launched an invasion of the Soviet Union. So, people were no longer as enamored with Public Enemy No 1. My last show detailed the St. Paul shooting.

"Tell us about the shooting, Evelyn."

"I used to sit in my jail cell that wasn't any bigger than a pantry and wonder how I ever stood up during all those wild days when we had to sneak around like a lot of alley cats for fear we would get caught.

"For instance, the day after the shooting with the police in St. Paul when Johnnie sat there in the back seat of the car frowning and holding his leg, and waiting for me to go and get help for him. For a minute I thought I couldn't get up off the seat of the car. I felt sure that if I got out and started down the street, I'd get a bullet in my back before I got two feet away. Facing the fear took practice, but I went.

"I started running down the alley and John shouted, 'Take it easy…' and I slowed down. He didn't want to attract any attention in broad daylight."

"So where did you go?"

"I ran in the back way of Eddie Green's apartment and brought him out to the car. Then Beth came down, and John asked her to take me for a ride while Eddie was getting a doctor. I guess he thought it was dangerous and he didn't want me to get caught too if there was going to be trouble.

"We drove around for an hour or more and then came back and waited for a little before the doctor was brought up. He was Dr. Clayton May. Then we got in our cars and I rode with Eddie. We drove around and stopped at a place on Park Avenue., and they took John to get treated.

"The doctor said he'd be all right. This doctor later went on trial with me for harboring Dillinger. He said on the witness stand that John and Eddie threatened him with machine guns and that Eddie followed him to see there wasn't any tip-off. Somebody else will have to tell that story."

"So, Eddie was shot and killed that day, right?"

"This place was where the doctor's nurse lived. She was Mrs. Augusta Salt. We stayed there for three or four days waiting for John's knee to heal up. But it wasn't safe. We had to leave. I guess we got out just in time. They killed Eddie Green just after we left. The police shot him down in the street.

"Where to? We couldn't go to another place in the Twin Cities. The police were looking in every house there for us. We couldn't go to Chicago. They knew the neighborhood where John used to stay, and they were waiting for him there. So, John picked the one place where nobody would think of looking for him. He went home. He went back to his father's farm.

"I argued with him about that. I didn't think it was safe. But he said, 'Listen, Billy. Who's smarter—me or the cops?'

"I could not argue with that one. It took us two or three days to get there because we had to drive around quite a lot. We didn't go places where we thought there might be danger. John couldn't get out and walk any place because he was limping pretty bad and that would be a dead giveaway."

"Was that the first time you met his family?"

"His dad was glad to see him when he got to Mooresville, and we had a real celebration. All his family came down to say hello. His half-brother, Hubert, was there, and his sister, Mrs. Hancock, came down from Maywood, Indiana.

"John's dad said he ought to keep out of trouble, but John just laughed. We took a lot of pictures. John had one taken with his wooden gun. He still thought it was a joke the way he got out. He gave the gun to his father as a present.

"It wasn't safe to stay around the farm long. John was careless. He'd go out and sit in the yard with his sisters and play games where all the neighbors could see. I guess the only reason they didn't turn him in was they were afraid. Anyway, we left there on the ninth of April and drove to Chicago."

"So, the next part is a bit of a mystery. What were you going to do?"

"Well, we were going to settle down. We talked about it a lot on the way up. John thought he could do it now. He had plenty of money. He thought Chicago was as good a place as any."

"He gave you money, right, for a divorce?"

"We wanted to get married and John gave me the money for a divorce suit against my husband, Welton Sparks, who was in Leavenworth. John and I had been in love with each other for a long time now — nearly seven months. And more than that, we got to know each other. John couldn't trust many people, but he could trust me.

"It sounds kind of silly now, but that was the talking plan. We couldn't settle down, so John talked about getting plastic surgery. Then we'd run off together somewhere exotic. We were going to head into Chicago while Johnnie took care of some business and then we were leaving. There was no use deceiving ourselves. We were going to get caught sooner or later. I got it sooner. We had just got into Chicago and I walked right into a trap. It was the last time I saw him in person, but the idea kept me sane in prison for a while until they killed him."

(In the next and concluding chapter of her life with John Dillinger, Evelyn Frechette describes her own capture while Dillinger, the most hunted man in the world, waited a block away.)

The show ended shortly after I had lost interest and it was time for me to move on with the next phase of my life without Johnnie. I'd been traveling for nearly five years, seen all I wanted to see around the country and talked about life with Dillinger over and over, I started to get the details mixed up repeating them so many times. By this time, the FBI had other interests and they stopped surveilling me. I was ready to go home.

Chapter Seventeen:

I Grieved!

The time I spent with "Crime Does Not Pay" taught me many things, some of which I already knew and other things maybe I'd been better off not knowing. But all in all, the money was good, and I got to get my message out to the world. Johnnie was more than some gangster; he had a conscience and genuinely cared about people for the most part. He was a normal guy, who got a bad rap by the courts, FBI, and coppers.

    I'd grieved for almost five years and was ready to move on with life, one that was more or less filled with peace and out of the spotlight. The only place I was going to find the solace I needed was on the reservation. Yes, many of my people had shunned me for my involvement with the Dillinger Gang, and it would take time to regain their trust. Nonetheless, it would be well worth the effort. I finished the last

Friday night show, got some dinner, and headed for home. It was more than a three-day drive since I did not like to travel much at night alone. I have to admit, the independence felt good. It was the first time in my adult life I was unattached to anyone. However, I had not lost all hope in finding love once again.

The first night I drove about fifty miles before stopping for the night. I passed a few Burma Shave signs and entertained the idea of homemade pie and could not resist. The hotel reminded me of a few we stayed in on the run from the FBI; it was nearly impossible to go anywhere and not think of Johnnie or our times together. He was truly one of a kind. When I walked into the office, there was a magazine on the table with an article about the Dillinger Gang. I could not help to notice and grab it on my way out the door after check-in.

The desk clerk walked me to my room and asked, "Oh, I see you found the magazine about Dillinger?"

"Yes, I did…."

"I can't wait to read it, we just got it yesterday."

"Well, I'll be sure to return it in the morning."

"Thanks, can you believe all that? It would have been cool to meet John Dillinger. You know?" I thought about her statement for a moment and contemplated answering her but chose to stay anonymous.

"I agree… he seemed like a nice guy."

"I know, right? Well, have a good night. If you need anything, please ring the front desk. If you want dinner, I am sure we can find something in the kitchen for you."

"Uh, sure that would be great. I'll be up in a few minutes after I freshen up."

I could not wait to read the article and see how many lies were written about what happened. I'd learned the conspiracy theories and tall tales ran wild when it came to Dillinger. I hoped that the roadshow cleared up some of the myths. I guess trying to evade hearing something about Johnnie was going to be impossible, as long as I was off the reservation anyway.

As I started to read the article it was obvious their outlook of what truly happened seemed bleak, just like most of them. I only read about one page and took the magazine back with me before dinner. Luckily the desk clerk was gone when I laid it back on the table. The last thing I wanted was to explain my reason for bringing it back early. My dinner was absolutely wonderful, the best food I had eaten in months. And the pie was homemade, just as reported. After dinner, I took a walk before retiring for the night. It was a beautiful summer evening, the cool air started to settle in, and it felt like home. The sensation brought me back to being a young girl playing in the field of flowers just outside of our town. If you can call Neopit a town, it was more like a village or clearing with a few huts. However, it was home. No matter where I went, it was the one place that kept me sane.

I got up before dawn the next morning and headed for home. I had one more day before being back in Wisconsin. On my way out of town, I grabbed some snacks and filled up the gas tank. In those days, it was not smart to travel without essentials, like plenty of water, food, and clothing. I noticed while driving across the country that the times were changing. The towns were expanding, and many of the rural areas now had power and water. The country was finally overcoming the depression, and dust bowl. It had been a rough ten years during that time. But people were finally coming back home to their houses, and industry was rebuilding. It was the start of WWII and the country was booming with military contracts and such. I enjoyed my drive home seeing the changes coming about.

On my last night heading home, I stopped at a small motel on the outside of this quaint little town. After checking in, I walked across the street to the only restaurant in town. It was packed, so I had to wait outside for almost thirty minutes. While I waited a nice, good-looking man walked up and asked if the seat next to me was taken. I admit, his charm caught me off guard. Our conversation lasted the whole thirty minutes, then he invited me to have dinner with him. I was eager to have some company and accepted.

At first, I was hesitant, since the last man I had any intimate contact with had died, and the other one was in prison. But Wally seemed pleasant; he did not ask too many questions about my past, and that made me happy. We talked for several hours, and he kept my attention.

"So, Evelyn, where are you from?"

"I am from Wisconsin. As a matter of fact, that is where I am headed back. I have been traveling for about five years and am ready to go home."

"Travelling, that must be nice…."

"It was part of my job, I guess you could say. But time to move on with my life."

"What kind of work do you do?"

"I was part of a traveling roadshow. We did interviews with famous people."

"Well, that is cool."

"So, how about you?"

"Huh, well you know like you, I'm from here and there."

"No, I mean where were you born?"

"Actually, I am not sure. My mother died when I was young, and my father left to find work shortly after that, and I ended up in an orphanage. But they sent me to school, put clothes on my back, and kept us fed. I guess it could have been worse."

"Yes, I know all about being in a boarding school. I was sent to one at five in South Dakota."

"What happened to your parents?"

"My father died when I was very young, and the government rounded us up and sent us to the Indian Boarding Schools. They kept me there until I was eighteen."

"So, you are Indian, wow. I've never known a true Indian."

"I don't tell many people about my heritage. But since we have similar backgrounds, you might understand?"

"Yeah, you could say that. It's no problem for me."

"Good, I am happy to hear that," I told Wally my destination and how to find me if he was interested. In some ways, I was excited to see more of him, but on the other hand, having my freedom was nice as well. In this case, it was up to fate if he came to find me.

I pulled out the next morning just before dawn, with no more communication from Wally, so I just figured it was for the best. On my last day, I decided to drive straight through home. I had written my mother and sister telling them to expect me between the tenth and thirteenth of June 1941. It was about 10:00 p.m. when I pulled into my mother's house. She was up as usual; some things never change.

I knocked on the door. "Oh my, Evelyn…. I am so happy to see you. Come on, do you need some help with your bags?"

"No, I'll get them. Give me a hug first, it's been far too long."

"Come on now…. Sit, let me get you some coffee or tea?"

"Yes, some tea would be nice, thanks." We talked for hours; it was almost dawn before I finally went to bed. I can honestly say it was the first good night's sleep I'd had in many years. Being home with my family took away the pain of the last five years. It's funny how mothers are the single most wonderful outlets to cure any ailment. It is true time heals all wounds, but age gives you the wisdom to deal with the lingering effects.

I slept almost sixteen hours; it would have been more if a visitor had not shown up to see me. "Evelyn, there is a man here to see you."

At first, I wondered who could be here to see me, and then I realized who it was. "Oh, that must be Wally." She looked puzzled. "He was someone I met the other night having dinner. Tell him to give me a few minutes to get dressed, please?"

"Of course. He is handsome." She smiled.

My mother invited him inside and they sat in the kitchen drinking coffee while I got dressed. It surprised me; I never expected to see him again. "Hello, Wally, it's very nice to see you again."

"Evelyn, sorry to drop in on you, unexpectedly. I just wanted to see you."

"No, it's okay, we were up till almost dawn talking. I have not seen my mother in years. Well, how about something to eat and we can take a drive?"

"Yes, that would be lovely."

My mother jumped in, "Evelyn, sit, let me. You've had a long trip."

"Thanks, Mom…. It's nice to be home."

"I am happy to have you here as well." We had bologna sandwiches with some chips, a staple in those days. Then we headed out for a nice afternoon drive. It had been a long time since I'd seen the reservation. We were gone for about three hours, and by the time we got back, it was like I'd known Wally for years. He stayed with us for dinner and left at about 10:00 p.m. We agreed to meet the next day and go for a picnic.

After he left that night, I went straight to bed. I think the exhaustion from my trip was catching up. The next morning just before sunrise, I heard the roosters crowing, a sound that always made me smile. I can remember collecting eggs and cleaning out the coop as a young girl. My sisters and I would fight over whose turn it was, and of course not being the oldest, it was always my turn. As the smell of freshly brewed coffee filled the house, I made my way to the kitchen. Mom was in front of the stove cooking me breakfast, some things never change.

"Mom, when we are done, what chores do you have? I'd like to help you while I am here."

"Oh, honey, don't worry. I can do it."

"Mom, I know you can but please let me help." She nodded. We sat at the table laughing and talking like children. "Come on, we have to get chores done, my gentleman caller will be here soon."

"Oh, again today?"

"Yes, we are going on a picnic. I thought maybe down by the old stream."

"I always loved that place. It's been years since I walked down there as well."

I finished my breakfast and got up to get chores done. "Where do you keep the basket, Mom, for eggs?"

"In the side closet right there by the back door."

"Thanks, I'll be right back."

"Alright, but watch the white one, she likes to try and sneak out through the gate."

"Yes, ma'am…." She smiled.

When I headed out back, I could see her peeking out the backdoor watching me. It's true, parents never see their children as adults. I turned and smiled to make sure she knew I was watching. I could feel the peace settling in and knew coming home was just what I needed to heal. Once the chores were done, I went back inside and made sandwiches, grabbed some chips, and lemonade to drink. Plus, Mom still had the old picnic basket we used as kids. The memories flooded back when I saw that old thing. We used to get so excited to have our Sunday afternoon picnics. There is something about sitting under a big shade tree in the fresh air eating lunch with your loved ones. I can still remember the last one before Daddy died like it was yesterday. Some memories never fade.

Wally showed up right on time, noon, just as we planned. "Hello, Wally… come on in. It's nice to see you again. I have everything ready to go."

"Oh, good. Where is your mom? I wanted to say hi."

"She is lying down. We can talk later after our drive."

"Is she alright?"

"Oh, yes, she gets up very early. And by noon she gets tired. Unfortunately, we are not getting any younger." He nodded.

"So, where to?"

"Well, grab the basket and follow me. I hope you don't mind walking?"

"No… how far?"

"About a mile to the creek. We used to haul water from there when I was a kid. I can remember my brothers carrying the buckets on their shoulders to the hut."

"Did you say hut?"

"Yes, we lived in huts back then."

"Oh my, that must have been freezing in the winters."

"It was. We all huddled on the floor beside the cooking stove in the center of the room."

"So, it was all one room I take it?"

"Yep! There were six of us until Daddy died. My mother used to cook, clean, make our clothes, and everything before we were shipped off to boarding school. It broke my heart that day. I watched her with tears rolling down my cheeks. I did not see her again until I turned eighteen."

"Wow! That is horrible. It's obvious she loves you very much. I have only heard stories about the Indians. When I was a kid, they told us to stay away from them, because they were dangerous. I do remember the raiding parties that went out on the reservations hunting to kill any Indian they found."

"Well, I can't imagine growing up in an orphanage was much better?"

"Huh, no. They were horribly abusive. Many times, the beatings would keep me from sitting in a chair for days. I have to say, I am glad to have been born a boy. I could hear the male workers raping the girls at night after everyone else went home."

"Yes, that happened to us as well, but one subject I'd rather not discuss."

"Oh, sorry…. I'm guessing?" I nodded. "How old were you?"

"It was not while I was in boarding school. I was walking along the road headed to the Reservation and four men stopped. And you know the rest. But I got pregnant and because one of the men had syphilis, my baby was born with bad birth defects and I could not raise him. A lady from the Brooks Farm and Beulah Home contacted me and said they could raise him for me. I was told because of the syphilis he would not live long anyway. It was one of the hardest things I have ever done. After the birth, the doctors told me I could never have any more children."

"Evelyn… I don't know what to say. What happened to your baby? Did he live long?"

"I am not sure." His questions choked me up. I had not talked about Billie in years.

"His name was Billie. I got to see him for a few minutes before they took him away. Many years later actually, while I was in prison—"

"Wait, you were in prison?" I nodded.

"That is for another day. Anyway, I heard that Rev. Edward Brooks turned out to be a serial killer. He murdered more than twenty-five children. When they finally caught him, the babies were found buried in shallow graves wrapped in newspapers in the dunes along Lake Michigan, near Beulah MI. Many of them were poisoned or beaten to death. My Billie was one of the babies."

"I'm stunned, don't know…."

"You don't have to say anything. It's alright, it's nice to get it off my chest…. He claims to have been doing God's work. His tenure lasted for more than sixty-five years."

"Sixty-five years, he was doing this kind of stuff?"

"I don't know about all those years but many of them, I am sure." We both got quiet for some time. I did not know if my honesty scared him away, or if we were going to move forward. In many ways, it was nice being with someone who was not on the run from the coppers. "Have I scared you away?"

"Oh, no…. I am just trying to digest all the things that you have told me. And I am sure there is more, like being in jail."

"Good, I have enjoyed our day. When the time is right, I will tell you more. Now, what about you?"

"Same here, I will tell you in time. But for now, it's getting late and I have to report to work in the morning."

"Work… what work?"

"Okay, don't laugh…." I shook my head. "I am a door-to-door salesman."

"Really, like someone who sells encyclopaedias or vacuums?"

"Yes… that is me."

"I can say that I have never met a door-to-door salesman. Hey, it's work, nothing wrong with that. How long have you been doing that?"

"Not very long, a friend got me the job."

"Well, good luck."

"What about you?"

"What do I do? Well, with the money I made from my traveling show days and my reservation money, I don't have to work. I am not rich or anything, but it's enough to get by."

"I think that is great. You are lucky." I smiled.

"Well, if you are ready, we should go; it's a long walk back."

Wally and I walked back hand in hand. We had connected in some way, I felt like we understood each other on some level. I bid him adieu that evening and he told me he'd be back in about two weeks.

Chapter Eighteen:

The Spying

The next two weeks were like a whirlwind; spending time with Mom was unexplainable. She nursed me back to health, mental health that is. I did not realize how much damage had been done from my time with Johnnie and being in prison. It even gave me time to reconnect with God and my faith. I'd been running for years, not only from the coppers, but the FBI and life in general. When the Great Depression hit and then we faced the Dust Bowl, the US shut down. There were no jobs unless you were part of the elite, which meant either starving or steal what you needed. I am not saying stealing is right, but the men did what they had to do protect their families. On my way back home, passing the old abandoned farms was like being in the Sahara Desert or something. The houses were buried in the dirt, cars left broken down on the side of the road, and families living in small tents alongside the roads. Then for anyone living in town, yes, they had food banks, but again, it mostly went to the wealthy, and by the time you stood in line, there was no guarantee anything would be left. People started forming lines days before the doors opened. And don't think it was any easier on the reservation, since the railroad and Wild Bill Hickock or other men like him slaughtered the buffalo by the thousands. The worst part of that was, the meat could have been used to feed people suffering from the depression. Instead, it went to waste rotting in the lands of America. As a matter of fact, I can remember seeing piles of buffalo hides as tall as the hills around them, or the pastures riddled with dead carcasses. The sight just made me sick, and the tears would roll down my cheeks. So, needless to say, America had a lot of healing to do.

By the time two weeks had passed, I was ready to see Wally again. I hoped he would show up. In those days, one could only hope. Not everyone had a phone or would let you use it to call anyone.

It was Tuesday morning that week when Wally showed up at my mother's house. I met him at the door with a large smile. "Hello, it's so nice to see you again."

"It's nice to be seen. Oh, I brought you something…." I waited with bated breath. He pulled a bouquet of flowers out from behind his back.

"Flowers, oh they are beautiful. Thank you, come in. I will get a vase."

"I hope that was not too forward, bringing you flowers?"

"No, it was a wonderful gesture. So, how was your trip? Get a lot of sales?"

"Sales…." He paused for some time.

"Yes, sell any vacuums or encyclopaedias?"

"Oh …. I did sell one vacuum." His vagueness raised my suspicions. "I'm sorry, it's been a long couple of weeks. I drove most of the night to get here and need some sleep."

"Oh, you had me worried for a minute. If you want to lie down on my bed, please do so."

"Thank you, but I can sleep tonight. I would rather spend my day with you. What's on the agenda today?"

"Oh, just boring stuff like going to town for supplies. Would you like to come along? Mom has a hard time going these days, so I like to go for her."

"I thought you'd never ask…. Are you ready now?"

"Yes, once I finish the chores."

"Chores? I haven't heard that word in many years. What do we have to do?"

"If you want to collect eggs, I will get the henhouse cleaned out."

"Sure, lead the way. I have never collected chicken eggs before." I looked puzzled at knowing someone who had never collected eggs. "I am from the city, remember; our eggs came from the grocery store."

"Oh, yeah, okay. Well come on, you're going to today."

It took the better part of an hour to collect the eggs and clean the coop. Mom had almost 100 chickens. She sold the eggs once a week to the grocery store, or anyone else. It was a nice way to supplement her income. I got a kick out of Wally, watching him run around gathering the eggs. You could only hold about twenty eggs in the basket before going over to empty it and fill the cartons. He worked like a trooper for the first twenty minutes or so, then he got bored. I could see the angst in his demeanor. Mom came out a few minutes later and took over while he rested on the side-lines. At the time, I just took it as sleep deprived. Besides, living on a farm is not the life for everyone. You have to be a special person to do farm work; it's dirty, never ending, and not always the best pay. We finished up and headed for town, and the trip would take most of the day. Mom usually went for supplies once a month when she got her money. Wally drove that day, he wanted to get his car looked at by the mechanic. He told me it had been making a funny noise. So, he dropped me off at the store and headed for the garage. I gathered all the supplies and bought a soda for a treat. Most of the stores back then had sitting benches out front, so women could wait for their husbands to bring the car. I waited for more than an hour before Wally came back. He explained to me that the mechanic had to replace some part on the front axle. However, he seemed different. "Hey, doll, are you ready?"

I looked at him. "Doll?"

"Sorry, don't you like that? It's just a pet name." I shook my head.

"Okay, noted. Here, let me help with these groceries."

We loaded them up. "Hey, before we leave, I need to stop at the pharmacy, is that alright?"

"Sure, sure.... Are you okay?"

"Yes, just things for my mom. I'll only be a minute." We were headed on our way home within the next twenty minutes. "So, I hope today was not too boring for you."

"No.... I like just spending time with you. It does not matter what we do."

"Good, I was hoping you would say that. Can you stay for dinner?"

"Tonight, no, sadly... I have an appointment at 8:00 p.m. in town. But I can come back in the morning?"

"Yes, that would be nice. I can show you around the reservation; where I went to school and stuff."

"Okay, that would be fun. I look forward to it."

We talked the whole way home; Wally was turning out to be a great find. My mother liked him and that made me happy. I wanted him to meet my sister; however, she would not be home for a few more weeks. He left as soon as the groceries were unloaded, and admittedly, I was starting to miss him after he left. We dated for almost three months; he came over for several days in a week and then would be gone for weeks at a time. The schedule worked fine with me. I was not willing to give up my freedom just yet.

On our third month anniversary, he wanted to take me on a trip for the weekend, so we could celebrate alone. I agreed and thought it was a good time to be alone. We did not travel too far, just on the far side of town at a nice hotel. "Are you sure you can afford this?"

"Yes, why do you ask?"

"It's just expensive to stay here."

"Please, let me handle my own money affairs."

"Yes…. I am sorry."

"Don't worry. I don't know about your other men, but I know how to make money."

His comment caused me concern. "I did not mean anything by that, just asking."

"No, I am sorry. I was out of line. You have a right to ask. Come on, let's just have some fun." I agreed.

We checked in under an alias, it was like déjà vu. I had to keep quiet, he did not know of my past. It was one secret I was intent on keeping for now.

Chapter Nineteen:

Time Heals All Wounds

The saying is right, time heals all wounds. I had moved on with another wonderful man. Wally had a normal job, came home every other weekend, and things were starting to look good. I felt like life was becoming normal. It had taken many years; my people were finally beginning to build a life for ourselves. We had established a government, who started crafting work and a stable lifestyle on the reservation.

After our wedding engagement, we decided to get married after the holidays. We had planned a big wedding in St. Anthony's but since Wally was not religious, he felt very uncomfortable, so I opted for using a justice of the peace. My sister stood as a witness; it was a nice ceremony, definitely better than my last marriage. We went on a honeymoon; it lasted three days. I wanted to revisit Florida, but our money situation could not afford such a trip, so we decided on a nice hotel in Wisconsin.

The drive felt like the good ole days. We filled the trunk with essentials and took off for our adventure. I snuggled in next to Wally driving and sang along with the radio, even the weather cleared up for the few days we were gone. All seemed blessed, just as planned. It had taken Wally since we met to open up about his childhood. Most of what he said was true; however, not all. His father was a good man between his drinking binges. As he stated, they could last a month or a few days, there was no consistency except with abuse. The death of his mother was called suspicious, and his father, he told me just disappeared. After that is when the state sent him to an orphanage. At that point, his life took a turn for the worse. A member of the staff liked little boys, so for the next five years every evening, he came and took him to a "special" room to spend quality time. Wally says he made him perform all sorts of sex acts on the man, then he returned the favor. When he tried to resist, he was threatened with his life or being evicted to live on the streets. The day Wally turned eighteen, he left and said he never looked back. I can say, in all the years I was in South Dakota, no one ever molested or raped me. It was only after I left that things got worse.

Our conversations lasted most of the first few days we were in Wisconsin. I don't think that Saturday we even left our room. We stayed tucked in under the sheets, making love and talking. Wally became a different person after talking to me. He was finally able to get that stuff off his chest; he never said otherwise, but I was the first person he ever told his story to. The horror he must have faced is unimaginable. In those days that was a common occurrence, and no one talked about the incidents with anyone. You suffered in silence or ended up in some hidden quarry where no one would ever find your body. In my own way, I loved Wally. He was a troubled soul but there were parts of him I found soft and tender.

We had a marvelous weekend, but I was ready to go home. I'd been back on the reservation for some time now and no matter where I traveled, it was the only place that gave me security. It's funny how when you are a kid the world seems like a big playground and you can't wait to see it all, then as you age the only place you want to go is home.

I'm not sure my new husband carried the same sentiment for the reservation. He seemed to get very anxious if we spent too much time in solitude. So, to compromise, I gave him his space. Things went along well for most of the next year. America was slowly changing; our involvement in WWII exploded the economy. Wally's business was growing very fast, and he was making money hand over fist. I had no idea how much money a door-to-door salesman could make.

On one of his workweeks, he came home early on Thursday morning, very distraught. When I asked what happened he seemed angry, highly volatile. I had not seen that side of him, and it worried me.

"Wally, what happened? You were not supposed to be here until tomorrow."

"What does it matter when I come home unless you have another man here?"

"No… of course not. What's wrong? You seem very upset—"

"I am… enough said. Stop nagging me."

"I did not think that I was. I'm just wondering why you are here on a Thursday morning, angry and drunk."

"So, what if I am drunk? I felt like having a drink."

Our argument continued for almost an hour. We shouted and yelled without accomplishing anything. He finally left in a hurry with no explanation. I had no idea when he'd come home, or if he was coming back.

My mother hid in her room the whole time, the incident really scared her. "Evelyn…." she called from her doorway. "Is he gone?"

"Yes, Mamma. It's alright."

"What in the world was that all about?"

"I don't know. Your guess is as good as mine."

"So, he never told you, even when you went outside?"

"No, he told me to stop asking, or else. Then got in his car and took off."

"Oh, Evelyn, maybe we should call someone? Tell the police."

"Mamma, I am sure he will cool off and explain everything when he comes back."

"I hope you are right…."

I knew she had a point and it concerned me as well. But the last thing I wanted was for her to worry or be afraid in her own home. I went on with my day and tried to calm my fears before he came home again. Needless to say, he stayed away for almost ten days. I could not believe what happened; it took us by complete surprise. Mom and I were sitting in the kitchen talking after dinner when he stumbled in the door. At first glance, I thought he was a stranger. He had dirt covering his face, he stunk like urine and was stumbling drunk again. As I jumped up to greet him at the door to the kitchen, he collapsed on the floor.

We rushed over to aide him, but he was completely unconscious. I was sure he passed out drunk or there was something else wrong with him. Mom and I did our best to drag him over the couch, and we'd wait to see if he woke up, or we'd be calling for the mortician in the morning. He woke up about four hours later, completely disoriented as to how he got home or on the couch. I explained to him, he came stumbling in the house and collapsed.

"Wally, what happened, where have you been? It's been ten days since you left."

"I don't know exactly, it's all a blur. I am so sorry for the way I acted…. You did not deserve that. My sales had been kind of slow recently and the boss called me in his office and explained he was giving my route to the new kid. Tried to tell me he was a better salesman and had new and innovative ideas. It made me mad. He said I was going to be transferred to another area."

"Well, that's not so bad. It's still work…."

"No, but I would only be able to come home to you once a month. I can't be gone that much."

"Wally, yes, I agree. But right now, finding work is difficult and you should make the change."

"Oh." He jumped up. "So you want me gone all the time now?"

"No, I never said that…. Look, it's just work and not forever. Maybe I can come with you sometimes. We can travel together."

"I would like that, but family traveling with you is not allowed."

"It's not like I'd be working or going to houses with you. I would stay at the hotel."

"No… no, that won't work. Please stop pushing the issue." I could see his demeanor changing again quickly. The last thing I wanted was another outburst.

"Fine…. I understand, do whatever you like. I will support your decision."

"Good…. Can I please get some dinner?"

"Yes, if you promise to go take a shower."

"Agreed…." He looked down. "I look pretty bad, huh?" I nodded.

Wally went into our room, got some clean clothes and took a shower, while I made him some dinner. Mom came out after he went into the bathroom. "It seems he has calmed down?"

"Yes, I am not sure what caused that incident, but he seems fine now."

"Let's just hope it stays that way."

"Agreed."

Mom went and retired for the night, while I sat with Wally in the kitchen while he ate. It seemed as though it was his first meal in days. I ended up making him two plates of eggs and sausage. The next several weeks went off without a hitch, and Wally was back to his normal self. I knew he was getting bored staying home all the time, but happy, nonetheless. A few days later, someone called the house for him, which seemed odd because it was the first time since I'd known him that he had a phone call. It was a man on the phone and they asked for Walter Wilson.

"Hello…." He listened intently. "Yes, sir, right away. I will see you in the morning."

"Well, that seemed like good news."

"It was my boss. I had given him this number to call in case of an emergency. He said that a young kid who was going to take my place quit and I can have my old route back."

"Oh, honey, that is wonderful. So, you are going to work tomorrow?"

"Yes, bright and early. So, I guess you'll be getting rid of me every week once again."

"I guess I will…. Why don't we go celebrate on your next days off?"

"Great idea. You pick, I don't care what we do." Our night was calm, soothing even. We made love and Wally left about 5:00 a.m. I was happy to see him content again.

We moved forward as if nothing ever happened, and he even started calling me in the middle of the week just to say hello. I honestly believed we made it over the hurdle. Our lives were peaceful until right before summer that year, when he came home early one Friday afternoon drunk. He was in a foul mood; just said he had a bad day. He told me his sales had been down and the boss was on his case. Later that evening after dinner, he went into the living room and sat down in the chair while Mom and I took care of nightly chores. We were outside for the better part of an hour, but when we came back inside, Wally was sitting in the same place I left him. I tried to talk with him but had a very one-sided conversation.

"Wally...." He only acknowledged me with his eyes. "Is everything alright? You have me worried."

"I already told you the problem, how many damn times are you going to ask? Get over it, woman." I had learned my lesson, so we just left him alone.

I went to bed at about ten after reading for a while, then about midnight, I heard the front door slam closed. It startled me, so I got up and went into the living room. Wally had either gone to the mini-mart for liquor or he brought it home with him. As I approached him from the side of the chair his eyes were black as coal. I saw evil in them unlike I'd ever seen before. It sent chills clear through my soul. He just glanced over at me and scowled. I turned and walked away. Needless to say, I did not get much sleep that night. The next morning, I got up about 4:00 a.m. when Mom did so I could check on him; he was plastered in the same place I left him the night before. The only difference was, he never budged, like he was in a trance. This carried on for four more days. I'd never seen anything like it, nor do I want to ever again.

After the fourth day, I sent Mom to my sister's. I was terrified he might hurt her. She hated leaving me, but it was the only option. On the fifth morning, I walked into the living, took off my ring, and threw it at him. "I am done, no more of this. I don't know what's wrong with you but no more. I want you out of this house. Get your stuff and leave now, before I call the police."

A few seconds later he jumped up like his butt was on fire. "Evelyn…. Please, forgive me. I don't know what happened to me." His excuses went on and on for almost thirty minutes, but I'd had enough.

"No…. No, you need to leave and don't come back. I won't live like this. I want you out."

He looked like a kid whose dog just died, "Please, Evelyn, give me another chance, I am sorry. This won't ever happen again, I promise." I must have lost my mind that day; something rushed over my body to give him another chance.

We talked again for hours and I called Mom and told her to come home. However, she never trusted him again. I can say that deep down, I did not either. All went well over the next few days he was home. He left on Monday morning as always;

however, something had changed between us. The kind of change that never fades.

In the next few mornings after he left for work again, I started feeling ill. At first, I thought it was the flu; however, when the symptoms did not fade it was time to see the doctor. They had told me years ago that sometimes syphilis can re-emerge. So that had me worried. Mom and I took a drive to town, and while she did the shopping, I visited the doctor, only his news was something I never thought possible again.

I walked over to the store and met her at the car. "Evelyn, how did the appointment go? You don't look so good."

"Mom…. I'm pregnant."

She looked baffled. "You're what?"

"The doctor said about eleven weeks."

"You are positive?"

"Yes, I heard the heartbeat. They told me after Billie I could not have any more children."

"What are you going to do? Are you going to tell Wally?"

"Mom.... How can I not tell him? It's not like he won't find out."

"Well, I was not certain you were going to stay married."

"I know… and that thought crossed my mind but for now, yes. We are going to work through this." She cocked her head. I should have listened.

It took me the next ten days trying to figure out how to tell Wally about the news. I had no idea how he might take this information. My mind swirled with thoughts, one being I wished it was Johnnie coming home in ten days. I stayed to myself for several days. I had to calm my fears.

Wally surprised me on Friday afternoon with flowers and chocolate. He seemed genuinely excited to be home, so I figured it was best to get it out right away. "Wally, it's so nice to have you home. But we have to talk…. Come sit on the couch with me." He looked worried. "Wally…. I am pregnant."

He started laughing. "You're what?"

"It's not a joke…. I am pregnant. I went to the doctor and heard the heartbeat." The room went silent, and he just stared at me. "Are you okay? Please don't go out on me again." He jolted.

"I'm not. This is just unexpected. Can I think about this for a while?"

"Think about it? It's not like buying a car or something." He looked at me, confused. "I can't go back and get unpregnant."

"I know, sorry. Look, I just need to be alone; I'll be back."

"Where are you going?" I asked.

"For a drive…. I'll be back later."

Well, his later turned into 2:00 a.m. and so drunk he could barely walk. I ran into the living room and helped him into the bedroom before he broke something or woke Mom. We made it into the room, and he turned to shut the door. His stupor changed instantly. "We are not having a baby."

"We what? I don't understand. As I said earlier, I can't go back and get unpregnant. If you think I am going to have an abortion you are crazy...."

"Let me make one thing clear: You will get rid of that baby, or I will."

The terror shot through my system; I backed my way to the door. "Where do you think you are going? And don't even think about yelling for mommy." I stopped. "So, what's it going to be? Me or the doctor?"

"Please... don't—we can work this out. You can leave, I will raise the baby on my own. Mom is here and my family will help. You don't have to do anything."

"Really, how is that going to be possible? You are my wife. Do you think because of that baby I will just leave, or divorce you?"

"Uh," I stuttered. The evil in his eyes poured out like water. "I want to have this baby, please don't make me do this."

He looked at me and smiled. "Then I am going to enjoy this…."

Wally took off his belt and beat me until I was unconscious. After I passed out, he stopped hitting me and scurried out the door. I came to a little later after my mom found me when she woke up to use the bathroom. She helped me to bed and called the doctor's office. I could hear her talking on the phone. "Doctor, my daughter's been hurt, can you come right away?"

The doctor showed up about an hour later with lots of questions. "Evelyn, what happened here tonight?"

Before I could say anything, my mother interrupted. "Her husband beat her because she is pregnant."

"Mom…."

"Evelyn, is this true?" I nodded.

"Where is he now?"

"He left…" I whispered.

"You need to be in the hospital. I want her there in a few hours."

"Fine. Mom, will you drive?"

"Of course, let's just follow the doctor. I can come home and get some things for you later."

We followed the doctor to the hospital. They rushed me into surgery right away, but unfortunately, I lost the baby.

Chapter Twenty:

My Baby's Gone

In another turn of events, the worst happened again. It seemed that no matter where I went or who I met things had a way of ending badly. I started to believe there was an aura of evil that followed me around.

The incident with my first son nearly killed me, and now I faced the loss of another child. He was essentially murdered like my Billie. If it had not been for my mother and sister, I might not have survived to write this book.

When I woke from surgery, seeing the faces of my loved ones ripped my heart in half. I was never one who believed in revenge, but this almost pushed me over the edge. However, my upbringing and faith helped me understand that only God has the right to revenge. We must keep the faith and believe the righteous will prevail in the afterlife.

I stayed in the hospital for almost three days; they had a hard time stopping the bleeding. Even then, I was bedridden for nearly a month. My sister came to stay with us for a time to help keep a watch for Wally. But he made himself scarce. I hated myself for being so stupid again, trusting a man to be what he claimed. Don't get me wrong, but I had been lied to by men all my life. Johnnie and I loved each other, and he would never have hurt me as Wally did; however, he lied to the world for much of his life. It began the first night we met when he introduced himself as Jack Harris. Then everywhere we went it was another alias, to the point we were not safe anywhere without being recognized. I admit the lifestyle was exciting to some extent. Only the running gets exhausting, and Johnnie had come to the same conclusion. He wanted out as well, and we even made plans to escape the life on our way back from his family farm, and before I was arrested. This was another case, and I'd had enough of all men for a while. The time recuperating made me realize I saw the signs with Wally deep down but ignored the signals. It was easier to explain them away with excuses, and now that reasoning cost my next child their life, a regret that would stay with me for the rest of my life.

By the end of the next month, spring was coming, and the weather started to warm up, thank goodness. All was quiet on the home front while I healed, and I wanted it to stay that way. So, as soon as the doctor released me, I decided to travel. It was time to take care of some things that had been eating at me for years. Since Johnnie died and I got out of prison, I stayed clear of everything to do with him or that life, because the FBI was surveilling me. Now, since I wanted to keep my family safe, the last thing I needed was allowing Wally to harm my mother or sister. I could finally take care of some issues and know they'd be left alone. Not to mention, they did not deserve the chaos that I brought into their world.

I felt good about my decision to leave home for a while; it gave me time to see the county by myself. In the past, my travels had been with a man who determined our destination. It was the beginning of the war and women, in general, were taking off their aprons and putting on the pants to fulfil the jobs men had done since society began. We were finally standing up and getting a chance to show the male-driven economy that women are just as capable as any man.

Since the day I left my Billie with the nurse of Beulah Home, a hole inside my heart could never be filled. Then when I found out that he had been brutally murdered on the news, it ate at my soul. In many ways, this time gave me the ability to make things right for him. I left a basic itinerary with Mom and headed out the next Monday morning after the doctor released me. My first stop was Beulah, Michigan. I knew the place was closed but figured the city hall would have records on where all the babies were born and maybe some info on each of them. Since I moved around so much with Johnnie, any paperwork that may have been mailed, I would have never received it. Plus, I wanted to see the countryside before we were locked down due to the rationings.

Then as figured, shortly after my return home, President Roosevelt halted any unnecessary travel. People were allocated three gallons of gasoline per week. They even stopped production of durable goods like new housing, vacuum cleaners, and kitchen appliances. Most of the population started moving in with close friends or family due to income levels and supplies. The government even put a limit on how much you could make a month.

On the reservation, women have always played an important role in the tribe's survival. It was only after Western culture took control that Native Americans got a bad rap. Suddenly, we became dangerous, uncivilized human beings because our choice of living is different. And it all boiled down to that simple fact; we were different. I have always had an issue with not being accepted because my beliefs are not the same as a Christian person. We are all children of God and should be treated as such.

My drive to Michigan was uneventful. It took me the better part of one day, as I did not drive as fast as some people. But I got to see all the wonderful

Victory Gardens. We had heard about them in the papers and how they were helping to feed America.

By May of 1943, there were 18 million Victory Gardens spread across 12 million cities. Of course, none of this was new to me being Native American, as we have always grown our own food. One of my favorite things to do was farm and garden along with hunting and gathering the necessary items for survival. My people have been self-sufficient since the beginning of time.

I checked into my hotel right about 9:00 p.m. and walked across the street to get some late-night dinner. It was the only restaurant open in town. I had already asked directions to the courthouse, so I would be ready in the morning bright and early when they opened at 8:00 a.m.

The restaurant was closing but I managed to talk the waitress into a club sandwich and cup of coffee. One cup of Joe never tasted so good. I felt like a new person, finally being able to get Billie what he deserved. I wasn't there for him during his short life, but I could be there for him after his death.

The thought still made me sick to my stomach, how someone could do such a horrible thing to an infant or child.

In my suitcase was a pen and paper, so I decided to write my mother a quick note. She would be worried, and I promised to write. I bought a roll of stamps before leaving home, which by the way were outlawed for purchase as the war continued. They were considered unnecessary commodities. My money was limited and making a phone call was expensive.

I arrived at the courthouse promptly at 8:00 a.m. The receptionist met me at the door opening the office. When I explained my situation, she was very aware of the case and said many women had come to ask the same questions. She took me into this small conference room and handed me a box filled with files on each baby. Since most of their parents were unknown, the only defining characters were the quick notes made by the coroner. It surprised me because the hospital knew my name and such.

It took me hours to go through every file and read the gory details. I placed the ones that looked plausible aside and continued through the rest one by one. After a few hours, the desk clerk came in asking how the search was going, and I explained there were serval good possibilities. We chatted for a bit and I got a fresh cup of coffee. When I had gone over the stack and narrowed it down to five files, I looked up and realized it was 2:00 p.m. already. So, I took a break and went out on the front steps and ate my lunch. In those days, you brought food and drinks wherever you went. One never knew when your car might break down or get in an accident. I had even come across people who were stranded and needed supplies.

It turned out to be a beautiful day: the sun was shining with a slight breeze cooling the warm rays. I sat on the steps clearing my eyes, I'd been crying for hours. It was getting hard to see with my eyelids swollen closed. I could feel those babies' souls yearning for some comfort. If I had been rich, I would have bought headstones for all of them.

When I went back inside, the clerk told me they closed at 4:00 p.m., so I would have to make a choice or come back the next day. I sat down and looked at the five files left and started narrowing them down one by one. The best place was to start with the dates, and that left two possibilities. As I read the details, one description caught my attention. The coroner wrote the baby had a cleft pallet and seemed to have been very sick before his death. I knew he was my Billie; however, I made one mistake and looked through the rest of the files, when I found photographs. It took everything I had not to throw up. Billie was found wrapped in a newspaper, with his skull caved in by a baseball bat. *Oh, my God!*

I took the file and packed up the rest in the box, so the clerk could make me copies. Then she directed me to the cemetery where all the babies were buried in unmarked graves. She told me they have records according to the police reports what grave each baby had been buried in. It was almost four when I left the courthouse and was ready for a break. The whole day gave me a splitting headache and left me completely exhausted. So, I hit the hotel for a hot bath and some sleep. By the time I was done, not even food sounded good. Somehow, even though it turned out to be a horrific day because of the images I saw, I came to peace with what had happened. It allowed me to move on, knowing I had done the right thing.

When I arrived in town, I had seen a funeral home, so I decided to find out about the headstones. After breakfast, the sun was shining, and I decided the walk might do me some good. It seemed like a nice, small American town. I spoke with the funeral director and of course, he knew of Rev. Brooks all too well. So, I explained my situation and he agreed to work with me on purchasing a headstone. It did not have to be anything extravagant, just serve the purpose.

He took me out in their warehouse to show me what kind of inventory they had. On the back wall behind some granite headstones was a small, black wrought iron cross with some decoration in the center around the plaque to engrave a name. It screamed my name. The man explained it had been specially ordered by someone years ago and they never came in to pay for it. Under the circumstances, he gave me the cross for free and just asked if I would pay for the engraving. It was a done deal.

I ended up staying one more day while the engraver finished the cross. When we were done, the man offered to drive me out to the cemetery and show me to the graves. I was grateful for the company. The whole scene caught me off guard. Thankfully, I was able to maintain my composure during our visit. But now that I knew where he was, I decided to go back the next day when they erected the cross. It would give me some time to visit with him. Over the years I had watched him grow up in my head; he would have been a man by now. *Billie, no matter where this life takes me, you will always be in my heart.* By the time I reached the car, I was sobbing uncontrollably. I guess it had been pent up inside for years.

When the funeral workers left the next day, I made a sandwich and headed for the cemetery and had a nice picnic with Billie. I knew it would most likely be the last time I visited this place, but he knew his mother would always love him. My next stop would be Chicago.

Chapter Twenty-One:

The Spying Has to Stop

My next destination happened to be Chicago, the Windy City. Since my arrest, it was the last place I wanted to be seen. However, many years had passed, and it was time to visit Johnnie and see where he was killed. Maybe even see a baseball game, a woman's game that was. Since our involvement in WWII, the owners of some baseball teams decided to fund counter entertainment for the masses. In 1943, an all-women's professional league was started. It is when the name baseball was changed to softball.  The best pitcher on record was Helen Nicol who won the Triple Crown with 31 innings, 220 strikeouts, and an average 1.81 run average. The average player made between $8 to $12 a week. It was officially canceled in 1954. Many women in America cheered, because they wanted to go back home and live out of the spotlight.

The drive from Beulah to Chicago was only about eight hours, an easy trip compared to my drive from Florida to Wisconsin in the dead of winter. I had been very angry with Johnnie over that decision, but he could not deal with the jealousy. When I hit Wisconsin, my heart leaped.

The closer I got to Chicago, it drew me back to the times Johnnie and I spent together, and our trips across the country. One morning when Johnnie and I woke up, we were in this seedy motel and he wanted to go for a country drive. So, we packed up the car with food, drinks, a blanket, and love. We drove for nearly four hours on this old country dirt road. He regaled me with stories of his youth; one tale was about his first baseball game. I'd never seen him come to life like that. His eyes sparkled; he truly loved the game. It was all new to me living on the reservation, but he promised one day we'd go to a baseball game. Well, he may not be with me in person, but I knew he'd be there in spirit. I was getting excited to see Chicago once again, only on my terms this trip.

I remembered one hotel on the outside of town that we stayed in several times that was a clean place, quiet, and the owners were very nice. I always believed they knew Johnnie's true identity, just never said anything. It would be a good safe place to stay this time as well. The idea of visiting Chicago as a tourist seemed foreign, although it was a nice change of pace.

When I arrived in town, it was early afternoon before rush hour traffic. I was excited to see the hotel still standing and open for business. It seems the death of a famous gangster did wonders for their business. I pulled in out front and took a deep breath, not knowing what to expect. The second I stepped inside the lobby it was plastered with images of Johnnie, and one of me and him outside captured by a reporter for the *Chicago Times*. I almost walked out when the owner noticed me and it was a done deal.

"Mrs. Smith!" he shouted.

I smiled. "You caught me. But it's Evelyn now."

"Sure, just joshin'. It's nice to see you again. Are you in town to stay or just passing through?"

"Visiting actually, I wanted to stay here if I can? It was always a good place."

"Oh, yes— please come on."

"Thank you, how much is it a night now?"

"Nothing, it's on the house."

"No, please, can I pay something?"

"Absolutely not, you are my guest. We always liked Johnnie and knew he got a bad rap. Come on, I have your old room all fixed up." I nodded. The idea of staying in our old room hit me hard. I did not know whether to cry or laugh.

He unlocked and opened the door. "Is there anything else I can get you?"

"No, I am good. Thank you."

"If you change your mind, just ring. Stay as long as you like."

"Maybe a few days?"

"Sure, sure whatever. Have a good night. I do have snacks in the lobby if you want any. I know ding dongs were always your favorite."

"Ah, you remember that. Okay, I might just take you up on that. Is the old theater still standing?"

"Oh, busier than ever now. It's a tourist attraction. Even has a sign out front."

"Oh, what they won't do for money." He nodded.

"Goodnight, Ms. Evelyn."

"Thank you."

I dropped my suitcase on the bed and looked around. It was just as I remembered, except for the plaque on the wall: "John Dillinger stayed here." *The best times of my life had become a tourist attraction.*

The evening came and went. I walked down the boardwalk and did some window shopping. It was nice to see all the new fashions. I even went into the thrift shop where I bought the dress, I was wearing the night we met. I got a thrill and did buy a new blouse. Johnnie would have giggled at me picking through the racks looking for the cheapest dresses or shoes. He used to tell me, "I don't care what it costs, you're my baby."

It had been more than five years since I walked the streets of Chicago, but it looked mostly the same. However, I was anxious to see the theater. Although, a woman walking the streets alone in the city at night is not smart, so I decided to wait till tomorrow. A hot bath and dinner sounded great. *Maybe I'd treat myself to a sandwich and a ding-dong.* By morning I was chomping at the bit to head out. It was a good drive out to the cemetery where Johnnie was buried, and I figured if I arrived early the crowds might be smaller.

I passed the theater on my way out of town along with the tavern where I was arrested, not memories I cared to relive. The drive also took me past Wrigley's Field just the place to get tickets for a baseball game. Since I did not have to pay for my room, I could afford a ticket to a game. The drive to Hillside Cemetery was about two hours if I did not stop along the way, so it would be very late when I got back to Chicago.

    The closer I got to Indiana the weather started to turn for the worse. It sprinkled on the windshield as I hit the state line. Nonetheless, nothing was going to stop me from seeing Johnnie today. I had a trunk full of raincoats and an umbrella. However, God must have been watching over me because the moment I pulled up to the cemetery the sun came out and it warmed up. I had forgotten how fast the weather changes in this part of the country. There were only a few people at Johnnie's grave, and they left shortly after I walked up, maybe the tears in my eyes showed my true feelings. If they only had known my identity. The cemetery had placed a bench on the south side of Johnnie's gravestone, so I sat and talked with him for over an hour. It felt good to get some things off my chest. At one point, it felt like he was sitting on the bench next to me, smiling with  that cocky grin of his. *Johnnie… I miss you. I hope someday we meet again.* I always hated the fact we never got to say goodbye, it haunted me. The cemetery was almost empty when I left except one black sedan parked on the other side of the lawn, which seemed odd to me at the time. However, I went on my way and never gave it another thought.

It was nearly midnight when I got back to Chicago and most everything was closed, except the red-light district. The buildings made me think of Ann, "the woman in red." *Was she still alive and in the States?* I hit the room and passed out on the bed; the last few days had been exhausting. Spending that time lifted a weight off my shoulders that I'd been carrying around for years. It was almost eleven when I woke up the next morning to the maid knocking on my door. I grabbed a few clean towels and sent her off until later. It was time to have some fun. I had been dealing with some heavy stuff over the last few weeks and needed to relax.

The sun was shining, a rare sight in Chicago. So, I decided to take a walk. My first stop was Wrigley Field and then the Biograph Theater. I had been schooled by Johnnie about the  place. Wrigley Field was built in 1914, originally called Weeghman Park after Charles Weeghman who founded it in 1915, and it was bought by the Cubs in 1916. Ernie Banks called it "Mr. Cub." It is the second oldest field next to Fenway Park built-in 1912. The red marquee sign is its signature memory piece. I can even tell you it's only 600 feet above sea level. The field is called a jewel box ballpark, which was popular in the early twentieth century. It was renovated in 1937 and English Ivy was planted alongside the field. It was one kind of ivy that could withstand the harsh Illinois winters. They even still have one of the last hand-turned scoreboards. Plus, there are fifteen flags: one for each National League team. The order of the flags on the pole was their current ranking.

I almost decided to pass on going to a game, until I saw the stadium in person. Then the thrill hit me, a real-life baseball game, or should I say softball game. The next game was in two days, hosted by the Rockford Peaches. I had a bounce in my step heading back to the Biograph Theater, and a good thing, because I needed the boost. By the time I reached the theater, it was as if I'd gone back in time. I could see Johnnie coming out of the theater, he loved movies. They made him feel like a normal person. We lived on the run twenty-four-seven and had barely any time for

any form of entertainment. Most of the movies we saw were gangster movies or copper shows and I didn't care for them, but it was what made him happy. I guess much of my life had been living for someone else. I always took it upon myself to be a caregiver to the people around me, at least that is what I told myself. I'd struggled to try to find myself searching for a place to fit in. Western culture took my natural heritage away from me; the only way of life my people had ever known was yanked out from under us and we either conformed or were killed. Those that did fight were left on the reservation to starve to death because the government killed our food sources. Sometimes the atrocities made me sick. When I went back home after many years of being away, and the boarding schools were closed, the young children that came home had no one waiting for them. I was lucky enough to have known my parents. Many of the children were taken as infants or young babies, and their parents were either killed or left on the reservation. Western culture was so dead set on destroying the Native Americans that all the birth records were destroyed. These children were dumped off in the middle of nowhere to fend for themselves. Thankfully, we all stepped up and cared for them, but it ruined their lives. They wander around lost, with no way to find their families. I hated that fact. It was funny when Johnnie was alive, he understood the difficulties my people faced. We connected on some level, anyway. I belonged somewhere, but now he's gone, and I am alone. Although, this trip had helped me grieve and come to terms with his death. I truly believe that some people are born in the wrong generation. They just can't fit in anywhere or conform to the demands of society. Nonetheless, he would never have wanted me to be sad, he was filled with too much life. So, no matter what, I would find a way to continue just as he would have wanted.

It seemed surreal to be standing in front of the Biograph Theater. I'd seen the pictures of his body lying dead on the sidewalk, so I knew where he was shot. The thought brought tears to my eyes again, standing in front of the sign. The scene suddenly became all too real. He was gone, and never coming back. I could still feel his arms around me, holding me in close. Our souls just fit. We could and did talk about everything. I think he knew me, and I knew him better than we knew ourselves. A sudden chill came over my soul, and I had to get out of there. The area was filled with bad energy. The moment I hit the edge of the theater, a calm refilled my soul. Anyway, tomorrow would be a new day, and I'd had my fill of sightseeing.

    The office was still open when I walked past, so I grabbed a few ding dongs and headed for some solitude. Besides, it had been a few days, since I'd written a note to Mom, so that would keep me busy for the night. I decided to just take it easy the next day, and rest. Then, Saturday afternoon was the softball game. I was very excited to witness growth in America: women playing sports.

    The next morning, I got the notion to call home and check-in. But since the only phones were in the local post office and general store, there was a board on the wall where people could leave messages. When the person came to town, they'd check the board. It was Saturday and I knew Anna, my sister, would be taking Mom to town for supplies on Tuesday. She'd take eggs and veggies to sell at the grocery stores, then use the money for monthly supplies. I'd be in town until then, so I could call back before leaving.

I went into the office to ask if I could use the phone and call home. Of course, the owners had no problem. "Thank you, I won't be long."

"No problem, Evelyn, take your time."

I knew the calls were expensive, so I just left a coded message: "Hello, all good. I am in Chicago, going to see a women's softball game, and heading home on Tuesday. How is everything, any issues with Wally? I'd love you to see ya soon."

I got some strange looks when I mentioned Wally, and the last thing I wanted to do was explain. So, I told them he was my sister's boyfriend. "Thank you.... Have a great day. I am heading to the softball game."

"Oh, you will have a blast, they are great!" I was happy to hear him say that.

It had been a long time since I did anything for myself or just have fun. Until now, everything I did was for and with someone else, but this time it was for me. I brought a pair of jeans, a blouse, and flats. The manager, Jerry, gave me a baseball cap to wear for the game. He said it was customary. So, I proudly wore the cap and prepped for my afternoon of fun. Johnnie would have loved the idea. It felt good to be doing something fun, and just forget about life for a few hours. I decided to drive over to the stadium since it might be late when the game ended and I didn't like walking in the dark alone.

When I stepped out of the car and walked up to the stadium, they were playing happy dancing music and I felt like a new person, sporting my jeans and baseball cap. As I approached the ticket stand, I got the most wonderful surprise. At first, I had to take a second look to be certain, but Sally noticed me first.

"Evelyn!" I heard her yell.

"Sally…. Oh my gosh. Is that you?"

"Yes, how are you? I have not seen you since before Joh—" she paused. "Well, you know."

"No, you have not. I know…."

"So, are you back in town for good? I miss you."

"No, just a visit. You work here now?"

"Yes, part-time ticket taker. Hey, when I am done do you want to hook up?"

"Oh, I'd love that. Come find me when you are done. My seat number is on there."

"I will…. Man, I am so glad to see you."

I smiled. "Me too. See you soon."

I could not believe it, seeing Sally at this softball game today. We had become friends when I was with Johnnie. She worked at the dinner and dance hall with me for a long time. I guess it was worth coming to the game after all today. There was a hop in my step to the bleachers. On the way, I grabbed a Coca-Cola and hot dog; there is nothing like a real Chicago style hot dog with onions, mustard, and sauerkraut. It had been years since I had one. It was proving to be a good day.

Sally arrived just after the National Anthem and first pitch. "Hey, girl, have a seat." She giggled and laid her head on my shoulder. "This is such a treat. I am so excited to have seen you here today. And to think I almost skipped coming today."

"Well, fate made you have a change of heart. I love that hat and the new look is great."

"It feels good. Jerry at the hotel let me borrow it for today. Said it was his lucky hat. I guess it worked."

"Yep! I agree. So, what happened to you?"

"You don't know?"

"No, the last I knew Johnnie was killed and you disappeared."

"Wow, I can't believe you didn't know. I was arrested and sentenced to two years in prison."

"Are you kidding? For what? You were not involved."

"They got me for aiding and abetting a fugitive. Johnnie's attorney fought for me, but we failed."

"Oh, I am so sorry. How did that go?"

"At first, I was terrified. But then I just learned to adapt. Besides, it was nothing compared to the Indian boarding schools they sent us to. So, I guess it was preparation. Then afterward, I traveled with the Crime Does Not Pay show for about five years."

"Oh my gosh, so you are famous now."

"Not hardly… I just did it to stay out of trouble. The FBI surveilled me for years."

"The FBI? You're kidding! They are crooked, aren't they? Just like most of the coppers around here."

"I think so, but enough bad talk. What have you been up to? Are you married?"

"No, was dating a guy for a few years. But I caught him cheating on me...."

"Oh, that's horrible."

"Eh, it's okay. He was a loser anyway."

"So, how are you otherwise? Did you ever finish school?"

"Yes, but I have not been able to get a job. I got my nursing certificate but unless you have the experience, they won't hire you. But, now with the war starting, I might get my chance."

"Well, that is great. I am proud of you."

"Now, tell me about you. Anyone special in your life now?" I cocked my head. "Oh, I know that look...."

"I did not date anyone for a long time after Johnnie died, it broke my heart. You know we had plans to run away. He wanted out, was going to do one last job and we were leaving town when I got arrested. Yeah, I met someone about a year ago and we got married. Then after we got married, he started to change. Suddenly drinking all the time and would come home drunk, and started smacking me around. A few months ago, he put me in the hospital, and I lost my baby."

"Oh my God…. Evelyn, I am so sorry. How far along?"

"About eleven weeks. I had just been to the doctor and heard his heartbeat."

"I don't know what to say…. I am so glad to see you." I tried to choke back the tears, but it was to no avail. "Let it out, girl. I can't imagine how hard that must have been. You have been through so much. If my man had been gunned down in the street, well, I don't know."

"Thank you, Sally…. You always were a good friend."

"Thank you. So where are you living now? Maybe I can come to see you?"

"I would love that, anytime, you know that. On the reservation with my mom. She is getting older and it's hard for her to do all that work alone."

"I am sure she appreciates that. So why are you in Chicago?"

"I have some things to handle, and I wanted to see where Johnnie died and visit his grave."

"Well, I for one am delighted to see you. When do you leave?"

"Oh, I don't know, a few more days anyway…."

"Good, we have to go out, to a movie or shopping. I can take you around town and show you all the new stores."

"Yes, that would be great. I have not seen anyone from those days since I was arrested. Oh, it's so nice to see you. I have often wondered what happened to everyone. This has been such a good trip. Thank you, Sally, for sitting with me today."

"You bet…. I have missed you and every time I drive by your old apartment; I think about you."

"Oh, yes I'd love to have a tour of all those places and see what things have changed."

"You bet; I am your personal tour guide. What time do you want to meet in the morning?"

"How about nine? I will be at your disposal all day. I don't have any other plans; except Tuesday afternoon I have to call the general store to see how my mom is doing and make sure Wally has not bothered them since I left."

"Then it's set. We are going to have a blast. I can't wait. I have to run, but see you in the morning." Sally left, and even though I had missed most of the game, it was worth every minute.

Chapter Twenty-Two:

You Can't Go Back

The next day after seeing Sally, I decided to take my mother up on her advice and stop to see some old friends. Sally and I parted ways. Chicago was great, but not one place I cared to stay any longer than necessary. I had learned over the last several years, there's no place like home. *I sounded like Dorothy...*

I had heard through the grapevine that *Opal Long* was still in Chicago. She was the only one of the Dillinger Gang women who ever liked or trusted me. The rest just tolerated my presence because of Johnnie.

He always said, "Just ignore them, they are jealous." It usually made me feel better.

Opal was different. The papers stated, "Opal Long didn't earn the nickname 'Mack Truck' for nothing, but I'll bet no one called her that to her face. She was a big, strong gal. Not only was she a prolific shoplifter, but she also hung out with the Dillinger Gang— part of the group because of her husband, Russell Clark. She kept house and cooked for the gang— just like any quiet homemaker would do. In reality, she was far from quiet and obedient. When the police showed up to arrest, she attacked them, and later she was arrested. Opal Long may have been a lot of things, but she wasn't a rat. Not a word did she tell the coppers about the activities of the notorious Dillinger Gang!"

I always giggled by their assessment, because they hit her right on target. Opal happened to be born the wrong gender. But we got along well, we understood each other. I would never have made it back to Chicago from Tucson if she had not been with me. The stupidity of youth. She was born on

March 20, 1906, in Texas, as she told me once. Opal never talked about her past.

After we returned from Tucson, she worked tirelessly to raise money for Clark's appeal. I can remember her visiting him in Lima Jail, begging Johnnie for the money to pay an attorney. When Clark was arrested, they blamed her and they all abandoned her, especially after Eddie Green's death. But I knew Opal, she was no 'Stool Pigeon,' and they should have known that. They finally arrested her on June 2, 1934, with her sister Pat Carrington. The same agent who arrested them got me: Larry Streng. Since she had no money, she admitted to harboring Dillinger and Hamilton. The judge sentenced her to six months in the workhouse in Minneapolis.

Once you spend enough time in Chicago with a notorious outlaw, you learn ways of finding out information, so finding her was easy. Opal stood out in a crowd, and I hoped she hadn't changed.

I walked up to the door and knocked. The door opened. "Oh… my God, Billie!" she screamed.

"Yes…. I see you have not changed…."

She looked puzzled. "What does that mean?"

"You are just as bold and brilliant as I remember." That got her to smile.

She grabbed my arm. "Get in here, girl, you never know who's watching out there." I cocked my head. "No, I am not in any trouble, those days are behind me now. I just don't trust those coppers now any more than I ever did. I never expected to see you again, what are you doing here? The last thing I heard you were on the Reservation."

"I was, well I am. I came to take care of some business and decided to come and see some old friends before I went home."

"Wow, you look great! I am so happy to see you. Oh, shame on me, would you like some coffee or… something stronger?"

"Coffee, that would be fine. We went out last night, so it was enough for me."

"Where did you go?"

"The Olympic Lounge."

"Oh, that place will never be the same as in the Johnnie days…."

"Yes, I agree. They used to have pretty good food and stuff, but it's not the same."

"So, what have you been up to since you got released?"

"Well, I moved back home with my mom. Then got married—"

"Congratulations…." I shook my head. "Bad?"

"Yeah, you could say that. The last time I saw him he beat me up, and I lost my baby."

"You were pregnant? Where is he, that scum…."

"Thanks, but hold up there skipper, he is dead."

"Good girl, you took him out."

"No… I did not, but I think some of my tribe did. I got word last Tuesday, the paper said it was a suicide…. I can't see Wally doing that. He was harassing my mom, sister, and me, which is one reason I left for a while. I wanted him to leave them alone."

"Honey, you should know by now, there is only one way to handle a man like that. Did you learn nothing from Johnnie? You know what he would have done—" I nodded.

"Okay, well, enough about me. What about you?"

"Not much to say, I am still here in this shithole, married again."

"Married to whom?"

"Do you remember my sister, Pat?"

"Of course," I replied.

"She had a friend, Ruby Ickes. Well, she introduced me to Dewey Elliot. We have been married for years now."

"Did you have any kids?" She shook her head.

We talked for hours; I had not laughed that hard in years. She told me stories I had never heard. Before I realized it, it was almost 4:00 p.m. and I was ready to take a bath and get some rest. It had been a long several days. Opal begged me to stay for dinner, but she knew I no longer fit into that crowd. She gave me a big bear hug and said goodbye. We both knew it would be the last time we'd meet. Before I got to the car, tears streaked my face. It felt good to know I was not completely forgotten. My hotel was about three miles from Opal's house, so I decided to take the long way around and see some more of the old neighborhood. I hit three streets from Opal's house and had just made a right turn back to my hotel when I saw flashing lights behind me. My heart nearly jumped out of my chest.

I pulled over and rolled down my window. "Miss, please step out of the car?"

"Did I do something wrong?"

"Please, just step out of the car, Ms. Frechette." The terror shot up my spine, he knew my name.

"Yes, sir," I replied.

"I need you to come with me down to the station."

"What am I being arrested for, officer?"

"We will talk about that at the station."

After patting me down, he put me into the back of the police car and headed for the station. "What about my car?"

"It will be impounded; you can get it back when you are released."

"I have not done anything…. Please, what is this about?" He refused to say another word, just told me to be quiet.

I knew the whereabouts of the police station, and our destination was not the local precinct. However, I knew my questions would go unanswered. About twenty minutes later, we pulled around behind this unmarked brick building. He got out and walked me inside these big revolving doors. It was no police station; I knew instantly it was an FBI headquarters.

The officer took me into a small conference type room and sat me down in a chair with handcuff rings on the side. I had a bad feeling in the pit of my stomach. A short while later, one very familiar face entered: Larry Streng. However, time had not been kind to him; a curse for his crooked behavior.

"Well, Ms. Frechette, we meet again."

"I guess we do, what do you want? Why am I here?"

"You need to ask such questions?"

"Yes, I have done nothing wrong…."

"I beg to differ. We have been watching you since you arrived last week."

"You have been watching me—for what?"

"At first, I was not even sure it was you until my men followed you to the cemetery. No one else fitting your description would sit at John Dillinger's grave as you did."

"I am here taking care of some business and stopped to see a friend. The last I checked that was not illegal."

"No… but when you are conspiring with criminals that is a different story."

"What criminals?"

"Well, that is privileged information."

"I have nothing to hide, and not done anything wrong. You need to let me go."

"Now, now, Ms. Frechette. When the time is right, I will let you go. Right now, just sit tight and don't go anywhere." He smirked.

I sat in that room for more than four hours waiting for him to come back. A copper would come in every so often and offer me a sip of water. When Agent Streng came back he did not look too happy.

"Well, now let's get down to business."

"Yes, please do."

"What are you doing in Chicago?"

"I already told you. I came here on business and visited a friend."

"And what business would bring you from the Indian land?"

"None of your business, it's personal." The next thing I knew, my head spun to the right when he bashed me across the face.

"Huh…." I screeched.

"Now, are you going to answer me or not?"

"I did not squeal the first time you arrested me and won't now, but I have nothing to hide."

"Then why are you here?"

"Fine— I came to put a headstone on my son's grave—"

"Your son's grave? What son?"

"Well, Agent Streng, you must be slipping, not knowing I had a child."

"Don't get smart… or—"

"Or what, you are going to hit me again?"

"Don't push me, Ms. Frechette. Don't push me."

"You have to get some new lines. I heard those same phrases many years ago."

"I mean it." Another man came into the room and whispered something. "I will be right back."

"Okay, I'll be right here." He grinned.

I waited for the next several hours for him to return and no one ever did. In fact, I sat in that room for the rest of the night. Then about 7:00 a.m., a female came in and took off my handcuffs. She escorted me to the door. My car was sitting in the parking lot. The keys were in the ignition. I had no idea what happened or why they arrested me, but it was a wake-up call to get the heck out of Dodge.

The real surprise came when I got back to the hotel. Jerry met me at the office door, and I thought he was going to cry. "Jerry, what happened, are you okay, your wife?"

He nodded. "The coppers were here last night…."

"You don't say…." He looked at me. "They arrested me last night and held me in this old building all night."

"Evelyn, I am so sorry; they had a warrant."

"They searched my room?"

"Yes, and made a mess. I tried to stop them."

"It's okay, Jerry. I know there was nothing to hide. Just some clothes."

"Yes, that is what they told someone on the radio."

"What were they looking for, do you know?"

"I have no idea…. But once that was over, they just left."

"Well, I am going to take a shower and pack. It's time to go home, so if I owe you anything, please let me know. I will come in before I leave and give you the key."

"Oh, no ma'am, you don't owe me anything. Again, I am sorry."

"Please don't worry. It's been a pleasure to stay with you. If I am ever in town again, I will look you up."

"Yes, any time. Evelyn, you are always welcome." Jerry and his wife were wonderful people

After the car was packed, I checked out and returned the key, hugged them, and hit the road. I just prayed for safety getting out of town. If I never came back to Chicago it was fine with me. The scene had not changed in more than six years. When I stopped at the last gas station on the way out of town, filled up, and got some snacks, I took a deep breath when I saw the sign that said leaving Chicago. My life with Dillinger was officially over. It was time to go home and make a new life of my own, not based on anyone else.

Chapter Twenty-Three:

The Women of My Past

The information in my head about the inner workings of the Dillinger Gang was extensive. No one had a clue of how much Johnnie had told me, or what I picked up along the way. It would be a curse that I had to live with, and my fame spoke for itself. But on the other hand, Johnnie taught me how to survive. When we met, I was a young girl enamored with a handsome, charismatic man who paid attention to me. My life changed forever that night, only I never looked upon it as a bad thing. The media made the Dillinger Gang out to be bloodthirsty criminals; instead, we were just the opposite. We lived in a time when just surviving daily was difficult, and no one's future was guaranteed. So, we lived each day as if it was our last, because many times that was reality.

After my trip to Chicago ended, I had taken care of the things that plagued my soul for many years. It took a huge weight off my shoulders and I could think straight once again, but none of the mess in Chicago with the agents was going to stop me from living my life. I owed that much to Johnnie. My travels around the US lasted for many years. I still wanted to touch base with many old friends; some were connected with Dillinger, and some were people I met along the way.

My travels over probably twenty years are too extensive for me to tell you about each one. So, I wanted to highlight the ones that had a major impact on my life.

It was believed that the 1930s gangster's molls were heartless, uncaring, selfish individuals who lived only for pleasure. I personally blame J. Edgar Hoover (the FBI Director) for his smear campaigns. The propaganda displayed us as soulless women who cared for nothing except a few strands of stolen pearls.

The first was one of my dearest friends,

Opal Long

Opal Long Alias (Bernice Clark).

Opal Long was one of the most caring, considerate women I have ever met. She was the most loyal. Opal had one sister, Pearl Elliot, who essentially brought her into the gang. She described the times as exciting.

Opal lived with Russell Clark and Charley Makley. She cleaned and cooked for them regularly. I can remember her cooking Charley's favorite '3-minute eggs.' The caregiver in her poured out for every one of us to see. When we had a big dinner, Opal would give up her seat and let everyone  else sit, while she either stood next to the table or ate in the kitchen. I went to eat with her many times so she wasn't alone.

The one thing I commended her for the most was putting everyone else ahead of her own needs. She prided herself on loyalty to the gang members, or "the kids," as she called them. It's easy to tell when someone is faking, and Opal was not one of them.

She was a large, red-headed woman filled with love for her family. The only thing I got her to tell me about herself was her birthday, March 20, 1906. She claims to have been born in Texas. However, it's a big state so that could have been anywhere. If anyone asked, she said, "The past cannot be changed and I don't dwell on it, ever."

Opal worked tirelessly as a waitress during the day and taking care of the gang members at night. We could always count on a homecooked meal and hot coffee.

I remember when we got arrested in Tucson, Opal fought hard with the coppers. She even broke one of the officer's fingers. They beat her up pretty good for that. After her arrest, the gang thought she was the one who talked and it was what got Eddie

Green killed. Johnnie thought she sang to get her Clark's appeal money.

Louis Piquett, the gang's attorney, never lifted a finger to help with her trial. So, because of that, she was charged with harboring Johnnie and Hamilton. She refused to give any information about the gang that would have made her life easier. In other words, she never became a "stool pigeon." She ended up back in Chicago.

Patricia Cherrington

Patricia Cherrington

Patty was a great girl, always happy and very smart. She had so much talent, loved poetry and music, and had once entertained the dream of attending college. She was born in Arkansas on September 26, 1903.

Patty's talents helped her to make a much better living than the rest of us. She worked in the nightclubs as a chorus dancer, and when prohibition hit, she took a job in the speakeasies as a dancer. However, when her health turned bad and she suffered from a malfunctioning gall bladder, she turned to finding men who could support her medical issues.

John "Red" Hamilton

Copeland was the first of our gang she dated. Then she moved on to Hamilton. Their relationship blossomed when she nursed him back to health after being shot in the East Chicago Indiana Bank robbery.

Patricia loved her men— all of them. I did not know at the time; she was writing to Welton and Art Cherrington while they were in prison. And she always visited Copeland while he was in Michigan City prison. Loyalty among men was not her strong suit.

I do think she did love Hamilton and felt bad she had to learn of his death in a letter from Johnnie.

When John Hamilton died, she was arrested soon after for harboring them in Little Bohemia.

Once in prison, along with her sister, Opal "Bernice Clark" Long, Patricia was abandoned by Piquett. Again, because of money, she had to plead guilty and was sentenced to Alderson Industrial Reformatory for a short time. When she was in prison, she wanted to have surgery, but the risks were too great, so she declined the procedure. They moved her to Milan Federal Facility in Michigan. Hoover called it a "Steel cell for female incorrigibles." After her release in 1936, she was again tried under the federal harboring law. Only that time it was for harboring Hamilton and Johnnie during the visit to the home of Hamilton's sister.

I found out later that she was tried twice because the incidents happened in two different states. Her first conviction was for a crime that took place in Wisconsin; the second, for a crime that took place in Michigan. Polly died in 1949 at forty-five because of health problems. Johnnie told her, "You are a good piece of company."

Polly Hamilton

She is one person I will never forget, one of the women who had a hand in getting Johnnie killed. Her claim to fame was on July 22, 1934, at the Biograph Theater. There was an incident in Gary, Indiana in the 1920s, but no one knows her role in the matter. Polly was married to a policeman named Roy Keele who divorced her, stating it was due to neglect They did not have any children. I admit when she started calling herself 'Dillinger's Countess,' it made my blood boil. No one knows for sure if she worked for Anna Sage as a maid, business partner, or prostitute, except she had a claim on his death. She was the only one who managed to avoid serving time in prison.

After the shooting, she went on the run for some time. Polly ran from the scene and jumped on the northbound train to Wilson Avenue, which was about twenty minutes. Then she took off on Wilson to Broadway Street and disappeared into the darkness. Later she showed up at 1209 ½ Wilson

Drive at the diner where she worked. After speaking with a co-worker, she called and asked Maxine to bring her a change of clothes. They were at the Malden Plaza Hotel. But Maxine was scared to get involved with anyone from the Dillinger Gang. So, she called the police and spoke to Captain Duffy of the Dillinger Squad. The police traced her calls and wound up at an empty apartment.

Polly remained on the run for some time. Captain Stege, a copper in Chicago, arrested Anna Sage with her son on July 24th, 1934. Since Polly was still hiding, Anna negotiated her reward for Dillinger's capture. Then the double-crosser called Polly and convinced her to surrender to the police. The coppers hid them both for a few days in Detroit before they returned to Chicago.

She left Chicago for a short time but returned after things had calmed down. Polly got married and lived on the North Side until she died in 1969.

Helen Wawryzniak (Helen Gillis) Baby Face Nelson

She was quoted as saying, "I knew Les was going to die, and I wanted to stay with him as long as possible."

I remember her as being very naïve, a nice girl, but we had nothing in common. Maybe because none of us liked Baby Face Nelson. He was an unstable sociopath.

Lester Gillis Alias Baby Face Nelson

Helen and Lester met as teenagers and got married when she was sixteen. In the first year, she got pregnant. Then during the next year, she had another baby. By the time Helen was twenty, her husband was Public Enemy No 1. The coppers had a shoot to kill order on him for a long time. In this case, she was an innocent bystander, stuck in a dangerous world with two children to raise.

After Johnnie connected her to Baby Face, her anonymous standing vanished. Before long, pictures of her surfaced all over. During the Little Bohemia raid when I was in prison, Helen was arrested and later released on parole. The mistake she made was meeting up with her husband a month later. Then when he died, they revoked her parole. She died in 1987 and is buried in Chicago next to her husband.

Mary Kinder

Mary, like boyfriend Harry Pierpont, was quiet and somewhat shy until she got to know you. At one time, much of her family was serving time in prison: her brother Earl, her husband Dale Kinder, and Harry. Then her other brother and brother-in-law, William, was also arrested for bank robbery.

I remember she told us that her father had committed suicide, and Mary and her mother found the body. A shotgun blast to the head.

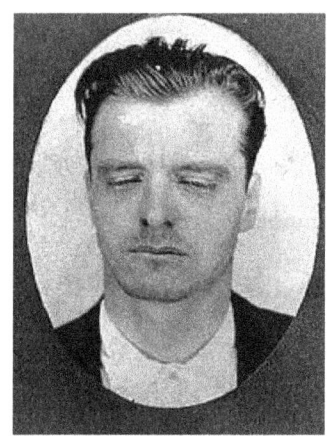

When Harry was convicted and sentenced to death, Mary joined the gang of escapees and remained loyal in trying to shelter Harry. She spent the money she earned on his defense as they prepared him for the electric chair. By then, she started traveling and giving interviews in some of the same shows that I did.

Mary lived until May 22, 1981, but died of emphysema and heart disease. I do remember her struggling with alcoholism for most of her life. She died penniless, and the sad part, buried, without a marker.

Sally Bachman

We only met one time and I don't remember much about her. Johnnie kept me away from this gang, they were dangerous. I know their tactics kept him awake at night. Sally was incorporated into the Baby Face Nelson gang by John Paul Chase in the last desperate days before Nelson was killed.

All I knew was she lived in San Francisco where she sold tickets to commuters across the Bay. One night, some rough men in a black sedan invited her for a ride. Needless to say, Sally never went back to work. None of us can say how we would have reacted in that case.

Sally and Chase traveled as far east as New York City, then back down to Nevada. Chase was later convicted for the death of Agent Samuel Cowley, who died with Ed Harris at the shootout in Barrington. It also claimed the life of Baby Face Nelson. It was relatively easy for Helen Gillis to tie Chase to the murder of Special Agent Sam Cowley.

Chase was sentenced to life in Alcatraz. As he adjusted to life on 'The Rock,' he could hear the birds singing, as Sally sang her tune putting the rest of the gang behind bars. The decision to sign the deal forced her to squeal on everyone. Believe me, the press had a heyday. She took the stand on March 29, 1935; all the men were indicted: Nelson's friends Anthony "Soap" Marino, Louis "Doc Bones" Tambini, Vince Markovich, Frank Cochran, and Anna Cochran, and Jack Perkins with his wife, Grace Perkins. Her story told a long line of mayhem, in it were no words of glamor.:

"We traveled across the country. We always parked along some riverbank and camped and bought our food in some town and cooked it in camp. We went to some restaurants and ate and brought food out to 'Baby Face Nelson.' He never went into a restaurant."

Helen made sure she paid for deserting her husband on his death bed. Her testimony, delivered in the back offices of the Feds, placed John Paul Chase at the Battle of Barrington and ensured his conviction and life sentence. It was relatively easy for Helen to tie Chase to the murder of Special Agent Sam Cowley. When they had ensured the convictions, she returned to private life, but lived throughout her days in fear of retribution.

Sally did the same tour as me, the "Crime Does Not Pay" show. She went as John Paul Chase's girlfriend with a story to tell. She transformed her traumatic experiences; it was Sally Bachman all the way. But she never asked for pity and was tough to the end of her life.

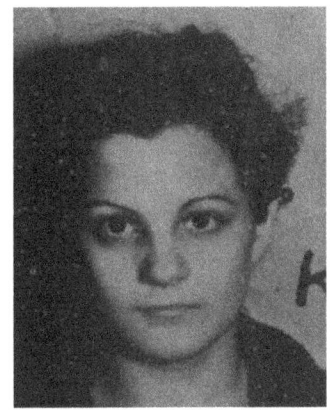

Marie Comforti

Oh, Marie… Homer Van Meter took Marie on as his girlfriend in May, 1933 after he was paroled. All we knew was she graduated from elementary school. In those days, it was immoral not to be wed and live or travel with a man, so we all posed as their wives.

During the Little Bohemia Lodge Raid, Marie was one of the three women captured. They interrogated her for days until she agreed to give information, but upon her return, Homer never trusted her again. In retaliation, she blamed him for abandoning her, as he suspected she talked to the FBI.

Homer Van Meter

Marie was tough as nails, she never showed remorse for any of the coppers who were killed and that got her in trouble with the agents. They gave her no special treatment; she was sentenced to one year. Then, again after her release, she was arrested and charged for the same crime. The different federal jurisdictions gave the right. She was the only woman among us to be charged twice.

In 1933, women did not have the same options as men, and instead of getting a higher education, they had to just find a job. It was the one benefit I have of being a Native American. Marie worked like many of us at a Chicago 'Five and Dime,' which offered lipsticks and small trinkets to neighborhood women and girls shopping with pennies. At the height of the Depression, it was next to impossible to get a job; no one had any money. They only ones with money were the gangsters.

Van Meter was killed exactly one month after Johnnie, which left Marie penniless. So, she turned herself in to a copper on the street corner.

Kathryn Kelly

Another woman that I only heard stories of but never met in person. Kathryn was born Cleo Brooks in Saltillo, Mississippi in 1904. We heard she changed her name to Kathryn, believing it was more glamorous. She got married, as many of us did, very young. At fifteen, Lonnie Frye became her husband. They later had a daughter named Pauline.

Kathryn built a name for herself being arrested several times for shoplifting in Fort Worth and a robbery in Oklahoma City. Her sheet included prostitution and receiving stolen goods. Her actions were passed down since her mother operated a bootlegging operation and she had two uncles serving time in Leavenworth for counterfeiting.

In the late 1920s, she was working as a manicurist and they say she created the image of Machine Gun Kelly. She purchased the first Tommy gun that Kelly ever owned, and she made him practice. I know she handed out the spent cartridges as gifts to friends.

Kathryn fell in love with George after meeting Anderson in Oklahoma City. They ran off together, taking Anderson's new Cadillac and his prized English bulldog. After Kelly's release, they headed off to Minneapolis. In September 1930, they got married. Later they were both arrested and arraigned on the same day, and both of them pled not guilty to Charles Urschel.

Kathryn told the Memphis police chief, "I'm glad we are both arrested because I am not guilty, and I can prove it. I'll be rid of him and that bunch. I don't want to say anything about that guy Kelly, but he got me into this terrible mess. and I don't want to have anything more to do with him."

The judge did not buy their claims and sentenced them both to life in prison. Kathryn told the authorities that if she weren't housed with her mother, she would use her influential friends to get herself released. When Kathryn was transferred to Milan, Michigan she wrote poetry and articles for the prison newspaper. She eventually became the assistant editor.

They were both released the same day on a $10,000 bond. Her mother's health was bad, so she was placed in a nursing home. Kathryn stayed close, she found work as a bookkeeper and eventually became a recluse.

Paula Harmon – (no picture available)

Paula was a sweet girl but a bit high strung. I have no idea when she and Fred Baker met but she came around every so often. They arrested her in Cleveland after an incident in a hotel bar, and she had a nervous breakdown. She was held from September 5, 1934, to the twenty-fifth, by none other than the Feds.

When they finally released her, she took off to Wynona Burdette and Gladys Sawyer's place and hid. She was arrested again *Fred Baker* shortly thereafter and hospitalized for a twenty-four-hour suicide watch. Paula got out and headed for Port Arthur, Texas to her parents' home, and she was interviewed again at their home. Over the next few months, her condition got worse, and they admitted her to the local mental hospital. It happened days after Fred and Kate Baker were killed.

They kept her for the next year and a half when the FBI interrogated her again in 1936. *Oh, they never let up....* Paula was finally released to her parents' custody in bad health. She made good money sewing for the town residents.

Vi Mathias

Vi and daughter Betty

Vivian was an attractive, thin farm girl who looked way too meek to work with Verne Miller bootlegging. When she was sixteen, Vivian, or Vi as her friends called her, eloped with Stanley Mathias, an employee on her father's farm. Stanley was convicted of murder, and Vi and their child went to Minnesota where she met Verne Miller.

It was his association with Alvin Karpis and the Barkers, however, that set the wheels in motion that would end with making Miller the most wanted man in America. Miller skipped bail and on the run is when he met Vi. She willingly joined him in his rapidly growing bootlegging business. The pair worked hard, and from 1926 to 1929, they were the leading bootleggers in the Twin Cities and known for their high-quality (and fair) casino operations in

Montreal, Canada. They were making a good living, but Miller wanted more, and in 1930 he moved to bank robbing.

He joined forces with such veteran robbers as Harvey Bailey, Tommy Holden, Jimmy Keating, Frank "Jelly" Nash, and George "Machine Gun" Kelly. They robbed banks throughout the Mid and Southwest. After her participation with Miller in the Kansas City Massacre, she was arrested. Mathias was taken into custody and later pleaded guilty to charges of harboring and concealing Miller. In a statement coerced through intensive interrogation for twelve days and nights, she told the FBI who was involved in the Massacre. Miller's bloody body was found along a roadside ditch.

It's amazing how when we age our priorities change dramatically. I learned that traveling was something I found exciting, but it also made me aware of the wisdom I gained through the experiences I endured. Many of the women I went to find and visit were not much different than I remembered as a young girl. In most cases, after a short time, there was nothing more to talk about. They were either stuck in the past, or had absolutely nothing in common with me, or maybe we never did, I don't know. Nonetheless, the traveling gave me a chance to see the world without being chased, shot at, or under pressure to maintain someone else's happiness. I had finally found peace in my life and no longer needed the company of another person to be content.

Evelyn Frechette – Life after Johnnie

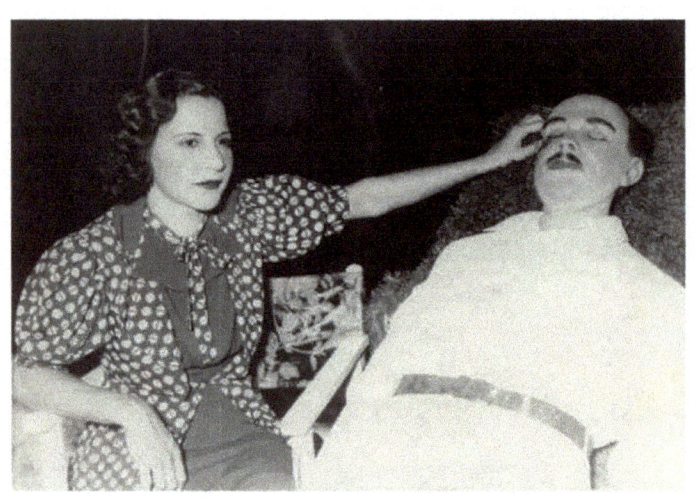

CRIMINAL RECORD

As Ann Martin, #2376, arrested Police Department, Tucson, Arizona, January 25, 1934, charge, fugitive from justice; disposition, released January 30, 1934.

for harboring a fugitive and obstructing justice.

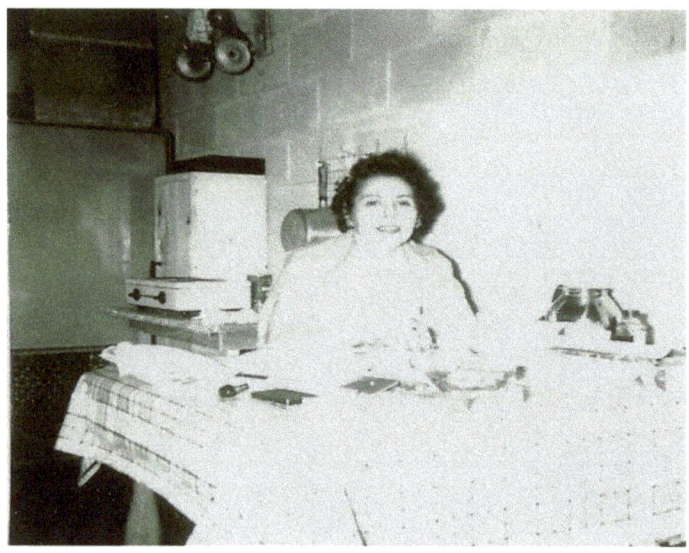

Evenly Frechette and Art Tic House

IDENTIFICATION ORDER NO. 1221
April 6, 1934.

**DIVISION OF INVESTIGATION
U. S. DEPARTMENT OF JUSTICE
WASHINGTON, D. C.**

Fingerprint Classification

24 27 W I 18+
 4 W OO 15+

WANTED

MARY EVELYN FRECHETTE, with aliases,
ANN MARTIN, EVELYN SPARK, EVELYN FASCHETTI, EVELYN FRISDETTE,
GRACE EDWARDS, MRS. JOHN DILLINGER, "BILLIE".

OBSTRUCTION OF JUSTICE.

DESCRIPTION

Age, 26 years (1908)
Height, 5 feet, 3 inches
Weight, 110 pounds
Build, slim
Hair, black – wavy
Eyes, brown
Complexion, pale
Scars and marks, mole on right cheek, pit scars on face
Remarks: full round face, hair may be dyed light red.

RELATIVES:

Mrs. Mary Frechette Sprague, mother,
Neopit, Wisconsin.
Mrs. Anna Borden, sister,
Neopit, Wisconsin.
Mrs. Frances Frechette Schultz, sister,
5013 North Paulina Street,
Chicago, Illinois.

CRIMINAL RECORD

As Ann Martin, #2174, arrested Police Department, Tucson, Arizona, January 26, 1934, charge, fugitive from justice; dissertation, released January 30, 1934.

Evelyn Frechette is wanted at St. Paul, Minnesota, for harboring a fugitive and obstructing justice.

Law enforcement agencies kindly transmit any additional information or criminal record to the nearest office of the Division of Investigation, U. S. Department of Justice.

If apprehended, please notify the Director, Division of Investigation, U. S. Department of Justice, Washington, D. C., or the Special Agent in Charge of the office of the Division of Investigation listed on the back hereof which is nearest your city.

(over)   Issued by: J. EDGAR HOOVER, DIRECTOR.

Dillinger's Sweetheart Named In Probe of 'Baby Farm' Deaths

Michigan Attorney General Orders Inquiry at Beulah Institution Where 25 Infants Died; Evelyn Frechette's Child Among Them.

Lansing, Mich., Jan. 23 (AP).—An investigation was ordered today of an institution at Beulah, Mich., described by Attorney General Harry S. Toy as a "baby farm," where at least 25 babies died, including one born to Evelyn Frechette, once the sweetheart of the late John Dillinger.

Circuit Judge Fred S. Lamb, of Cadillac, Mich., will open the investigation at Beulah tomorrow, the Attorney General said.

Edward L. Brooks, sr., proprietor of the institution, readily admitted today that he had attended the Frechette girl. However, he insisted it was "several years ago and only after a Government agent brought her to my establishment in Chicago and asked me to do it." The baby lived only a few weeks, he said, dying after he had brought it and the mother to the Beulah farm.

State health department records revealed that a child was born to Evelyn Frechette in Chicago in 1928, but that it died three months later at Beulah and was buried in the "Beulah Cemetery." The name of the father was not given.

Health department authorities also stated that 17 certificates had been found in the files relative to deaths of babies at Beulah and that some of them were signed by Brooks as undertaker.

Brooks said he did not know when he treated the Frechette girl that she was an associate of Dillinger.

"There is spite work behind the charges that my place was a baby farm," he declared. "I have consciously done nothing illegal and they can go as far as they like with their investigation."

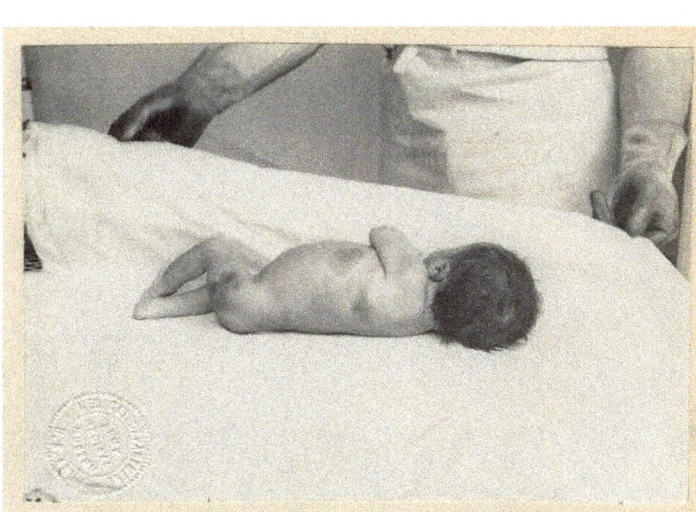

Infant with Syphilis

Evelyn Frechette – FBI Surveillance

C. GRAINGER KORNEGAY, President
JOE E. McLURIN, Treasurer

MOULTRIE B. BURNS, Vice President
FRANK H. HEATH, Executive Secretary

DIRECTORS:
WARD C. BELCHER
DAVID KIRSCHNER
W. F. NETTLES, Jr.
AUSTIN SHEHEEN
H. D. KIRKOVER
BASIL BRUCE
GUS BELEOS
D. J. CREED
D. M. MAYS
J. O. ZEMP

CAMDEN AND KERSHAW COUNTY

Chamber of Commerce

CAMDEN, SOUTH CAROLINA
April 8, 1937

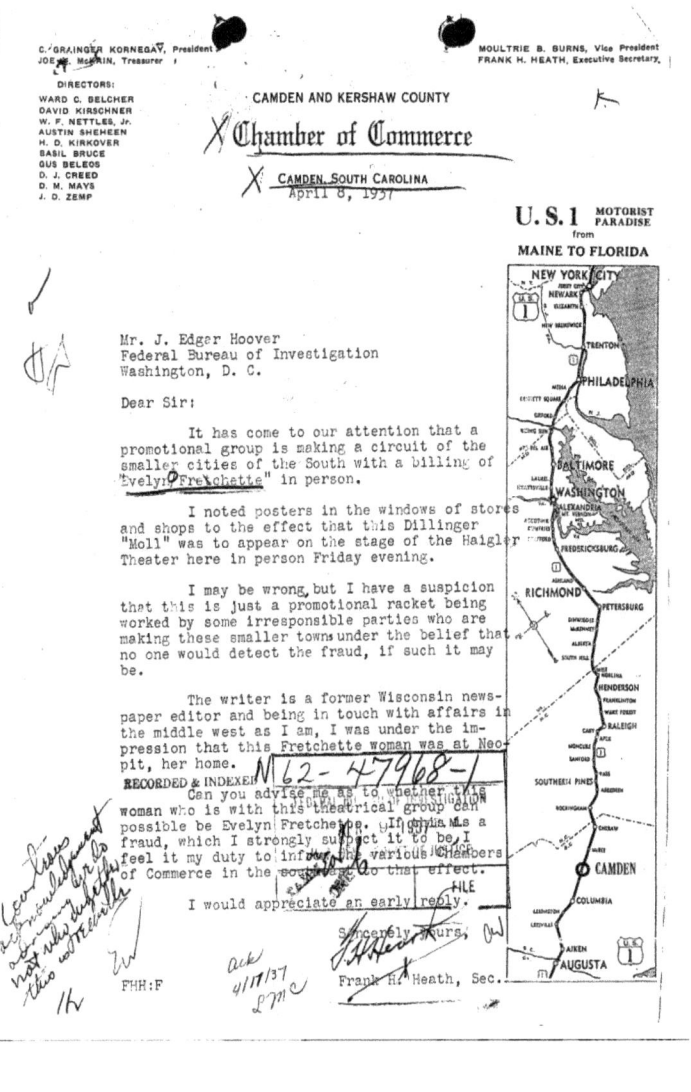

Mr. J. Edgar Hoover
Federal Bureau of Investigation
Washington, D. C.

Dear Sir:

It has come to our attention that a promotional group is making a circuit of the smaller cities of the South with a billing of "Evelyn Fretchette" in person.

I noted posters in the windows of stores and shops to the effect that this Dillinger "Moll" was to appear on the stage of the Haigler Theater here in person Friday evening.

I may be wrong, but I have a suspicion that this is just a promotional racket being worked by some irresponsible parties who are making these smaller towns under the belief that no one would detect the fraud, if such it may be.

The writer is a former Wisconsin newspaper editor and being in touch with affairs in the middle west as I am, I was under the impression that this Fretchette woman was at Neopit, her home.

Can you advise me as to whether this woman who is with this theatrical group can possible be Evelyn Fretchette. If she is a fraud, which I strongly suspect it to be, I feel it my duty to inform the various Chambers of Commerce in the south to that effect.

I would appreciate an early reply.

Sincerely yours,

Frank H. Heath, Sec.

FHH:F

EMH:JDlF
62-47968-2

RECORDED

May 5, 1937.

Mr. J. B. Drury,
Federal Bureau of Investigation,
4244 U. S. Department of Justice Building,
Washington, D. C.

Dear Mr. Drury:

I am in receipt of the pamphlet entitled "Public Enemies - U. S. War on Crime," which you recently purchased at the Johnny J. Jones Shows in Washington.

It was thoughtful of you to submit this pamphlet and I want to thank you for this courtesy and also for your comments concerning the appearance in one of the side shows of Evelyn Frechette.

Sincerely yours,

John Edgar Hoover,
Director.

CC-Washington Field

Federal Bureau of Investigation
United States Department of Justice
Washington, D. C.

TDQ:A   Date May 3, 1937.

MEMORANDUM FOR MR. TOLSON

Mr. Peake, formerly employed by the Washington-Herald, telephoned and wanted to know if the Director was in the city and whether he would meet Evelyn Frechette if she called at the Bureau this afternoon.

Mr. Peake advised she was in the city playing at a carnival and had expressed a desire to meet the Director and go through the Bureau. I informed him the Director was absent from the city and the date of his return was uncertain and that apparently this was an attempted publicity stunt on the part of Miss Frechette. He denied this and wanted to know who could meet her if she called at the Bureau and was informed that I knew of no one who desired to meet her.

RECORDED
&
INDEXED.

62-47968-3

FEDERAL BUREAU OF INVESTIGATION
MAY 7 1937 P.M.
U.S. DEPARTMENT OF JUSTICE
FILE

Signature

Federal Bureau of Investigation

United States Department of Justice

P. O. BOX # 1525,
PITTSBURGH, PA.

May 29, 1937.

Director,
Federal Bureau of Investigation,
Washington, D. C.

Dear Sir:

In reference to the deceased John Dillinger, it has been ascertained that the Johnny J. Jones Carnival and Circus, appearing in Pittsburgh, Pennsylvania, during the current week, has as a sideshow attraction a unit known or billed as "Crime does not Pay" the main feature of which is Evelyn Frechette, described as a gangster-girl and gun-moll of John Dillinger.

Miss Frechette gives a general discourse on her association with John Dillinger and answers questions put to her by the audience. In answer to specific questions from the audience she stated among other things, that Dillinger had two "mobs" composed of six members each, not mentioning names; that she did not know who actually killed Dillinger, inasmuch as she was in a Michigan prison at the time; that she did not personally know the "lady in red" as John had "taken up with her" while she, Frechette, was in prison on charges of "harboring John Dillinger".

This information was submitted by Anthony M. Frahlich, stenographer of this office, who attended one of the performances and who states that the girl is really Evelyn Frechette, identified from pictures in the possession of this office.

The above is furnished to the Bureau in the event that Frechette's location may be known for purposes of interview, or otherwise, if desired.

RECORDED & INDEXED 62-47968-4

Very truly yours,

R. J. UNTREINER,
Special Agent in Charge.

LMC:MC

RECORDED & INDEXED

62-47968   1   April 17, 1937.

Mr. Frank H. Heath,
Executive Secretary,
Chamber of Commerce,
Camden, South Carolina.

Dear Mr. Heath:

    I am in receipt of your communication dated April 8, 1937, in which inquiry is made as to whether Evelyn Frechette is making a circuit of the theatres in the various cities of the South as a theatrical attraction.

    Please be advised that this Bureau is not informed as to the present location of Evelyn Frechette, and I regret, therefore, that I am unable to advise you as to whether the information to which you refer in your letter is reliable.

                      Very truly yours,

                        John Edgar Hoover,
                        Director.

cc Charlotte

APR 17 1937

Federal Bureau of Investigation
United States Department of Justice

Washington Field Office, Room 4244,
Washington, D. C.

April 28, 1937.

Director,
Federal Bureau of Investigation,
Washington, D. C.

Re: EVELYN FRECHETTE.

Dear Sir:

As of possible interest to the Bureau there is attached hereto a thirty page pamphlet entitled "Public Enemies - U. S. War on Crime".

This book was purchased by Mr. J. B. Drury of this office at the Johnny J. Jones Shows now playing at 18th Street and Benning Road, N. E.

One of the attractions at this carnival is a side show entitled "Crime", featuring a real "Gun Moll", Evelyn Frechette.

Mr. Drury informs that the manager of the show asked Miss Frechette a number of questions and told something of her life; that it was the usual practice to allow members of the audience to question Miss Frechette. He was particularly careful to distinguish between Evelyn Frechette and "The Woman in Red", Mrs. Anna Sage, advising that the latter had been deported to Rumania. This booklet sold for ten cents and is reported to have been written by Evelyn Frechette while in prison.

It is understood that the carnival is operating under the auspices and for the benefit of the Tall Cedars of Lebanon, a fraternal organization.

Very truly yours,

GUY HOTTEL,
Special Agent in Charge.

GH:EB
Enclosure.

U. S. WAR ON CRIME

"BRING 'EM BACK"
ALIVE OR DEAD

DESPERATE BATTLES and
SCIENTIFIC DETECTION
of
BOOTLEGGERS
GANGLAND
PUBLIC ENEMIES

Instructive Discussions

Edited and Copyrighted, 1935
By Max Stein

STEIN PUBLISHING HOUSE
521 S. State St.
Chicago, Ill.

BORDER BANDITS

After the end of the Civil War, as the result of lax Border Law, the still sparsely settled "Wild West" produced gangs of picturesque gunmen who "Died with their Boots on" such as Jesse and Frank James, The Younger Brothers, The Dalton Brothers, Bella Starr and her Cherokee Indian husband. Bob Ford who killed Jesse James, Red Kelly who killed Bob Ford. These and other killers such as Billy The Kid, a product of New York slums who went west to fight Indians he had heard about, occupied the headlines of the Press for many years.

Their bold ideas of robbing banks, trains and rich travelers, and the bravery of the U. S. and State Officers who persistently battled these outlaws at the risk of their lives, were never surpassed in romance. Because of the fact that press headlines have never featured them, the names of brave officers have been forgotten by the public.

In the so-called "gay 90's" and the early part of the 20th Century a prison sentence was dreaded, not only for its hardships, but generally because of the strain and lasting disgrace it brought upon members of the immediate family. Welfare Societies were formed during these years to educate prisoners and bring about reforms.

When the war in Europe broke out in 1914, a new era was begun. Financial conditions had been very

THE NEW ERA

bad. Suddenly money was easily earned without hard work. Many adventurers joined the colors of one of the warring countries.

The advent of the U. S. into the War in 1917 intensified the quickly changing situation. Men were removed from quiet communities and contented work to become hardened to bursting shells, blood, misery, crippled limbs. The world became filled with shell-shocked dissatisfied individuals who wondered how and why this all came about, tracing the cause to an invisible master-force at the top, so flexible, so vast, that no finger could point it out.

It was during this time, when men and women were occupied with the largest event in the world's history that reformers, with the aid of "Big Business" leaders, amended the U. S. Constitution to prevent the use of Liquor as a beverage; a principal argument being that only sober people are safe with intricate machines.

After the Armistice of Nov. 11, 1918, as the American Nation's heroes returned from countries that have no illusions about the pleasures of home life, they found a changed homeland. Their gathering places were vacated, many of them with "closed for one year" signs on the doors; while housewives simply could not understand why it was a crime to crush fruit to make wines.

No revenue to the state was necessary in order to make beer or stronger drink, but if anyone were

WARS OF THE GANGS

caught doing so a jail sentence or possibly a bullet from an investigator was the result. So-called "snoopers" were ridiculed and held in disgrace by fighting men who laughed at "the adventure."

Taxes increased. Work decreased. A law-making orgy just then seemed to infect the daily-grinding law makers. It was estimated that two million laws, each with penalties attached were being enforced. The country became a camp of law breakers. Bootlegging became an art that was not considered either criminal or offensive to the average citizen. Extremely alert and energetic men became "rum-runners." Outstanding among these were the large dealers, who had zoned agents. The amount of money supplied for prohibition enforcements, although mounting fast, were almost useless in face of the fact that a large majority of the public considered the whole "experiment" impractical.

Lack of law enforcement, Political corruption, and the breaking down of the Courts was the natural result. Juries would not often convict! Headlines of newspapers seldom even mentioned new inventions, social scandals or other news. Gang wars between zoned liquor agents, Political Murders, Bomb explosions, Battles with officers in which machine guns, armed boats, armored cars and airplanes were used on both sides, were common occurrences. Murdered men or women were found at almost any place. Police

LIQUOR LORDS

generally knew all the facts, but seldom had any proof for conviction. The cases in New York of Arnold Rothstein and "Legs" Diamond were National Scandals.

Among the first dramatic mystery murders to attract Nation-wide attention was that of Jim Colosimo at his widely known Cafe on Wabash Avenue, Chicago. He was popular, a free giver to charity. In Gangdom he was known as a Chicago leader of Liquor interests.

All that ever became public of the Crime, was that Colosimo hurried in response to a mysterious Telephone call. A few minutes later he was found with several bullets in his head. No one was ever tried for his death.

Similar mysteries followed in quick succession in the larger cities. Chicago newspapers featured the crimes of the followers of liquor Lords to such an extent that Public interest attached to them an atmosphere of romance, awaiting impatiently every issue of the favorite Daily Paper as do the readers of continued fiction in Periodicals.

Alphonso Capone and John Torrio, not long from New York, replaced Colosimo in the Newspapers. Every crime committed, every "ride" on which leaders were taken to their death, every "spot" on which someone was placed to be riddled with machine gun bullets was blamed on some Over-Lord or a rival.

Soup kitchens and Bread lines during the worst

THE MARCH OF CRIME

conditions of unemployment also were credited to money supplied by Capone. Charges were published of forced contributions from Chain Stores for this purpose. If fiction writers had previously circulated such horrible murder details being related as daily news items, public nausea would have relegated them to oblivion.

Early morning extras announced one morning that Assistant State's Attorney William H. McSwiggin was killed and his body found in a street in Cicero. Two men whom he had unsuccessfully tried for murder of a liquor lord were also killed in a car in Cicero about the same time. All the police could learn was that 200 bullets were fired from Machine Guns in a passing automobile.

"Who killed McSwiggin?" was a question asked for months.

Murder followed murder, but the death of O'Banion in his North State St. Chicago flower shop landed on Page One of newspapers all over the country. Many "rides" were taken in avenging him.

LIQUOR LORDS

generally knew all the facts, but seldom had any proof for conviction. The cases in New York of Arnold Rothstein and "Legs" Diamond were National Scandals.

Among the first dramatic mystery murders to attract Nation-wide attention was that of Jim Colosimo at his widely known Cafe on Wabash Avenue, Chicago. He was popular, a free giver to charity. In Gangdom he was known as a Chicago leader of Liquor interests.

All that ever became public of the Crime, was that Colosimo hurried in response to a mysterious Telephone call. A few minutes later he was found with several bullets in his head. No one was ever tried for his death.

Similar mysteries followed in quick succession in the larger cities. Chicago newspapers featured the crimes of the followers of liquor Lords to such an extent that Public interest attached to them an atmosphere of romance, awaiting impatiently every issue of the favorite Daily Paper as do the readers of continued fiction in Periodicals.

Alphonso Capone and John Torrio, not long from New York, replaced Colosimo in the Newspapers. Every crime committed, every "ride" on which leaders were taken to their death, every "spot" on which someone was placed to be riddled with machine gun bullets was blamed on some Over-Lord or a rival.

Soup kitchens and Bread lines during the worst

THE MARCH OF CRIME

conditions of unemployment also were credited to money supplied by Capone. Charges were published of forced contributions from Chain Stores for this purpose. If fiction writers had previously circulated such horrible murder details being related as daily news items, public nausea would have relegated them to oblivion.

Early morning extras announced one morning that Assistant State's Attorney William H. McSwiggin was killed and his body found in a street in Cicero. Two men whom he had unsuccessfully tried for murder of a liquor lord were also killed in a car in Cicero about the same time. All the police could learn was that 200 bullets were fired from Machine Guns in a passing automobile.

"Who killed McSwiggin?" was a question asked for months.

Murder followed murder, but the death of O'Banion in his North State St. Chicago flower shop landed on Page One of newspapers all over the country. Many "rides" were taken in avenging him.

THE ST. VALENTINE DAY MASSACRE

MYSTERY MURDERS

The next act that startled the whole world was the famous gangland Massacre on St. Valentine's Day, 1929. Seven victims were lined up facing a wall, with hands up, and shot down by two machine guns.

They were James Clark, Johnny May, Adam Kyer, Albert Weinshank, Dr. R. H. Schwimmer, Pete and Frank Gusenberg. The latter was still alive when taken to a hospital and had 27 bullets in him. It was alleged that an attempt was made to wipe out the leaders of an opposition liquor ring in their own headquarters, a Garage on North Clark St., Chicago. Two cars, thought by onlookers to be Police Cars, were seen to stop, one at the front and one in the rear of the garage. Two men in Police Uniforms and two others entered through the front door and two through the rear carrying several machine guns. There were probably 150 shots fired, nearly all of which tore into the seven men in the place. The "police" were then seen to return to their cars and drive away.

One man who later looked in curiously, gasped, "There's dead men all over the place." When the police came they paused in horror. A week later one of the cars was found partly burned. It had been faked to resemble a Police Squad Car. No other evidence useful as proof in Court was ever found. Chicago's reputation had received another serious blow.

Police estimate the length of life of a Gunman Racketeer at 31 years. Few have been known to live past 38 years.

"PINEAPPLES" AND GUNMEN

The "Pineapple" Period was probably the beginning of the government's entry into these Mystery Murders. Liquor Lords had become so important that they entered politics in a large way.

Bombs known as "Pineapples" were placed in the home of U. S. Senator Deneen and other Federal, State and City Officials and candidates for office.

Washington's leading investigators were sent to trace them, which ended in arrests for income tax violations.

U. S. Headline news was put aside one June afternoon when the newspapers found that gangland was not letting them go scot free.

"Jake" Lingle, Chicago's Ace Police Reporter with the Chicago Tribune was the victim. He was murdered in a crowded downtown, Chicago Railroad Subway Station—killed because he knew too much.

It was during the investigation of those who might throw some light on the murder that one of the "Big Shots" of Liquor was examined. He told the Police Lieutenant, "You brought me here, now take me back. They'll kill me before I get to Madison St." "Oh, I'll take you back," replied the Police Officer, Soon after leaving the station with three guards, on the best lighted block of downtown State St., Machine Gun Bullets began to blaze, killing a street car motor man and wounding a by-stander—just one more example of how cheaply life was held by these people.

10

U. S. WAR ON CRIME

The revocation of the 18th Amendment and the consequent legalization and licensing of liquor gave a legitimate standing to most of the dealers and manufacturers.

Several gangs quickly turned to Kidnapping, while others were already bold enough for Bank and Mail Robberies. Smaller bait was then attacked by Criminals.

Slowly a new Crime Cure Agency began to function. Criminals had been able to escape control because of Township, County and State Lines, but they now began to meet up with men trained by the Department of Justice—young lawyers and others educated with new clean ideas in the most modern methods used in every part of the world to ferret crimes.

With the aid of Congress and the President, the U. S. Government began to build a National Training Center in the field of Criminal Law enforcement Administration at Washington. Everything that science has to offer was put at the disposal of the department, with the result that the Federal Bureau of Investigation soon had on file over five million sets of finger prints—and decidedly rivals Scotland Yard's reputation of being the best equipped Crime Detector in the world.

THE CRIME THAT SHOCKED THE WORLD

Key to Illustrations: 1) Discovery of Empty Cradle; 2) The Ladder Breaks; 3) Baby is Found; 4) $50,000 Ransom Paid; 5) Marked Bills Traced; 6) The Trial.

THE "G" MEN

The excellent work done in the tracing of bills in the Hauptmann Case, also the scientific manner of tracing wood used in the kidnap ladder was outstanding unchallenged evidence used at the trial.

Other stories of fine detective work by government officials are being told. A story is told of Government agents who had traced one well known desperado to a small town. They wired the sheriff instructions to capture him and mailed six photos. The sheriff wired back: "I have the whole gang. Waiting for further instructions."

On Sept. 1, 1934, a new Federal Island Prison was opened in California. With the advent of new Scientific discoveries in weapons, Machines, radio and speedy communications, transportation and secret codes, the government watches and checks every suspect patiently and minutely.

In the following pages it will be seen that criminals are learning that the Government is in earnest, that the "Federal Dick gets his man, and that if he doesn't get him alive he 'brings 'em back dead.' "

DEATH DEALING MACHINE GUNS

The boldest defiance of law-enforcers took place June 17, 1933, while Detectives Grooms and Hermanson of the K. C. Police and Federal Agents Vetterle and Caffery re-enforced Chief Reed of McAlester, Oklahoma and Federal Agents Smith and Lackey who were bringing FRANK NASH, an Oklahoma Train robber back to Leavenworth from which he had escaped.

The seven officers surrounded Nash outside of the Union Station. Friends of Nash had enlisted the aid of CHAS. (Pretty Boy) FLOYD, already notorious as a killer, VERNE C. MILLER, ex-convict and gunman and other aids.

Floyd and Miller, coming from two directions with machine guns, boldly ran toward the car in which Nash was held prisoner shouting to the officers "Up! Up! Put 'em up." Detective Grooms fired, wounding Floyd, who yelled "Let 'em have it," instantly killing Detective Grooms, Caffery, Hermanson and Chief Reed who lay scattered in the street. Prisoner Nash, seated in the car, was killed. The gangsters got away during the excitement.

VERNE MILLER'S body was found Nov. 20, 1933, nude, almost unrecognizable on a highway near Detroit. A Chicago Liquor Lord who was found dead, supposedly was killed by Miller, and Police records charge his death to this claim.

PRETTY BOY FLOYD was shot to death by Federal and County Officers Oct. 22, 1934.

KANSAS CITY MASSACRE

PUBLIC ENEMY NO. 1

John Dillinger, known during his brief career as Public Enemy No. 1, was born in Indianapolis on June 28, 1902, and came of Quaker stock. Although his mother died when he was three years old, his childhod was a normal, happy one. He went to grade and high school, as well as Sunday School.

At 14, John decided that he no longer wanted to study, and decided to work instead. For a while thereafter he did work as a machinist, but soon he bought himself an old automobile and began to drift around, worrying his family until finally his father bought a farm in Mooresville, Indiana, in order to take him away from city influences.

Open spaces appealed to John; he worked hard and ambitiously. When he was 18, an escapade in which he temporarily "borrowed" a prominent citizen's car caused his arrest, humiliating him so much that he ran away to join the navy. This was on July 23, 1923. Five months later the rigid discipline annoyed him to the point of desertion. Later he was dishonorably discharged.

At 20 John Dillinger married his childhood sweetheart. Five months later he and a companion whom he had met at a pool room slugged and attempted to rob a Mooresville grocer. He was then sentenced to ten to twenty years in the Indiana reformatory. His companion was sentenced to two years. This unequal decision was believed to have turned him against society.

BANK ROBBERIES AND MURDERS

After two unsuccessful attempts to escape from the reformatory he was transferred on July 15, 1929 to the Michigan City penitentiary. His wife then divorced him.

From the time that he was freed on parole on May 22, 1933 until he was shot he put into practice much he had learned from companions he had met at Michigan City.

Fred Fisher, manager of a thread factory in Monticello, Ill., was the first hold-up victim. The banks at Saleville, Montpelier, and Indianapolis were the first bank hold-ups to be credited to Dillinger; Saleville on July 17, 1933; Montpelier on August 4; that in Indianapolis on September 22.

As time passed, and he was successful in evading arrest, Dillinger began to plan for the escape of his friends Hamilton and Pierpont. His first attempt to toss guns over the walls of the prison failed, but on September 20 he had them enclosed in a package of merchandise consigned to the prison, and with the help of a conspirator, the guns reached the two convicts.

On the 25th of September he was arrested at the home of a girl friend in Dayton, Ohio, and taken to the Lima jail. He did not stay there long, however, because on October 12, three of his friends masquerading as Indiana deputies freed their leader and killed Sheriff John Sarver. Then they looted and robbed police stations, getting machine guns, pistols and bullet-proof vests.

REWARDS—ALIVE OR DEAD

Dillinger and Van Meter then decided to have their faces and finger-tips operated on. For this they needed money. So, on June 30 it is claimed Dillinger and four companions raided the Merchant's National Bank at South Bend, Indiana, obtaining $29,890, and killing policeman Howard Wagner.

The report finally was spread that he was seen oftenest in the neighborhood of Lincoln Avenue in Chicago. Federal agents continued to hunt him down. Then they received a tip from "A Lady In Red" that Mr. Dillinger had long wanted to see the moving picture, "Manhattan Melodrama," and that this film was being shown at the Biograph Theater on Lincoln Ave. on Sunday evening, July 22.

The trap was carefully laid. "G men" had studied his peculiar gray eyes, his walk, his stride. His face had been changed, but they were warned before they left the government offices that "the only sure way to identify Dillinger was by the back of his neck."

Federal agents and police watched Dillinger enter the theater. They waited for him to come out. He stepped out of the crowd in the lobby, began to walk south from the theater—and as he crossed a nearby alley he turned, saw his pursuers, dodged behind some women into the alley and dropped—wounded three times in the abdomen and the upper part of the body—beyond the protection of his bullet-proof vest. He died at 10:45 P. M. July 22, 1934, ending a most eventful career that had lasted exactly fourteen months.

DILLINGER AND HIS GANGS

Key to Illustrations: 1) Flees G Men in Raid; 2) Shooting Their Way Out of Trap; 3) Raiding Police Station; 4) Bank Hold-up; 5) The Wooden Pistol; 6) Dillinger is Shot.

"G" MEN AND DETECTIVES AT WORK

A Greencastle, Indiana bank was robbed of $75,000 on October 23—after which Dillinger was believed to have driven to Florida. The state of Indiana was in a turmoil. The national guard was called out and a search started that would have done credit to a search for Jesse James or Pancho Villa, who thought he could indefinitely defy organized Governments.

John Dillinger next appeared in Chicago where he evaded a trap set for him by the Chicago police in a dentist's office, escaping with a woman companion through a rain of bullets.

Soon after, on November 20, another bank was held up in Racine, Wisconsin, to the amount of $28,000. The looted vaults of the Unity Trust and Savings Bank on West North Ave., in Chicago, yielded a great deal of jewelry and over $8,700.

At the next robbery on January 14, Dillinger, assisted by Pierpont and Hamilton, robbed the First National Bank of East Chicago, Indiana, of $20,000, and killed a policeman, Wm. P. O'Malley.

The bandits escaped, but ten days later Dillinger, Clark, Pierpont and Makley with three women were captured in Tucson. Three states: Indiana, Ohio and Wisconsin, vied for their extradition: Indiana for the murder of O'Malley; Ohio for the murder of Sheriff Sarver; Wisconsin for the Racine robbery. It was decided that they be brought to Crown Point, Indiana for trial on the charge of murdering policeman O'Malley. Later, Clark, Pierpont and Makley were turned over to the state of Ohio.

THE "WOOD GUN" ESCAPE

They held Dillinger at Crown Point for about a month. Then, on March 3, with Youngblood he escaped from the jail, using the famous toy pistol. It was after this escape by means of an alleged wooden pistol that the U. S. Police and Government started the most spectacular man hunt ever known in America. Eight of Dillinger's lieutenants were marked for death—by the electric chair if possible, or by gunfire if necessary.

For a while Dillinger was very successful at evading the police. On the 13th of March he and Hamilton were traced to Mason City, Iowa. On that day $52,000 was taken from the First National Bank. On the 15th they received medical treatment at St. Paul. There a new gang was formed including Van Meter, Tommy Carroll and Lester Gillis—better known as "Baby Face" Nelson. Dillinger and his sweetheart, continued to live in a good residential neighborhood in St. Paul until March 31—when they and Van Meter shot their way out of a trap set for them by Federal men and Police.

After April 22, when he and his gang again shot their way out of a resort on Spider Lake in northern Wisconsin, killing a federal agent and a CWA employee, he was apparently seen in many places.

On June 23—through special legislation, the federal government offered $10,000 in rewards for Dillinger and $5,000 for Nelson—who had killed agent Baum. In addition, Indiana, Ohio, Michigan, Illinois and Minnesota offered $1,000 reward each for Dillinger.

THE GANG'S ROUND UP

It is estimated that Dillinger's cost to society was over a million dollars; that over 12 bank robberies brought him more than $300,000; that because of him many more people were sent to jail; and that in addition the government and states involved spent over $500,000.

After the death of Dillinger, Government Agents determined to round up all those who aided him.

HOMER VAN METER died while resisting a trap set for him Sept. 22 at St. Paul, Minnesota.

CHARLES MAKLEY, a college man, who had escaped from Michigan City, Sept. 26, 1933, while serving a 10 year sentence for robbery, was shot and killed when he and Pierpont tried to escape from Columbus Ohio Prison, where he was held for execution.

HARRY PIERPONT, escaped from Michigan City Sept. 26, 1933, while serving a 10-year term for Bank Robbery. He gained a reputation as a deadly "quick trigger" man. He was executed Oct. 17 at Columbus, Ohio Prison.

"BABY FACE" NELSON was shot to death Nov. 17, 1934, in a terrific gun battle at Barrington, Ill., during which Federal Agents Samuel P. Cowley and Herman E. Hollis were slain.

One man, in whose home it was claimed Dillinger's facial operation was performed, five days later fell from the 19th floor office of the Dept. of Justice.

BROUGHT TO JUSTICE

JOHN HAMILTON was the last of Dillinger's Lieutenants to be taken off the "active" list. His body was dug up in a quarry grave near Oswego, Ill. by federal agents on Aug. 28, 1935.

From the condition of the outlaw's body it was theorized that he had been dead for many months, and that he had evidently been killed even before the death of his leader, in July, 1934.

Rooming House keepers, attorneys, doctors, and others, both men and women in different parts of the country, who had assisted these gunmen, were also brought to justice by the Government and Police. Each received either a jail sentence or fine.

The Bloody Barrows, (Buck and Clyde) were first heard of on Aug. 13, 1928, when Buck was arrested in San Antonio, Texas, for the theft of a car. Although he was discharged for that theft, from then on the two brothers were in prison and out.

In 1932 Clyde was freed from a Texas Prison. He teamed up with Bonnie Parker "two-gun Moll." The two then became the center of a reign of terror in the southwest states.

ALVIN KARPIS has been accused by the Federal Government as a kidnapper of Earl Bremmer of St. Paul and murder committed during Bank Robberies.

THE DRUG EVIL

In May, 1935, to fight the drug evil, the government opened its first U. S. Narcotic Farm, a Four Million Dollar Institution comprising 1,100 acres in Lexington, Kentucky. It is administered by the U. S. Health Service to restore the shattered health of Drug Addicts, who will be treated as Medical Patients. Another is to be used in Fort Worth, Texas. Patients who otherwise would be in Prisons, are cared for here, also volunteers who wish to undergo treatment.

This is considered an ideal advance in the anti-narcotic movement for the prevention of crimes committed by those under the influence of the poppy seed.

The murder of Ervin J. Lang may well be charged to the influence of drugs dulling to the brain. Mrs. Dunkel, Lang's mother-in-law, apparently became his lover after the death of her daughter, Lang's wife. Her jealousy was aroused when Lang announced his engagement to a young lady. Mrs. Dunkel determined to kill him.

Mrs. Evelyn Smith, a close friend, married to a Chinese Laundry Owner, was induced upon a promise of $500.00 never paid, to help her. Mrs. Smith finally carried out the murder herself, carving off Lang's legs to enable her to remove the body, in which she claimed she had the unwilling aid of her husband.

Their casual matter of fact preparation for the crime confessed by them was cold-blooded and revolting. Justice Harrington, in sentencing each to 180 years imprisonment at hard labor, said, "It appears

SEX MURDERS

that throughout the commission of this crime you indicated a cold indifference to the possible penalty of death in the electric chair.

"Infliction of the death penalty and a swift execution would be an anesthetic to your consciences, an easy and painless passing from this existence. The punishment the court will inflict, will be a deterrent to crime, an admonition to criminals that you are suffering a living death, tortured by your consciences, while at work at hard labor behind the grey walls of the penitentiary, deprived of your liberty, for the balance of your days."

A series of "come-true" night-mares in the murder field seemed to happen in the near Chicago zone just about at this same time. They were all classified by Police under the newly titled "Sex Crimes."

Because she resisted the advances of her young companion, a beautiful girl was strangled in a vacant lot and her body dropped through a sewer catch basin, later discovered by city repair men.

A young man stabbed his sweetheart to death because they were tired of life and swore it was a suicide pact. "We went to the park to die. I first stabbed her, then gave her the knife, but she was so weak she could only cut my shirt with it."

There was a revolting murder of a pretty night club entertainer, whose lover sent five bullets into her, as she lay in her bed dying, with his name on her lips.

The "Wolf of Peoria" had annoyed girls for seven

BOY GUNMEN

years. One day a girl's nude body was found in a cemetery. At the trial, where he was sentenced to death, it was proven that when the girl had resisted, she was beaten, strangled, and killed.

A University Professor was forced to drive a man who he knew as Jones from Ann Arbor to outlying Chicago, where a brutal mutilating sterilization operation was performed upon him with a penknife, from which he died. He had recently married a nurse, whose former lover was accused of the crime.

It is estimated that now the majority of so-called bandits are young men or boys, who were raised during the "dangerous days," when reckless dare-devil bootleggers were glorified in the headlines. They have been attracted by the illusion of the romance and the big easy money of the racketeer just as some boys aim to follow in the steps of leading ball players, statesmen, merchants, detectives, etc.

Almost anywhere, any person may suddenly find that a boy with a gun is facing him. Their amateur bravado is not humorous and Police make short work of them, but because of their age, reform elements have prevented drastic action to end the evil.

It is known that most small children recognize no proprietorship nor damage until after a certain amount of proper training is given them. In kindergarten, the child who will not comply with rules; who lies, cheats, or persists in violence, disregarding the rights of others, requires personal attention to prevent

ANTIDOTES FOR CRIME

it from developing with these characteristics.

The boy of 12 or more whose erratic nature has not been checked by some good influence will have to be dealt with by society.

As the youngster grows up he discovers that complicated State, County and Township laws with different procedures, permit criminals to evade justice. They learn the methods of escape, trick to evade Law, sometimes with the aid of attorneys, politics, etc. All restraint is forgotten. After a few successful crimes; the misery caused to victims; the worry caused to their own relations; evasions from officers of the law; a frenzied belief that their life is normal soon brings a feeling that all is safe.

Capt. Donald Wilkie, formerly of the U. S. Service, claims the average in regard to crime have been as follows: 6 to 1 the Criminal was arrested; 12 to 1 if caught and tried, he did not go to prison; 124 to 1 if a murdered, he was not executed. As principal causes, he gave political drags, lawyers, red tape, perjury, simple alibis, etc.

As an antidote for evil, substitutes must be offered. Easy access to music and sports, as well as active participation in group organizations with leadership, such as the Boy Scouts offer can and does replace degrading interests.

It is imperative that the Agricultural success of men like Geo. Washington, Thos. Jefferson and others be intensively taught the young, upon which to base

BACK TO NATURE

their future. The U. S. A. has space for hundreds of millions of people. The ground is fertile, the climate and all other conditions are favorable for enjoyment of family life. With regulation and some labor, the land will do the work with the aid of nature. It is not necessary for masses to congregate in American centers to provide Industrial Competition for nations who have not the natural advantages provided to the Americas. American labor has no need to compete with lower scale foreign labor.

It is in these centers of population that so much unhappiness becomes possible. Unemployment, or employment at lower than living wage, unsanitary and immoral family conditions easily breed dissatisfied minds that rebel at unfairness and then either develop great fighting reformers to better things or they can develop into derelicts, brutes, growlers, or criminals.

As we observe plant and animal life we notice that where a life is added, whether it is insect or flower, provision for its existence is also at hand. It is only man who has food and shelter withdrawn, not that sufficient is not provided by nature, but his own laws prevent the use of necessities except by payment for it in money, which, of course, makes money and its attainment the goal of every human being.

Gradually as a major part of its war on crime in the U. S. the powerful hand of gov't has insisted that more humane methods be used, by further regulation of great interests that control so many of the require-

SCIENTIFIC CRIME DETECTION

ments of the people.

Social responsibilities being assumed by the government will prevent much poverty and discontent. Satisfied, home-building people are good citizens with no criminal intent.

"Back to Nature" may not be the slogan for every one, but Civilian Conservation Corps in charge of the U. S. Army, under suggestions of the A. F. of L., took 310,000 unemployed young men between 18 and 25 years old off the streets.

Many suggestions have been offered in the War on Crime, viz:

That all firearms be registered;

That every person be finger printed;

That all police officials take University Courses in Police Science, learning thoroughly Identification, Traffic, Psychology, Evidence, First Aid, Firearms, Drugs, Gambling, Prostitution, Penology, Physical Training, Law and other Police Matters;

That much stricter laws be enforced against public officials who serve criminals instead of the public;

Limit insanity pleas, also paroles;

Stronger penalties for repeaters;

That Corporations become subject to punishment for criminal offenses;

Avoidance of too many laws, or unjust law-enforcement;

That county jails be prevented from being crime schools;

30

CRIME DOES NOT PAY

That Drug and Drink Addicts be separated from criminal offenders and treated.

That the U. S. attack on crime is effective and thorough-going has been proven. It is, however, characteristically American, and soon new stories and plays will make new heroes and ambitions for the youth to emulate.

Certainly, if a young man now is squarely confronted with the situation "Shall I hold Human Life cheaply and follow the easy money of the gunman Racketeer to face Government agents who have been "Bringing them in dead" or shall I be a Law enforcer—a protector of neighbors and family," there should no longer be any doubt as to his answer. "CRIME DOES NOT PAY."

RESTRAINT

A cross word not spoken, a shot not fired, a stab not made, a suicide not attempted as the thought occurs, is an evil deed averted. Later, one shudders at the folly of the blunders or crime that might have been committed but for the use of "restraint"—a product of civilization not practiced enough.

The desire for thrill may be a cause of crime. Excess in drinking, speed or the desire to do something startling can be cured only by the exercise of restraint.

THE LIE DETECTOR

THE POLYGRAPH IN OPERATION A BLOOD-PRESSURE CUFF ON THE WRIST AND A PNEUMOGRAPH CORD AROUND THE CHEST OF THE SUBJECT WILL RECORD ON THE MOVING SCROLL ANY INDICATION OF A LIE

Made in U. S. A.

The Detective's Guide to Success

—BY—

C. R. WOOLDRIDGE

Author of

"Hands Up! in the World of Crime."

Tells you how to become a Successful Detective and Contains valuable Information, Instruction and Advice for Government and Guidance of Detectives and Police Officers.

PRICE 25 CENTS

MAX STEIN PUBLISHER
CHICAGO, ILL.

Chapter Twenty-Four:

War Games

In 1939, Germany invaded Poland, which ultimately started the beginning of WWII. Japan aimed at dominating Asia and the Pacific. Combined with support from the UK, the European Axis declared war on the US. So, on December 7, 1941, the US joined WWII.

Now, I am not a history major, but one thing we learned in boarding school was American history. Western culture deemed it necessary to civilize the Native Americans. So, when 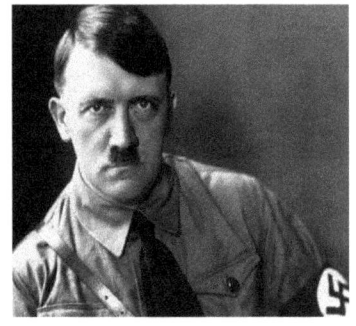 Adolf Hitler was unsuccessful in his attempt to overthrow the German government in 1923, he worked to become Chancellor of Germany in 1933. One of his first missions was to abolish democracy, adopting a radical, racially motivated revision of the world order, and soon began a massive arming campaign. In France, to secure its alliance, he allowed Italy to gain free access to Ethiopia. As the situation escalated, in early 1935 the Territory of Saar Basin was legally reunited with Germany and Hitler rejected the Treaty of Versailles, which sped up his rearmament program and upped recruitment to his army.

On January 1, 1942, the Allied Big Four, Soviet Union, China, the United Kingdom, and the US with other smaller governments, created the United Nations. In this charter, they overwhelmingly agreed to defeat Germany at all costs. The decision would change the world forever.

As the war efforts escalated, women at home in the US had to step up and take over male-dominated jobs to keep America running. One of our biggest issues was keeping the people at home fed while the men were off to war. So, by mid-1943, the [Victory Gardens](#) spread across the

countryside, to over 18 million at the end of the war. They even built one at the White House by the first lady, Eleanor Roosevelt. It boosted our morale. Of course, the bureaucrats in Washington complained about how this decision would hurt the food industry. But the country was only just recovering from the [Great Depression](#) and none of us were going to endure such an event again, this time we would have control over our food supply. Every person in America saw just how well the government did in keeping its residents fed during the Depression. So, I decided to take part in such a stupendous event. It was my way of giving back to my own people and the others who had suffered just as much as the Native Americans.

  I went to work immediately upon my arrival back home. My mother's place was the perfect spot for such a garden. Many of the people in that era on the reservation had never been taught to farm or did not have the ability. I had both the knowledge and ability to hunt, fish, and farm. I'd spent much of my life running, or struggling to fit in somewhere, so this was my chance to shine. It kept me out of the spotlight and I could help my people.

As the war progressed, it brought more than just food shortages, it also caused gas shortages. So, we were given ration books. The national speed was reduced to thirty-five 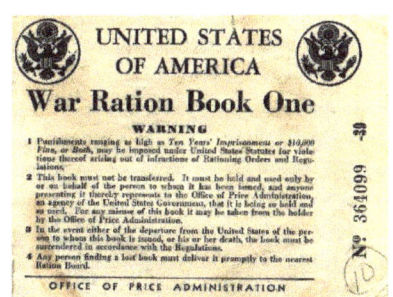 miles per hour and you had to prove that you only owned five tires or less to receive a gasoline ration card. Then we were allotted three gallons a week.

If you went to the store for groceries, they gave you one egg, a stick of butter, and one steak. Most of the canned food and non-perishables were sent overseas to the soldiers. And, we were shorted on rubber, metal, and clothing, to just name a few. In this case, we were much better prepared because of the Depression, and people had started storing essentials just in case.

We were even rationed on stamps. Families had loved ones in the war and wanted to write letters but we did not have the paper to make the stamps. You could only buy a book once a month.

Our tire supply in the US stopped for almost a year. The dealerships stopped selling cars and started selling bicycles. But, as conditions in the war got worse, they quit selling radios, phonographs, refrigerators, vacuums, washing machines, sewing machines, and typewriters. Then anything that had been packed in a metal can or container was switched to some type of bag or other material because all the steel went to build equipment. Our freedom was at stake: Hitler was progressing well at ruling the world, and his sights were set on the US.

We were rationed to half-pound of sugar and flour per week, and one-pound coffee every five weeks. I admit, one advantage that came about was women were no longer expected to wear silk nylons. The military needed the material for shoes, so we did without. Women quickly learned to love that shortage.

Please, don't think it stopped there.... We had meat, butter, and dairy shortages as well. So those people without farm animals were stuck with the grocery stores. Sometimes even the private farmer had to give up their milk for the war. The one surprising item that was not rationed was bread, until after the war was over. Then you could no longer buy wholemeal bread, just white bread, and many people complained it gave them digestive issues.

America had been fighting for survival during the Great Depression and it brought on a huge separation between the people and the government. But when the war began, we reclaimed our strength; patriotism hit the highest records ever. We were proud of our country. Some disagreed, but for the most part, life was good. Until we heard the news about the Holocaust. The news was so horrifying it took months for everyone to believe what we were being told.

It officially started in March 1933, but Hitler was able to keep it quiet until late 1938, when the information hit the world. The papers called it the 'Night of the Glass.' German militia turned Jewish businesses and residences into ghettos. They segregated them from society and began rounding them up. When the violence erupted, many of the Jewish people fled to Germany and came to America. The German government called it a necessary genocide to rid the world of a nuisance culture. Their choice of words sounded way too familiar. I will never understand the need to control others because of their culture, skin color, or beliefs.

As Germany continued to win the war, their death camps increased. Before long, they started filling railroad cars with people (humans) to have them incinerated. The paramilitary death squads murdered over 1.3 million Jewish people, and that was just in mass shootings and programs. All in all, more than 13 million humans were slaughtered. Sound familiar?

However, the issue started way before the war began: Protestant charities and some members of the German medical establishment pushed for a sterilization law that passed on July 14, 1933. It was called The Law for the Prevention of Hereditarily Diseased Offspring. The New York Times reported on December 21, 1933, "400,000 Germans to be sterilized".

In October 1939, Hitler signed a "euthanasia decree" backdated to September 1, 1939, that authorized Reichsleiter Philipp Bouhler, the chief of Hitler's Chancellery, and Karl Brandt, Hitler's personal  physician, to carry out a program of involuntary euthanasia. After the war, this program came to be known as Aktion T4, named after Tiergartenstraße 4. They targeted mostly adults, but the euthanasia of children was also carried out. So, between 1939 and

1941, 80,000 to 100,000 mentally ill adults in institutions were killed, as were 5,000 children and 1,000 Jews, also in institutions. There were also dedicated killing centers, where the deaths were estimated at 20,000. Overall, the number of mentally and physically handicapped people who were murdered was about 150,000.

By the time the Holocaust hit hard, the militia would march the countryside, ordering Jews to strip off their clothes and be shot on sight. Their corpses were thrown into a ditch on the side of the road. At first, they only aimed at locating men from ages fifteen to sixty, but later it went to anyone claiming to be Jewish. The Native Americans had faced this type of genocide since the seventeenth century. So, we had learned how dangerous the government can become.

In 1942, the president authorized an executive order that allowed the military commanders to round up Japanese people and place them in internment camps. Although the order did not state Japanese Americans, they were also included. If any of them lived in Alaska, they were ordered to leave. The government was eventually forced to pay restitution to those affected by racial prejudice, war hysteria, and the failure of political leadership. The hysteria got so bad that people started hanging signs on their businesses and homes stating, "I am an American".

After I left for the reservation that year, it was right at the start of spring, so the weather did not get good enough to plant until the end of May. By this time the shortages had begun, and travel was very difficult unless it was an emergency. Plus, we found the reservation to be a place of sanctuary. Then in 1942, due to the war effort, we lost another 400,000 acres for a gunnery range and they housed some Japanese American internees. As if Western culture had not caused enough chaos to the different cultures. In all at the time, there were 350,000 Native

Americans in the US and 25,000 of us served in the military. It is a higher percentage than any other minority.

By the time the war ended, the US was recovering from the world-wide task of defeating Nazi Germany and the eradication of many cultures. The resources were dangerously short and the last thing the government needed was to care for the Native Americans. Over 40,000 Indians worked in war-related industries and had already relocated to the cities and towns to assimilate with White culture. It had become a staggering task for the government to uphold. So, initially, the Indian Affairs commissioner began relocating Native Americans from two tribes to cities where jobs were plentiful and better than what the reservation could offer. Nearly thirty percent had already moved by 1960. In 1946, congress took the first steps to terminate the Indian Claims Commission. It started with rewarding Natives who contributed to the war effort and then setting up hearings to return stolen land since the creation of the USA in 1776. Then finally in 1953, Congress endorsed the house concurrent resolution that gave Native Americans the same rights as any other citizen in America. In the same year, public land was returned in California, Minnesota, Nebraska, Oregon, and Wisconsin.

[Senator Arthur Watkins](#) of Utah, an advocate for my people, claimed, "Following in the footsteps of the Emancipation Proclamation of ninety-four years ago, I see the following words emblazoned in letters of fire above the heads of the Indians— THESE PEOPLE SHALL BE FREE!"

They were the best words to our ears; it meant we were finally free from Western culture to live our own lives as we chose. Many of my people stayed living and working on the reservation because, at that point, it was difficult to find a job and live well on the reservation land. However, since I did not have to work and had my fill of Western culture for a lifetime, so the best place for me was to stay put where I felt safe. Besides, my plan to help became a huge part of my life for the duration of the war.

Since before we could walk, my mother had us either on her back or running around her in the open fields gathering food, hunting, and fishing. It had just become second nature to me by this point in my life. Besides, there is something spiritual about growing your own food. I love getting up every morning, watering, pulling weeds, and sowing seeds. In Wisconsin, our soil is conducive to growing anything. We get natural rainwater, heat to propagate the seeds, and temperatures to keep them healthy during the summer months.

My days consisted of gardening early, taking care of the livestock, and then fishing. Most of our meat came from the fish I caught. By that time, we had a freezer in the laundry room so we could store food for the winter. It beat gathering what you could find all winter; nonetheless, my fondest memories are canning with Mom in the kitchen during harvest times.

We would clear the counters, empty the cabinets and the cellar for room, and then can for almost a week straight. It was the most fun; we'd laugh and giggle like schoolgirls. I can remember her stories about being a child with her mother cooking and gathering. The one thing I do not miss is having to sleep on those grass-filled mats on the floor in that hut. Oh, the winters were brutal. Although Daddy was alive then, and I miss him sometimes, it catches me off guard. And before I knew it, tears were streaming down my face. I never had any pictures of my daddy, and there are days I can't remember what he looks like. It's devastating to think we could forget what a loved one looks like over the years.

The years passed and so did the war. We would run to the general store once a week and get our rations, and buy a newspaper to see what was happening on the war front. In May of 1945, we started to get reports that UN forces were gaining ground on the Nazis and Japan, and hoped by the fall it would be over. Our men were tired and anxious to come home. We were finally getting a foothold on things at home; the shortages were being eliminated and financially the US had gained a lot of ground.

Mom and I continued to work on the Victory Garden and help feed the people in our area. We went to town once a week with supplies for the general store and pick up our rations. My sister, Anna, had come to visit about the first of July that year. It was always a fun time with her. When possible, we would go to town and shop at the local thrift shop or see a movie. It had been especially hot that year; temperatures of over ten to fifteen degrees above normal. The green beans were ready for harvesting, so we gathered our necessary rations and got the rest ready for pick-up. Then, Saturday morning, Mom and I got up early and started canning; it would be Monday afternoon before we finished.

We'd been canning for two days. I got up Monday morning and made coffee and breakfast while Mama slept in. She was getting up in age, and I started noticing her slipping a bit. I went out and took care of the chickens and watered the livestock, and when I came back in, she was up and ready to begin our long day.

"Good morning, Mama. Did you sleep well?"

"Yes, thank you…. Is the outside taken care of?"

"Yes, chickens and livestock are watered."

"Well, then I guess we better get this done…."

We worked until almost lunchtime in the cool, but by late afternoon the kitchen got very warm. Mama started looking very pale and I thought she might pass out from the heat, so I convinced her to go rest and I could finish up. It took me about three hours to get the last twenty jars filled. Mama was up and rested by the time I finished; she was sitting in the living room. A nice breeze swept through the living room. "Oh, Mama, I am glad to see you up. How are you feeling?"

"Much better, I am sorry…."

"No… don't be sorry. I have it all done. Let me get you some lemonade, okay?"

"Oh, that would be wonderful…."

"Good, stay right there. I'll be right back."

I returned a few minutes later to find Mama asleep on the couch again. I walked over to wake her, "Mama…. I have your lemonade." I touched her shoulder. "Mama—" My heart stopped. "Oh, Mama— please no… don't leave me."

Chapter Twenty-Five:

A New Age Is Dawning

Life in America had become something no one had ever experienced. We fought to survive the Great Depression for over ten years, the Spanish Flu pandemic, and then WWII hit, which almost drove us to the brink of destruction once again, but now we were hitting all-time highs.

President Roosevelt called it "Arsenal of Democracy." He begged Americans to push and defeat the Axis Powers.  The patriots stood up, and we fought once again to overcome the oncoming forces. At the peak of the war, America was producing more munitions than any of the allies and enemies combined.

On the home front, the massive call for arms drove unemployment down to 1.2 percent, from 25

percent during the depression— still a record today. Our factories that had all been shut down were turned into production

facilities to produce munitions. On D-Day, Eisenhower took over the allied expeditionary force, and Detroit car plants shipped 50,000 vehicles and over 5,000 ships overseas to help fight the war. America came to life!

By the end of the war, Americans were ready to spend their money and live once again. We had been forced into poverty for too long and it was time to spread our wings. The troops were coming home to family and friends as heroes. Oh, the economists said that America would fall after the war, and we would be plunged back into another depression worse than the first one. But history proved them wrong, and we came out of the war more powerful and stronger than ever.

The morale among everyone was grand, new car sales, appliances, and home sales soared. Over 11 million cars were sold in the first year after the war. Plus, one out of every six Americans had a job. The pay was good, and people were happy. The home  contractors were building up to thirty homes a day in the early 1960s. I remember seeing articles that GNP sales went from 300 billion in 1950 to 500 billion by the 1960s. It firmly established the United States as the richest and most powerful nation in the world. We were loving life.

The 50s brought on the baby boomers, and in just a few years more than 3.4 million babies were born in the US. By 1964 there were almost 77 million baby boomers. But even with the eruption of joy from love throughout America, the civil rights movement just started to get a foothold. Native Americans sat back and watched the African American population progress through the same fights we'd faced for centuries. I remember hearing people say Black children were 'inherently unequal.' We'd been hearing that since before I was born.

In the early 50s, I got my first TV. It was exciting and took America to another level of information. Shortly after we started seeing the fight for freedom among the Black community, as we once had done. One woman stood up and she will always be a hero in my book: Rosa Parks. Anyone who lives in that era

remembers watching her fight for equality. In 1956 more than 100 Southern congressmen vowed to fight segregation. But the movement gained strength and after Rosay's arrest and twelve more years fighting, on November 13, 1956, the Supreme Court ordered segregation was unconstitutional.

My people had our freedoms granted in 1924, but it was not until 1962 were we allowed to vote. It took 136 years before we were granted full rights as any other White American. Our fight to vote was done state by state; Utah was the last to approve voting for Native Americans. However, not all Native Americans wanted their right to citizenship; they felt bonded to our sovereign nations.

This was one of my most favorite times for the music, it came to life with artists like Sam Cooke, Chuck Berry, Fats Domino, and Buddy Holly. We moved into the 'Rock 'n' Roll' area and it swept the nation. It was the first-time music had been directed at the younger generation. Of course, when Jerry Lee Lewis and Johnnie Cash came along, they got their fair share of criticism, mostly due to the erotic nature of the lyrics and dancing styles.

We also were exposed to TV shows like *I Love Lucy*, *The Honeymooners*, or *Leave it to Beaver*, the white picket fences and women at home cooking, cleaning, and raising children. It was the time of innocence. But let's not forget the infamous Elvis Presley: not a woman on this planet was not in love with him, including me.

By the end of the war and rationing past, I was able to travel. I'd spent years at home gardening and raising food to feed us and now it was time to see the country once again. I had not been to South Dakota since I was a kid and wanted to see it again with adult eyes.

The Flandreau Colony has been home to Indians since 1683. The burial mounds south of Trent contain Native American remains that date back centuries. The 1851 treaty ceded land from the Falls of the Big Sioux to Big Stone Lake. Then in 1857, the Dakota Land Company laid out a townsite northeast of the present site on the north bank of the

Big Bend. When the Santee families moved from Nebraska to take up homesteads, they relocated along the river as far as twenty miles to the north and south of the old townsite. They called the settlement Riverbend.

Fifteen original families walked from Santee, Nebraska, in March 1869 to South Dakota. One woman perished in a snowstorm on the walk to the Big Bend. They trapped, hunted, and fished for food and used hoes to begin farming. It took them years to improve their living conditions without any government aid.

I had been hearing stories about the school and how it had progressed since I was a student. Intimidation and fear were very much present in our daily lives.

I remember one of the first incidents: We would cower from the abusive disciplinary practices of some superiors, such as the one who yanked my cousin's ear hard enough to tear it. After a nine-year-old girl was raped in her dormitory bed during the night, we girls would be so scared that we would jump into each other's bed as soon as the lights went out. The sustained terror in our hearts further tested our endurance, as it was better to suffer from a full bladder and be safe than to walk through the dark, seemingly endless hallway to the bathroom. When we were older, we girls anguished each time we entered the classroom of a certain male teacher who stalked and molested girls.

Then back in the day, the government took women from their families and placed them into boarding schools as part of their vision of educating Indian girls in the hope that women trained as good housewives would help their mates assimilate. I often described those times as filled with deep misery for having my heritage stripped away, forced to pray as Western culture, and cut my traditionally long hair. But eventually, I came to terms with the past and learned the most we can do is learn and try not to repeat it.

It had been more than five years since my mother died and I'd put my grief aside to survive the war. However, things had returned to somewhat of a positive outcome and I needed to heal my soul. So, the best way for me was to travel.

As you get older the yearnings of youth fade; meaning having a mate at all times was not important to me. At one time we all need to have someone love us and hate being alone. But age changes your outlook on life. You learn to accept things and just go with the flow. My mother had spent the better part of her life in poverty. After my father died, she never remarried. I am not sure if she was ever with another man. It took me years to understand her reasoning and maybe I never will completely. The kind of love my parents shared does not come to everyone, and most of us struggle just to find someone we can stand to be with for any length of time. I had my share of those relationships, except Johnnie. We were soul mates, just met in the wrong era. I have never met anyone like him, nor would I ever again. It did not matter what we were doing, we read each other minds. In most cases, we finished each other's sentences. I loved him with all my heart, and he loved me.

 Since Mama passed, the time alone gave me ample spells to reflect on the past and put many things in place as I progressed with life. In many ways, for years I was angry with Johnnie for making the impulsive decisions he made and leaving me alone in this world to fend for myself. It was selfish on his part. On the other hand, he was not fit for the 1930s, they were too restraining for his soul.

 I spent almost a week getting the house ready before I left. Since Mom was gone, I had to deal with the chickens and livestock, then clear out the garden and get everything canned up for winter. I planned to be gone for a few months, which would put me back home mid-to-late summer.

 Johnnie had been dead for more than ten years and it was time to see Chicago again. The city seemed to have a draw on my soul. Maybe it was the one place I felt closest to him. Only this time, I had no intention of seeing anyone. My visit would be incognito. I had barely left the reservation in years; we were completely locked down during the war. And of course, the best way to travel those days was Route 66. It had been completed from Chicago to the Pacific Coast. I could start in the Windy City and head north up to South Dakota. After the war, businesses along Route 66 created automobile clubs where you could pay a yearly fee and stop at certain places for free. They provided water, fuel, wood, and best of all, showers or laundry facilities. Many of them even had small motels that were included in the price. In all my travels, this trip was probably my most favorite. It allowed me to see more of my people's country. Some of the cities had become dangerous to travel through or stay with the race riots going on, or theft and crime. I only planned to stay in Chicago one night. During the war *Gone With the Wind* had come out and because of travel restrictions, I could not go and see it. So, while I was in the big city, it was on my agenda. Of course, the only place to see it was the Biograph Theater.

The film was released in December 1939, and it swept the country as America's first real love story. It became the highest-earning film until that point and held that record for  more than a century. We all fell in love with Clark Gable. I'd never traveled much in the South, so it always fascinated me, it was like a different world down there. The movie gave me a great insight into life in the South without having to visit. Besides, the South was not one to accept minorities.

I hit the city limits of Chicago and felt like I had entered the twilight zone. There were new housing developments everywhere. Many of the old buildings I remembered were gone, and new ones had been put in their place. I remembered another out of the way motel just a mile or so from the Biograph and decided to see if it was still standing. The last thing I wanted to do was have anyone recognize me.

The motel had been remodeled but was still standing, and it looked like a nice place. So, I pulled in and registered for one night. The movie started at 8:00 p.m. and I hoped since it was not a premiere showing the crowds would be lighter. That was not the case. I stood in line for more than an hour to get my ticket. I watched the people walking the street, and was immediately taken back to the 30s. The old Terraplane sedans with the new V8 were so fast for that time. I can't tell you how many coppers we outran. I have to admit, the ladies' attire was much classier in those days. We had button-down shoes, hats to match our clutches, and never went out of color with the season. The only time I ever wore my pearls was coming to see some gangster movie with Johnnie right here at this theater.

As we moved closer to the ticket window, I heard some women talking behind me. "Look, do you know this is where they killed Dillinger? I would like to have been here to see that." It took a few minutes for me to gather my thoughts.

I stood on the section of cement, closed my eyes, and took a deep breath. It broke my heart to know this is where Johnnie took his last breath. *At least I know his last thoughts were about me.* The idea that he talked about Anna was crazy. He used her as a supposed safe place to stay while he healed up from surgery. No one ever guessed she'd sell him out. *Stool pigeon....*

As we approached the ticket window, I heard the cashier say, "One ticket left." It must have been fate for me to be in that place. I paid and giggled to my seat; it had been years since I had movie popcorn and a sodie. Johnnie and I would always share a large popcorn and sodie, but that night I ate it all by myself. It was a good thing I brought tissues; that movie was an emotional rollercoaster. By the time I left the theater, my heart was filled with joy. It felt good to be in Chicago one more time.

The next morning before I left town, I had to stop by Wrigley Field and see the Rockford Peaches.

They were not playing but the team shop was open, so I bought a jersey. In the lobby hung a big picture of "Pickles". By the end of the war, she was a household name. My next stop was South Dakota.

    I was horrified on the drive to Riggs School because the day they released me I swore to never return. And I still was not sure what drew me back to that place. Maybe just curiosity, I am not sure. The streets were well marked by that time, and it was easy to locate. It had a long narrow entrance with the main building at the end stopping in a circular drive. Most of the main building was still standing; however, they had rebuilt much of the outbuildings. I was elated to see the steam cleansing houses had been removed, along with the lashing poles. I can still hear the screams of children crying as the teachers beat them until their backs were bloody. By the time my

flashbacks passed, I'd had enough and decided it was time to move on. I did not have the strength to go inside, for fear of never being able to leave again.

I figured while in South Dakota it was time to see the national monuments. Mount Rushmore was started in 1923 and finally finished in 1935. They hired a few hundred workers, most of whom were miners, sculptors, or rock climbers, who used dynamite, jackhammers, and chisels to remove material from the mountain. The men built a stairway to the top of the mountain where ropes were fixed. Then the workers were supported by harnesses attached to the ropes. The men built a stairway to the top of the mountain where ropes were fixed. Then the workers were supported by harnesses attached to the ropes.

The best part was the irises of the eyes were sculpted as holes. A cube of granite was left in each to represent the reflection highlight thereby  making the appearance of the eyes more realistic. I have to admit, seeing it in person was awe-inspiring. Most people had the same impression as me.

I knew the second monument of Crazy Horse was only started, but because I was Native American,  they let me come in and see the progress. Outside the main building, there was a white marble statue to resemble the completed project. The land used to build Crazy Horse is sacred to the Lakota Tribe. The place brought me to tears: I felt the ancients, their energy filled the air. It brought me the closure I had been seeking. When I left that sacred place, my next destination was home. It felt like I had come full circle and made peace with my maker. I ended up staying the night in a small hotel not far from Crazy Horse, something just told me to spend the night in this incredible place. My mother came to me that night, and her message was filled with love and everlasting life. I got up at dawn and poured a cup of coffee and watched the sunrise. I even took my shoes off to become one with Mother Earth. Native Americans believe we are all one with the universe, our spirits are carried along with the winds, warmed by the sun, and clothed in the light of the moon. I had no idea of my fate that lay ahead in the next few days.

Chapter Twenty-Six:

True Love Comes More Than Once

One of my greatest pleasures in life was traveling, but after a few weeks or months, I was ready to come home. *As I said before, there's no place like home.* I'd driven almost straight through the last leg of my trip. After I left Shawano my car started acting sluggish, but I was tired and wanted to go home so I just ignored the issue. I got about another mile up the road and the car died, of course. Anyway, I grabbed what I needed and headed back toward town. It was only a few miles, not far. However, it was late afternoon and the last thing I wanted to do was walk in the dark. The road I was on had some traffic and most likely someone would come along soon. Since being with Johnnie, I had learned to take care of myself.

I got almost out of sight from the car and I noticed some dust in the distance. A car or truck was headed my way. It came as a relief. When the truck pulled up, a nice-looking man in his mid-fifties jumped out, at least he looked young.

"Hello," I stated.

"Hello, do you need some help?"

"Yes, my car broke down up the road and I was walking back to town."

"Well, jump in, let's see if I can help. If not, I can give you a ride."

"Oh, thank you, my name is…." I hesitated, "Billie…."

"Billie, that is interesting." I thought here we go; he's going to recognize me. "Billie, I am Arthur or Art."

"It's nice to meet you, Art."

We jumped in the truck and headed for my car. "Do you live around here, Billie?"

"Yes, in Neopit. I have a house there."

"I have not seen you around here before …."

"No, I was on my way home and wanted to take a shortcut."

"Well, I am glad to have come along. This is a dark road at night."

"I know, and I am glad you stopped as well. Thank you."

"Of course, it's not every day a man gets to help a beautiful woman stranded." I blushed.

"Oh, no, but thank you."

We got back to my car, and Art jumped out, fully confident about fixing my car. It only took him a few minutes to determine the problem. "Billie, it looks like you are stuck with me a bit longer. Your car needs a fuel pump and is going to need a tow truck."

"Okay, let me just get a few things and we can go. Is that alright?"

"Yes, can I help with anything?"

"Oh, please, if you would get my luggage from the trunk?"

He looked. "Have you been on a trip?"

"Yes, for the last month. I love to travel."

"I know what you mean. Me too…. If you don't mind, where did you go?"

"Not at all. I went into Chicago to see *Gone With the Wind*. And then up to South Dakota."

"Those are very specific places, why to Chicago and then up to South Dakota?"

"I lived in Chicago for many years and wanted to revisit the Biograph Theater. Then I was in boarding school in Riggs and wanted to see it again. Plus, I visited some more of the reservation in that part of America."

"The Biograph Theater, isn't that where John Dillinger was shot?" My heart sank.

"Umm…." I paused. "Yes, I believe you are right."

"You know I used to work for fish and game as an officer and I think I met him once. He was with three other men looking for a cabin up here."

"Really…. I wouldn't know anything about that." I had to keep it believable.

"I was not sure until later, but after hearing all the reports it was most likely them. You know, he seemed like a very nice man. I mean, yes, he robbed banks but so did a lot of people back then. It was hard just surviving back then."

My brain was trying to believe everything he was saying, it seemed incredible. "I had heard that as well."

"So, you said you lived in Neopit? That is on the reservation, right?" I thought, *here we go….*

"Yes, it is…. I am part Native American. My mother was Native and my father was French."

"I see…. Are they both alive?"

"No, not anymore. My father died when I was very young, and my mom died just a few years ago. I took care of her the last few years she was alive."

"Both of my parents are gone as well, and my wife died in 1944. We had one son together. He works with me now."

"Did you say you were a fish and game officer?"

"I was for many years. But right before the war I retired and opened a barbershop. I found my second calling."

"Do you live around here as well?"

"Yes, I have a cabin on Shawano Lake. My grandkids say it's a magical place."

"Magical… sounds nice."

"I don't know about that part, maybe…. It keeps the rain off my head. I suppose it's not as nice after my wife died. I am not the housekeeper she was."

"I haven't met a man that was." I smiled.

"So, are you married?"

"Not anymore, my husband passed away many years ago."

"I am sorry…. Do you have children?"

"I had two children, both of them died very young as well."

"Oh, that is horrible. I cannot imagine losing my son. What about siblings?"

"Yes, I have two sisters and three brothers. I am very close to my sisters but brothers not so much. We are scattered all over the country."

"At least you have some family alive. We will be in town in a few minutes, would you like me to talk with the shop owner about your car?"

"Yes, that would be very nice. But not necessary if you have other plans?"

"Not at all…. I would be delighted."

"Thank you…. Will they give me a ride home after they pick up my car?"

"I am sure, but I would be more than happy to take you home. I promise I am not a serial killer or anything like that." I giggled.

"No, I am sure you are not. That would be very nice, thank you."

"Okay, it's a date then...." He looked at me.

I smiled. "It's a date."

At that moment, I had no idea what was happening, except he seemed like a nice man whom I felt very comfortable around. We met with the garage attendant and he agreed to pick up my car and take it to the shop, then call me when it was done. I signed his form and we headed home. It was apparent my detour was perfectly planned by fate. I have not had that much fun with anyone in a long time, especially a stranger.

"Well, I don't have much in the house since I've been gone for almost a month, but I can dig something up for dinner if you'd like to stay?"

"That is the best offer I've had in forever."

The house was in good shape when we got home. The next-door neighbor was picking up my mail, so that would be a stop tomorrow. "Well, I filled the cellar with canned goods before I left, so if you will excuse me, I will go get some vegetables for dinner."

"Yes, certainty, I can get some windows opened for air circulation. It's a bit stuffy in here."

"Agreed…. Thank you." I knew deep down this was the man I'd spend the rest of my life with.

"So, I grabbed some green beans and potatoes and I believe there are some steaks in the freezer. Will that work?"

"Oh, steak of course… sounds yummy."

I cooked up our makeshift dinner and we sat in the kitchen and talked for hours, it felt like meeting an old friend. He left just before 10:00 p.m. and promised to call when he got home. We made arrangements to meet the next day and go fishing. Then when my car was finished, he would give me a ride. It was official that night, I walked on cloud nine.

It took me hours to fall asleep; my mind raced with all the things I wanted to ask him. My only concern was being able to tell him the truth because hiding my past was impossible. So, I just figured the best plan was to face the fear head-on and tell him up front.

Art arrived at about 6:00 a.m. just as we planned. I had fresh coffee and breakfast made. I heard his truck pull in and met him at the door. "Good morning... please come in."

"Well, you look chipper!"

"I am, got some rest and a shower. I feel much better. Again, thank you for all your efforts yesterday."

"It was my pleasure. I am just happy to have met you. It's not every day you get to meet someone like you and just hit it off."

"I am glad you feel the same way, I was not sure how to tell you. The last thing I wanted to do was scare you off. But I do have some confessions to make."

"Confessions? You're married?"

"Oh, no, nothing like that… But it's about my past."

"So, you are the serial killer then?" He laughed.

"Gratefully, no, but…." I paused. Art looked concerned. "My real name is Evelyn Frechette." I waited for some response.

"And… so, you have a nickname."

"Well, yes, but I am the Evelyn Frechette that used to date John Dillinger." He got very quiet. "If you want to leave, I understand. The last thing I wanted to do was lie to you. It's just not something I announce to the world."

"No, I don't want to leave, unless you want me to?"

"Oh, no, I would very much like you to stay. So, you are okay with this?"

"Yes…" He paused. "It just took me by surprise. It doesn't happen to me every day that I meet a celebrity."

"Oh, no, I am far from that. Just a normal person."

"You are far from normal… or Dillinger would not have kept you in his company for that long. Thank you for being honest and telling me. Yes, that was one secret that needed to be told."

"I am so glad to hear you say that. I keep to myself these days, I do not want to be in the limelight anymore."

"My lips are sealed. Did you and John have children?"

"No, I had a child when I was very young, and he died. The doctors told me I could no longer have children, and then a few years ago, when I was married to Wally, I got pregnant again but lost the baby. I started using the nickname Billie after my first child."

"I am sorry to hear that. How old were you?"

"In my early twenties. I was raped by several men and got pregnant. The baby was born with some birth defects and died a short time later."

"You are a strong woman to have been through the things you have told me and turned out seemingly stable."

"I have had my ups and downs. But what else do you do but keep fighting?"

"I like your attitude." We ended up talking again for hours and skipped fishing altogether.

When you are in your early twenties the first inclination is to immediately end up in the bedroom but as you age, enjoying a man for their company is much more appealing. I learned this concept from my mother: she chose to spend the last half of her life alone. She knew finding another man that could fill Daddy's shoes would be impossible. It took me most of my life to figure that out; I'd spent much of my life either comparing every man I met to Johnnie or my father, and neither worked out very well. But the most astonishing part is that when I finally gave up trying and just learned to love myself, the person I was destined to be with came along. Don't get me wrong, I loved Johnnie with all my heart; nonetheless, our relationship existed on rocky roads. It survived because of youth, hormones, and excitement, and that's not a recipe for longevity. I know God put me on that road for a reason, he knew the plan way before me. It's why I stayed in North Dakota another night and took that short cut home.

The phone rang while we were talking. It was the garage; my car was fixed. "Was that the garage?" he asked.

"Yes, my car is ready. Are you sure you don't mind taking me to town? He offered to come and get me."

"Absolutely, I would love to take you. Besides, it gives me an excuse to spend more time with you."

"You are too kind…." He smiled. "And spending time with you is pretty special to me as well."

The whole day seemed like a dream; I thought finding someone else like Johnnie was impossible. But here I was sitting next to him in a truck. Again, someone, I had just met swept me off my feet. *I was the luckiest girl in the world, it was the best day of my life….*

Chapter Twenty-Seven:

I Brought My Toothbrush

On the way home from North Dakota, I dreaded coming home to an empty house. A short time ago, I was wishing for some freedom; running away from any man who was nice to me, and then when my wish was fulfilled, I begged for it to change. My marriage to Wally left me tarnished, it made me skittish. Then a few weeks after Art and I started dating, the fear hit me like a ton of bricks: *What if he turns out to be like my dead husband...?*

I almost walked away, figured leaving now would be better than getting hurt later. Then, in a few short hours, my answer came. I had been wondering why Art had not asked me to come over to his cabin. We had talked about the lake and its location, not to mention how much he loved living there; yet, he failed to ask me to come to his house. It had me confused and rather upset not knowing why.

The next morning, we planned to go fishing. He would pick me up at 7:00 a.m., and said he knew of a perfect place that had giant catfish. I was very excited to see this new lake since I'd lived in this area all my life. Art showed up right on time as usual with all his gear in the back and a fresh cup of coffee for me.

He kissed me. "Good morning, beautiful."

I smiled. "Morning, how are you? Did you sleep well?"

"As a matter of fact, no. My alarm went off, and you were not with me." He smiled.

"Oh, that is sweet…. I missed you as well."

"I have something to show you before we go fishing, is that alright?"

"Yes, of course, is everything alright?"

"Most definitely.... I should have done this a long time ago." I was hoping deep down he meant showing me his home.

"What do you want to show me?"

"It's a surprise.... We will be there very soon, it's on the way."

We headed off in the truck going in the right direction. "We are going to your cabin, aren't we?"

"I knew there was no way to surprise you."

"I thought there was something wrong, and you were avoiding it for a reason."

"There was a problem...." I flinched. "I am a terrible housekeeper." I laughed.

"You mean to tell me all this time, it was because your house was dirty?"

"Yes, and it smelled musty. My granddaughters always complain."

"Will they be there to meet today?"

"No, as a matter of fact, it will be just us. I'd like us to spend some alone time together." He stopped the truck, and turned to look at me. "Evelyn…. I am in love with you. Where have you been all my life?" My heart stopped.

I choked back the tears, "I—" He kissed me. Suddenly it got very hot in the cab of that truck. We headed to his cabin acting like high school kids. My mind raced with all kinds of crazy ideas, it felt good to be in love once again. We turned up the radio and sang along to our favorite songs; my concerns had been resolved and I knew I'd finally found a home.

The second we pulled in the drive; a peace came over me unlike I had ever felt. It was a small two-bedroom cabin sitting on the edge of the lake. The whole front was covered with windows and a full

wrap-around porch. Along the backside was a screened-in sitting room overlooking the lake. In the center of the wall was a door and staircase that led to a long sidewalk that meandered its way down to the dock. It was absolutely perfect! I fell in love immediately.

"Art, this place is beautiful! I might never leave here...."

"Good, because I don't want you to." He looked at me and smiled. "Come on.... Let me show you the inside. But don't say a word, I have been cleaning for weeks."

"Cross my heart." We giggled. I walked up the steps behind him, knowing I had come home this time.

Art opened the door and waited for me. It was everything I had ever imagined. The door opened into the kitchen and dining room with two steps down into the living room. Along the east wall was a large wood-burning stove, and on the other side sat the living area. Then a small hallway extended on both sides leading to the bedrooms. The kitchen side had the laundry room and cellar area. On the other end was the second bedroom and a full bath. In the middle of the living room was the door leading out to the screen room that overlooked the lake.

"Billie… Billie, are you alright?"

"Oh, yes, I'm speechless. This house is more than I could have ever imagined."

"So, you approve?"

"Yes, it's perfect. But agreed, it needs a good cleaning and some tender loving care."

"Whatever you want, tell me, we will get it done."

"Just some decorations and cleaning. Maybe a few pictures?"

"Done…. Now, would you like to see the lake?"

"I thought you'd never ask… lead the way."

"One more thing before we go, I have another surprise to show you. Come this way." Art went down the hallway to the master bedroom and opened the door. Out bounced a springer spaniel. "This is Nibber."

I started to giggle and got on my knees. "Come here, you...." He jumped in my lap and we became the best of buddies. "I love dogs, I used to have an English bulldog."

"Now I know you are a keeper." He smiled. We headed out for the dock, Nibber right on my heels.

The dock was a bit wobbly, but I did not mind. "Are you ready to fish?"

"Yes, let's go get the poles."

"No, you stay right there. I'll be right back."

I plopped down and took off my shoes and socks. The cold water felt good in the summer heat. Art returned promptly. "Here you go," he handed me my pole.

I laughed at him watching to see if I could bait a hook properly. "What are you looking at?" I asked.

"Wanted to see if you were going to bait that hook by yourself."

"I have been fishing since I could walk. It's one of my favorite pastimes, plus good for eating."

We fished for hours, and it felt comfortable. Nibber lay on the dock next to me and went to sleep.

"Evelyn, I thought we could go to the barbershop tomorrow and I can introduce you to my son. Are you okay with that?"

"I would love to meet him. Will he be okay with our arrangement?"

"Yes, he will be fine. Are you okay?"

"As long as we can keep my past between us."

"I agree, it's no one else's business."

We fished all afternoon and caught enough fish to feed us for a month. I even cleaned and scaled the fish right alongside Art. He was highly impressed. "Now, just wait till we go hunting. I am a good shot."

"You have yourself a date. I'd like to see that." We laughed. Art showed me his chest freezer, it was filled with enough meat to last two winters.

"Since we caught all these fish, how about a late lunch?"

"Sounds wonderful! I will do the veggies and you get the fish?" I asked.

"Of course, how do you like your fish?"

"My favorite is sautéed in butter, garlic and onion, then lightly simmered until it's done."

"Perfect! Just perfect." We ate lunch and cleaned the kitchen. Art took my hand and led me to the bedroom; conversation was no longer necessary.

I woke up the next morning just before dawn. Art was still sleeping, so I decided to go make some coffee and breakfast, since he had so graciously made it for me several times. After the coffee was brewed, I put the eggs and sausage in the pan to keep warm and walked out to the screen room. It had been a long time since I sat next to a lake and watched the sunrise. I was almost finished with my cup when Art woke up and came out to join me on the porch.

"Good morning, beautiful…. How did you sleep?"

"Wonderful, next to you—"

"Great." He walked over and knelt next to my chair. He had a very serious look in his eyes. I was not sure what to expect. "Since the moment we met, I knew I never wanted to spend another day of my life without you by my side. Then after feeling you next to me last night, I did not want to wait another minute. The tears streamed down my face. "Evelyn Frechette… will you marry me?"

I stared at him speechless for a few minutes. "Art…. I would love nothing more than to marry you. Can we go now?"

"Yes, we can go to Chicago and see a justice of the peace. Is that okay with you?" I nodded.

"I just need to go home, get some clothes, and change. I cannot marry you in jeans and a blouse."

"Oh, so you would rather be naked and marry me?" He laughed.

"Well...." I blushed. We ate breakfast and headed for my house with Nibber in tow.

The ring Art gave me was gorgeous. I was not sure how he found time to shop for jewelry like this, or if it had belonged to his wife that died. Either way, I never asked, it didn't matter. Our wedding anniversary date was September 8, 1965. When I left Chicago the last time, I never had any intentions of going back again, and not this soon.

We stopped at the first courthouse just inside town and made it right on time. They were closing in one hour, and it took some convincing to sway the judge. He wanted us to come back the next day, but we promised to never tell anyone. The last thing either one of us wanted to do was stay in Chicago overnight.

I had been saving a beautiful chiffon beige dress for some special occasion, and this fit the bill. So, I grabbed my mother's brooch, bought a bouquet of white daisies on the way into town, and my garter belt was blue. All the bases were covered. Art had a nice beige suit and bowtie to match. It was a nice touch and fit his personality. When the judge said, "I pronounce you man and wife," they were the most beautiful words I had ever heard.

Art looked relieved when we left the courthouse. I think it made him at ease introducing me to his family. Just knowing we were married made everyone more comfortable; living together back then was a sin if you weren't married. By the time we reached home, it was nearly 2:00 a.m. We were both exhausted and hit the bed to sleep for a few hours. Our honeymoon could wait for a few days.

I admitted to some trepidation about meeting his son, daughter-in-law, and granddaughters. But Art assured me they would be good with us being together, just give them time to adjust on us getting married so soon. I understood that part, the shock had not sunk in with me yet.

We left the house at about 7:00 a.m. to open the shop at 8:00 a.m. Nibber sat next to the door; Art said he never went to work without him. I understood wanting to have your dog with you at all times. It was a bit after 8:00 a.m. when his son arrived, so I made myself busy cleaning and making the coffee.

Art came over and took my hand, "Ward," he paused. "This is Evelyn, she is my wife. We have been dating for a few months and got married yesterday."

"Uh…" The shock covered his face. "Hi, Evelyn?"

"Yes, or Billie…."

"Is that a nickname or something?"

"Yes, in a way."
"It was her son's name, he died very young."

"Oh, I am so sorry."

"No, that was a long time ago. It's very nice to meet you. Sorry to spring this on you like this."

"You could say that, but if Dad is happy then so be it. I am glad to meet you."

He turned to set his stuff down. "Dad, can I talk with you for a few minutes?" I knew how that conversation might go.

I could hear them whispering, *Are you out of your mind? Do you even know this woman? She could be some fraudster or something.* Then everything got very quiet. Ward came out of the backroom. "I am sorry, Evelyn, please forgive me?"

"Nonsense, for what? You are just trying to protect your dad. Yes, this was sudden, but I do love your dad, and would never do anything to hurt him. I promise."

"Thank you, you seem like a nice person." I smiled.

"Look, if you guys need some more time to talk, I can go outside or take a walk?"

"No, please stay," Ward said. "I am good now. Besides, I guess we better get to know each other."

"Fire away, ask whatever you like. I am happy to tell you everything."

Ward and I sat and talked most of the morning between customers, and by the time the day was done, we had become good friends. Art, I know, must have taken a big sigh of relief.

"Now, Ward, what about the girls? What are you going to tell them?'

"I'd like to introduce them soon."

"Yes, how about this weekend?"

"We can come over to the house. I think that might be best." We all agreed.

On the way home, I told Art I needed to go home and get some things. But I would be spending the rest of the week cleaning and getting the house ready for them to visit. He agreed. I went home the next morning, called my sisters, and started packing up my stuff. I only had the things in my bedroom, the rest of the house belonged to Mama. I met them the next morning, and we decided that Anna should move in and take over. She was single and it was very expensive for her to live in town. My sisters were very happy for me and just loved Art. They thought he was the cat's meow.

It took us three trips to move all my stuff over to Art's. And that gave me two days to get that house in shape for company. The porch was covered in dust and cobwebs, not to mention the musty smell. I worked my fingers to the bone till the weekend, but the house looked spectacular by Saturday afternoon. We invited them over to go fishing and then dinner. I didn't want to interrupt their normal family gatherings any more than necessary. Anytime a new person enters the scene it is always destructive in some fashion, and the last thing I wanted was for it to be a negative experience.

I felt like my pants were on fire all Saturday morning waiting for them to show up. Art laughed at me over my nervousness. "Will you relax? They are going to love you. I did, so why wouldn't they?" They pulled in the drive and I nearly jumped out of my skin when they knocked on the door

Art had told me his granddaughters' names were Barb, Sue, Kathy, and Sharon. I was not always the best with names, but I tried to get them right. Sharon came in first, and she seemed highly perceptive. Kathy came in right behind her, highly energetic but loving and kind. The next two, Barb and Sue, were very protective of their grandfather and drilled me with questions. Ward had told them I was the new maid, which fit the bill since the place looked fantastic. I was taken aback by not being introduced as Art's wife but understood his reasoning.

All the girls were dressed in play clothes and excited to go fishing but hesitant about baiting the hook and murky water. It made me giggle because I was raised in this stuff and many times took baths in the creek. Yes, it was fresh water, but not always. I guess there is a big difference between being raised in the country and the city.

We headed for the dock; Art carried the poles along behind. Ward and his wife sat on the porch and watched. I helped Kathy and Barb bait the hooks and helped them get started, while Art helped Barb and Sue. Once we started moving around on the dock it started to rock around and the girls got really scared. So, I suggested that Art go up on the shore while we fished. It was a lot of weight with all of us on the dock. Sue finally caught her first fish and jumped up, screaming for her dad to look and fell over the edge. Of course, the rest of the girls jumped up screaming that she could not swim, and out of the blue Ward came running down the dock after her and the whole thing collapsed.

    I turned to see Art on the shore laughing, and inside it was very comical. No one got hurt and it was just water. When I turned back around, I noticed the girls were panicking, so I jumped in and pulled three of them out. Ward had already gotten to Barb. In a few short minutes, the whole situation faded. They dropped all their attitudes and considered me their hero. The only one who took heat afterward was their grandfather for laughing. We got a laugh for years; needless to say, we had hamburgers for dinner instead of fish.

Over the next month, we painted the whole cabin and put-up new curtains. Plus, I got some pictures, one that the girls helped me pick out. It was fun taking them shopping and doing girl things. They were never the adventurous types, which did not bother me too much. It gave me something to do when Art had his all-men outings or visits.

After the experience with his family, Art and I needed some rest. He was upset about the dock and complained about having to rebuild it. But I convinced him it would be a great project for us to do together. In the meantime, I talked him into taking a road trip for our honeymoon. I had never been to the Pacific Ocean and since Route 66 was completed it would give us some time alone to see the countryside. He agreed and we packed up to hit the road after the cabin was all secured the next morning. The three of us were off on our first adventure.

Chapter Twenty-Eight:

Pacific Ocean Here We Come

None of us ever expected the outcomes that resulted in 1968. America had finally overcome the ravages of WWII and then we were plunged into the Vietnam War. The turmoil started on January 21, 1968, when the North Vietnamese army failed in their attempt to kill President Nguyễn Văn Thiệu. We held our breath wondering how long it would be before the US got involved. However, the Vietnam event was never officially called a war until many years later. It destroyed the country when it came to the soldiers coming home from the war.

Later on, that year, Martin Luther King was assassinated, which caused violent riots in the big cities. Most of them remained within Washington D.C. and of course Chicago and Baltimore. President John F. Kennedy worked tirelessly to pass the Civil

Rights Act of 1968, which was not completed until after his death by President Johnson in April of that year. The legislation was passed with bipartisan Congressional support and it prohibited housing discrimination based on race.

What many people did not know was the Civil Rights Act of 1866 had no federal enforcement provisions attached, so essentially it was null and void. It was not until 1968 when the federal government granted all rights to everyone regardless of race. It meant for the Native Americans a guarantee that we had the right to freedom of religion, and the right of habeas corpus— or the right to a fair trial by our peers.

The idea was that the Bill of Rights would protect Native American communities from potential abuse within tribal lands. It allowed for formal trial courts that extended the sovereignty of Native American reservations to include legislative authority. We had rights; the Native Americans' civil rights would be protected, but we would also be able to govern ourselves in sovereignty. It was called the grassroots movement.

On March 6, 1968, President Johnson signed an Executive Order establishing the National Council on Indian Opportunity (NCIO). President Johnson said, "The time has come to focus our efforts on the plight of the American Indian." If it was only that easy. Yes, the effort made a step in the right direction, but nothing changed for generations to come.

The times had changed in America after WWII: women were playing a major role in society and the completion of Route 66 made it easy to travel and see the country. It started in Chicago and ran through Missouri, Kansas, Oklahoma, Texas, New Mexico,  and Arizona before ending in Santa Monica. It went almost 2,448 miles. I can remember reading in *The Grapes of Wrath*, he coined it as 'Highway 66,' a symbol of escape and loss.

I remember during the Dust Bowl it was a primary road for people to escape the mid-section of the country. But the damage done to the road took years to repair. The businesses nearly died during the war with all the restrictions. After 1947 use of the highway began to explode with gas stations, motels, restaurants, and tourists shops. The song 'Get Your Kicks on Route 66' came out later that year.

Some trivia: In 1857, Lt. Beale, a naval officer, was ordered by the War Department to build a government-funded wagon road along the thirty-fifth parallel. Initially, the section was tested using camels for pack animals. The road became what is now Route 66.

I had wanted to see the Pacific Ocean for as long as I can remember. Johnnie had promised many times we could go but that never happened. When I met Art, one of the things I loved about him most was his dedication to me and our relationship. He worked very hard to make my dreams come true. Sometimes, I felt guilty because he was able to give more than I could. However, he never seemed to care. His agenda was to always make me happy. My relationship with Dillinger was one-sided in many ways. Yes, I needed the support financially and we fell in love, but that is not something you can build a longer relationship on. The fast times spent breaking the law were only going to end badly. I suppose I knew that right from the start.

The second most reason I wanted to do more traveling on Route 66 was that part of the road overlaps the northern section of the Trail of Tears. During the relocation of the Cherokee Indians in 1838 from their

homeland to their forced land in the southern Appalachians, many of my people died. A total of 60,000 Indians traveled that road. The relocation caused untold disease, starvation, and approximately 4,000 of them died. The tribes included Cherokee, Muscogee, Seminole, Chickasaw, and Choctaw nations, as well as their African slaves.

Although out of the horror, some heroism emerged from the Cherokee Tribe. One group of Cherokees, the Oconaluftee Citizen Indians, remained in North Carolina. All sixty families led by Yonaguska, Long Blanket, and Wilnota had land in their names under the Treaties of 1817 and 1819. They lived sober, industrious lives, and were able to successfully appeal to the North Carolina legislature to remain on their lands, mostly near the Oconaluftee River.

When the soldiers came to remove them,

three to four hundred Cherokees hid in the wooded mountains of Western North Carolina. In November of 1838, Tsali and his family killed two soldiers who were attempting to capture them. Tsali and his family became fugitives from the federal government. Aided by William Holland Thomas (Yonaguska's adopted son), the American soldiers found Tsali. After his capture, he agreed to give himself up and be executed so that other Cherokees would be allowed to stay in their homes in the mountains. A story developed from this event.

The Legend of the Cherokee Rose

In the latter half of 1838, Cherokee People who had not voluntarily moved West earlier were forced to leave their homes in the East.

The trail to the West was long and treacherous and many were dying along the way. The People's hearts were heavy with sadness and their tears mingled with the dust of the trail.

The Elders knew that the survival of the children depended upon the strength of the women. One evening around the campfire, the Elders called upon Heaven Dweller, ga lv la di e hi. They told Him of the People's suffering and tears. They were afraid the children would not survive to rebuild the Cherokee Nation.

Gal v la di e hi spoke to them, "To let you know how much I care, I will give you a sign. In the morning, tell the women to look back along the trail. Where their tears have fallen, I will cause them to grow a plant that will have seven leaves for the seven clans of the Cherokee. Amidst the plant will be a delicate white rose with five petals. In the center of the blossom will be a pile of gold to remind the Cherokee of the White man's greed for the gold found in the Cherokee homeland. This plant will be sturdy and strong with stickers on all the stems. It will defy anything which tries to destroy it."

The next morning the Elders told the women to look back down the trail. A plant was growing fast and covering the trail where they had walked. As the women watched, blossoms formed and slowly opened. They forgot their sadness. Like the plant, the women began to feel strong and beautiful. As the plant protected its blossoms, they knew they would have the courage and determination to protect their children who would begin a new nation in the West. Among my people, the land became sacred since so many Native Americans died. It was one thing I wanted to witness for myself before I died.

It still sickened me when I found out that some motels and businesses along the route banned African Americans the right to patron their establishments. It was not until 1936, when Victor Green, a Black postal worker from New York, published a book containing the businesses that accepted African American customers. As if their money did not spend like any other White person's.

President Eisenhower signed a federal aid Highway Act that was eventually the death of Route

66 in 1956. Then eventually, Interstate 40 took the place of Route 66 in many places, and most of the businesses died out.

We did, however, get to see *The Wizard of Oz* on one of our stops in Kansas. I had never seen it and since Baum backed women's right to vote, I wanted to see the movie. When the movie was first introduced it failed, but when MGM picked it up it grossed over 3 million in ticket sales.

My favorite everlasting phrase, "Toto, I have a feeling we're not in Kansas anymore." I for one loved the tin man.

I can't tell you how excited I was to finally see Santa Monica Pier. We had seen photos and heard stories about the building of the great pier. When it was initially built it was only to house sewer pipes and water breaks. But the spot became so popular that Charles Looff and his son financed the amusement park. Of course, Looff knew the draw of carousel rides and began that creation right away. It is now registered as a National Historic Place.

After that the Blue Streak Racer, a wooden roller coaster, was built. It was purchased from San Diego Wonderland amusement park that had gone bankrupt during WWII. At the same time, the Whip, merry-go-rounds, Wurlitzer organs, and a funhouse became part of the park. In 1938 they finally finished the bridge to Santa Monica Pier. The movie *Night Tide* had been released a few years prior. The park had been closed since the Great Depression; it did not reopen until 1943. Its new owners, a Venice banker, tore down the Blue Streak and replaced it with the Whirlwind Dipper. Art thought I had gone back in time to my grade school days when we finally arrived in Santa Monica. Our first stop was the beach. The last time I visited the beach was with Johnnie in Florida. And let's just say that was a stressful trip.

We checked into our hotel room and I changed into my bathing suit. The grey skies of Wisconsin don't offer many chances for a tan. All I wanted to do was sit in a lounge chair and sip umbrella drinks for the remainder of the day. Art just giggled at my enthusiasm. "Are you ready?" I asked. He nodded.

I grabbed the picnic basket and we hit the beach. Our hotel was right on the beach, so all we had to do was walk down the steps. The ocean breeze smelled just as I remember so many years ago. Art grabbed our stuff and I hit the water. I loved to swim but not in the ocean. It felt good to be free of the city and everything else stressful. The water had some strange effects on your soul.

When I came back to the chairs, Art handed me a drink and I plopped into the seat next to him. We laughed and just shared each other's company. I'd never seen the sunset over the ocean, it was the most beautiful thing I had ever seen.

The next day we hit the amusement park. They opened at 10:00 a.m. and believe me we were in line right on time. I had to do some real talking to get Art to agree to ride the Whirlwind. But I told him you only live once and he could not say no.

I remember looking at Art when they strapped us in, his knuckles were white. "Hang on, honey," I told him. We felt the car start moving slowly as we climbed to seventy feet in the air. The feeling was amazing, I felt my stomach fall as we hit top speed of fifty miles per hour, then in about five minutes, it was over. Art even smiled when we hit full speed, it made me giggle.

We spent the rest of the day eating till we got sick and going on the small rides. Only I rode the carousel horse alone. Art had enough fun for one day, so I agreed to leave and we took a long walk on the beach to see the sunset once again. We both had the time of our lives. It was late September when we got back home that year. I was ecstatic to see the girls. They were looking forward to spending the holidays with us. In a way, I was as well. I loved decorating and cooking and buying gifts. We left Santa Monica with a gleam in our eyes and a song in our hearts.

Chapter Twenty-Nine:

Holidays with the Family

We got home from California and I spent two days cleaning after we rested for a day or two. I admit, aging takes the energy right out of you. On Sunday morning we went to church and stopped at Ward's to see the girls. It had become a tradition, one I missed.

After we got back, Ward wanted to take a week or so off. He had worked by himself to maintain the barbershop while we were gone. So, I went with Art each morning and helped him in the shop. I realized we had spent nearly six months together and were never apart more than one day. Yet we somehow never got tired of each other, or had any arguments. I called my sister when we got home and met her for lunch one afternoon; we had a lot to catch up on.

I met her at the diner down the street from the barbershop. "Hey, sis…. How are you?"

She looked exhausted. "I am good, but working a lot of hours." My sister had gotten a job at the hospital with good pay. "But you look fantastic… maybe I need a husband like yours?"

"I think you might." we laughed.

I learned a long time ago that family is essential for anyone to find happiness. No matter how long we are apart, it's always the same when we meet again. I started going out to the old house once a week, helping her clean and take care of the place. It was the least I could do since she had always been there for me during all my life experiences.

The time flew by and before we knew it Halloween was upon us. I had taken the girls shopping for costumes, since both their parents worked full-time. We had a witch, princess, nurse, and Dorothy from *The Wizard of Oz*. Since the cabin was in the middle of the woods, Art and I went to Ward's house for trick-or-treating. It was something I had never done or participated in. Being involved with Johnnie, the last thing we wanted was kids knocking at the door. So, I got to experience the night just as the girls did. I walked for hours taking them door to door. The boys stayed at Ward's house. By the time we were done, all their pillowcases were overflowing.

As we prepped for Thanksgiving it was a major discussion because my people always had goose, and no one ever thought about turkeys. So, we eventually agreed on both, since I was certain the girls would not like the goose. I still can't believe we managed to get more than twenty people in that house for the holidays. Art and I planned to start preparing dinner three days before to have everything ready in time.

In the woods about a mile past the house was a small area where the wild turkeys always flourished. So, we headed out that Sunday morning at about six to snag us a bird. I nearly died laughing when Art missed his shot and I got mine. You would have thought the world had come to an end. Since I had never eaten or killed a turkey, Art took the lead. Believe me, they have way more feathers than chickens. We decided since the stove was small as was the kitchen, Art would build a smoker out back to cook the goose and pheasant. Then we had room to cook the pies, potatoes, and bread. I handpicked cranberries at a local farm to make the sauce. I was informed you need to have cranberry sauce with turkey. I was learning all sorts of new things.

One of our pastimes since 1924 was reading about the Macy's Day Parade. But it was not until the first TVs that we could watch the parade on Thanksgiving morning. Only that year we had a color TV to watch, and it was a special year because Snoopy made his debut. We had been reading about him and the red baron for years. Now we got to see him in person.

Sarah Josepha was the mother of Thanksgiving; she wrote a letter to the President in

1863 asking for the declaration of a federal holiday. In 1939, it was declared a holiday. Did you know, Jingle Bells was not a Christmas song, it was originally intended for Thanksgiving in 1859?

One thing Western culture carefully worked to hide was the real story behind Thanksgiving. Most Native Americans look at the holiday as a mourning of the day American settlers arrived on the Northern Continent. It led to centuries of oppression and genocide.

My people believe: Thanksgiving Day is a reminder of the genocide of millions of Native people, the theft of Native lands, and the relentless assault on Native culture. Participants in National Day of Mourning honor Native ancestors and the struggles of Native peoples to survive today. It is a day of remembrance and spiritual connection as well as a protest of the racism and oppression which Native Americans continue to experience.

One fact I remember the elders teaching us during fall solstice was in the first few years after settlers arrived here in America in 1621, they were starving. They would steal food from the Wampanoag graves to survive the brutal winters. Indians celebrated the gifts granted by Mother Earth's abundance. As such, our meals consisted of corn, beans, wild rice, and goose or some meat. And none of the things we expected to see on Thanksgiving existed, like pumpkin pie, since there was no butter, wheat, or ovens, nor would there have been cranberries. Potatoes existed but not in America at the time. Most likely their meals would have been fruits, vegetables, and fish.

In order for us to fit twenty people, we had to completely remodel the house. Ward brought chairs and an extra table, while I made a small spot for the kids in the living room, hence the kid's table. I cannot ever think of a more enjoyable time. Yes, I miss the autumn meals from

when I was small with my parents and siblings, but this was different.

    The day after Thanksgiving I started decorating for Christmas. Art always got a kick out of me. I would spend hours in the stores shopping for ornaments and lights. I wanted new things that fit with the times. Since the early '50s, America had been in a race with Russia for who could reach the moon first. Then when President Nixon took office, he believed it was in our best interest to beat the Soviet Union. So, the race sped up. Originally, the moon landing was set for early 1969 but it was changed to late December 1968. So, each night we started getting updates on the launch date. It was an exciting time for America.

    One afternoon, Art and I had to make a quick trip to town for some supplies before the weekend. The girls were coming to stay the night and go out on the boat the next morning. We left Nibber at home where it was warm; he would have frozen in the truck. In those days getting stranded in winter with the snow and weather was easy. We never left home without water, a change of clothes, and blankets.

It was almost dark when we got back home, and normally before we got inside Nibber would be at the door to greet us. I walked in and realized the house was very quiet. "Nibber.... Where are you boy?" He did not respond.

Art and I looked at each other, and we both thought the worst. He went into the bedroom. "Evelyn, come quick," he hollered. Nibber had passed away on the bed while we were gone. I cried for hours. The kids were going to be heartbroken.

Our furry friends become members of the family and when they die, we feel the same pain. I remembered all the dogs I had owned. Art and I carried him wrapped up in a blanket out back and buried him under a tree on the backside of the property. He told me there were four other Nibbers buried in the same place. We said some prayers and wished him safe travels in his next life. The next morning, I woke to a silent house. Nibber always greeted me with sloppy kisses. But when I rolled over, Art was already gone. It was odd for him to disappear without waking me. I walked into the kitchen and saw a note on the table: "Be back soon, I love you, Art." He had made coffee, so I sat in the kitchen crying into my cup for almost an hour.

After I poured my second cup, he pulled into the driveway. The snow had started to come down steadily. "Hey, you. Where did you go this early?"

"To get you a surprise."

"A surprise? But it's not Christmas yet," I sniffled.

"I know, but you needed some cheering up. So, I made a trip. Put your shoes on and come with me…."

I grabbed my coat and followed him, but I noticed something was odd when the truck was still running. He turned around. "Come on, it's cold out here…. Open the door."

My curiosity was piqued, and I reached for the doorknob when I heard something very familiar. "Oh, Art, where did you find him?"

"My friend up the road. He told me the other day; his bitch had puppies."

"He is beautiful. What are we going to call him?"

He laughed and turned away. "Nibber—" I rolled my eyes, that's just like Art.

The house came to life once again with the pitter-patter of a puppy, although the first week he kept us running with potty training. I had forgotten how much work babies could be. We enjoyed little Nibber immensely, he had a great personality. I was excited to take him hunting in the spring.

A few days later, Art went out and cut us a Christmas tree and one for the girls. We had a ball decorating both trees. They came over that weekend and helped me holiday the house. It was the first year that colored lights came out. One of the ladies in church hand-made Angel tree toppers. I was excited to pick it up on Sunday after mass. Plus, the holidays gave me a chance to dress up for shopping, mass, and gathering with friends and family. It was most definitely the best time of the year.

We decided to start celebrating with each other on the twenty-fourth, that way the girls had time with their parents on Christmas morning. Only that year was exciting since we gathered on the twenty-first and twenty-fourth.  Since the moon landing took place a few days before Christmas, we had dinner and then huddled around the TV. Now that was tricky since the screen was only about twelve inches and the picture was very blurry. They came back over on the twenty-fourth and we ate again, then opened presents.

I had so much fun buying a gift for them, especially clothes. Times were tough and raising four girls got expensive. Art and I got each one of the girls a dress and a pant outfit. I remember that year, them telling us we were hard to buy for since we had everything. But neither of us cared about getting gifts, it was more fun shopping. However, that year their gift was absolutely precious. They had made a ceramic cast of their hands. Then they painted it with lots of colors and wrote their names and date in the ceramic before it dried. It became my centrepiece on the coffee table.

The girls had become my surrogate children, they made my life worth living. I spent many early mornings on the porch wondering what Billie would have grown up to look like, and what he would have done with this life. My second child, I never knew if it was a boy or girl, so I always hoped it might have been a girl. My life with Art turned into something I never imagined possible.

Chapter Thirty:

I Said Goodbye

The day I met Art on that country road changed my life once again, just as it had changed the night I met Johnnie. We go through many phases in our lives, each one different from the last but equally important to create the person we are to become. If any piece of our past were to change, it would alter our future. So, when you live with regrets about your decisions it negates all the good things you accomplished. I learned that lesson not so long ago, and I paid for the feelings for many years to come.

Life is a gamble; we cannot possibly make the right choice every time, but what is the right decision? In the midst of the chaos that I lived every second of my life, I learned you must go with the flow or die trying. We all do the best we can with what is placed in our laps. Choices are made based on what you have at the time. It does not matter if it's right or wrong, what matters is what happened at that moment. At that point, it's up to you to find some balance or create another path that will redirect your life the way you see fit. Yes, I made some decisions that were not the best options, but the last thing I was going to do was beat myself up about it. I moved on and did the best I could under the circumstances. And guess what? It all came out in the wash. Life is what you make of it, period. You can choose to be happy or say the choice is up to each person.

I grew up on the Indian reservation in the lowest poverty that you could imagine, but we made do and lived each day as if it was our last. That concept I also learned from John Dillinger, a man I loved with all my heart. He lived to the fullest degree possible and was never going to let anyone get in the way of his goals. Now, not all his choices were the best, and yes, they got him killed. Nevertheless, he stayed focused on where he was going. Many people thought of him as a narcissistic bank robber that did not care about anyone but himself. Those impressions could not be further from the truth. I saw that man do more for people than anyone could ever imagine. It was the one thing that drew me to him, and I knew him better than he knew himself. It took many years to overcome the loss of a man I loved with all my heart, but in that grief, I found myself and took the best things from his life and moved on to make my life better.

The girls had a blast Christmas Eve and went home with a new light in their eyes for the future. I loved spending time with them more than almost anything in the world. They helped fill the gaping hole in my heart from not being able to raise my own children.

Art and I sat up almost all night talking about our destiny, the role that God played in our lives, and what we believed after we died. It was one of the most intimate conversations I had ever had with anyone. I loved him because of his honesty, and I always knew he told me the truth. Since many of my relationships were based on lies, it felt comforting to be with someone who based his life on the truth.

The next week we celebrated life, spending every moment with the ones we loved. None of us know when our time is up, so we need to make every second count. Christmas morning, we saw the sunrise and sat on the porch drinking coffee. Then finally we had breakfast and when total exhaustion set in, we went to bed, cuddling up warm and cozy. Nibber slept comfortably at my feet.

We decided to spend New Year's in town at the local hotel. They always had a big party. The invitation granted a nice steak dinner, dancing, and listening to the count down in Times Square. Old man winter blew in a horrible blizzard dumping a few more feet of snow, but we didn't care. In the midst of family, nothing else mattered.

A few days after the party, I got a cold and almost lost my voice. When the symptoms dragged out into two weeks, Art insisted I go make an appointment and see the doctor. I hated hospitals, although to ease his concern I went anyway. They ran several tests when they found my illness was more than just a cold.

It took several weeks for the results to come back and the diagnosis was not good. We scheduled another appointment. The second we walked into the doctor's office I knew it was bad news. "Please, sit down," the doctor said. "Thanks for coming…. I am sorry my news is not better."

"Doc, please… just tell me?" I asked.

"I am afraid it's throat cancer, stage three." I choked back the tears.

Art knew I could not speak. "Is that bad?"

"I won't lie, but yes. However, we have options. I can make an appointment in Green Bay for treatments."

"What are these treatments?"

"Evelyn, it would be chemotherapy."

"Is that my only option? What about surgery?"

"I am afraid at the stage of your cancer it would not be possible. If we had caught it sooner, I would have said yes. But now, no, I am sorry."

"Alright." I struggled to speak. "Can I think about this?"

"Yes, but I warn you, the longer you wait the less chance at recovery you have."

Art blurted out, "Yes, make the appointment, I don't want to lose you." I nodded.

In the back of my mind, I knew this was the end. The last several weeks with our talks it was clear God was telling me to make amends with my loved ones. Art took the news very hard. He had lost the first love of his life and now was losing the second.

By the time we got back to Shawano I really had come to terms with the outcome; however, what I dreaded most was telling the girls. It was going to destroy them. I remember the day my daddy and mother died. Their pain was real, and I hated causing the girls any pain.

It was close to dinner when we got back to town and knew the family would be home. So, dealing with the problem head-on was the best option. Ward answered the door and knew instantly something was wrong. "Hi, Dad, is everything alright?" He shook his head. "Please come in." I went in behind Art and we gathered in the living room. The girls came and wrapped themselves around me. "I have never been one to beat around the bush, so I am just going to say it. We went to the doctor today since you know Evelyn has been sick the last few weeks." He paused; the family looked worried. Barb grabbed my arm. "The doctor says she has cancer."

The room got deathly quiet. "No, there must be a mistake!" Barb yelled.

"No, baby…." I grabbed her shoulders. "Come sit down." She looked at me with tears in her eyes. "I am not mistaken; I wish I were." We cried together for a long time. I am not sure I have ever ached inside as much as I did that night.

The next morning the girls called and begged to go with us each time to Green Bay. They wanted to show their support. I gratefully accepted their offer; it would at least give me more time to spend with them.

We started the first treatment Monday at 6:00 a.m. Since the appointment was so early, we drove up Sunday night and stayed in a motel. I made it through the initial one with flying colors and thought it would be a breeze. I immediately started feeling better, somewhat tired but better; unfortunately, that did not last long. Before the second treatment, I was completely bedridden.

My sisters came to stay during the day while Art went to work. I insisted on him going to the barbershop, the last thing he needed to do was watch me die. On Tuesday evening when Art came home from the barbershop, I asked him to call the girls. "What, why?" he blurted out.

"It's time…" I whispered.

"Time for what?"

"I have to tell them goodbye, please…."

"No, not yet. You are going to get better." I shook my head.

"Please call them, we don't have much time."

I spent the next two hours hating to say goodbye. They all looked so sad, and all I could think about was how God had blessed my life.

Our priest came and gave me last rites, but after he left, I could see the  anger in Art's eyes. It tore me up inside to see the man I cherished in so much pain. He paced the floor trying to come up with a solution to fix this situation.

"Art," I called out to get his attention. "Come lay down next to me." It took him a moment. I know he was thinking that once he lay down my dying would be real. He finally obliged. "Please… don't; cherish our time together. Promise me you won't be sad when I am gone. Celebrate my life…. Send me off to heaven wrapped in love."

The tears welled in his eyes for the first time in the three years we were married; I'd never seen him cry. "Come hold me one more time, please?"

He grabbed hold of me with all his might. I looked up into his eyes and tried to explain my reasoning so he could understand. "I have been facing fear my whole life. There is so much anger in the world, I have seen it many times. The only thing I want in this room right now is love. I have but one dying wish: for you to hold me until I am gone."

The End
Fade to Black

Epilogue

The history of Native Americans dates back tens of thousands of years, with the original settlement of the Americas by the Paleo-Indians. Anthropologists and archaeologists have identified a wide variety of cultures that existed during this era. The contact with Europeans had a profound impact on their history.

It is generally thought that the settlement in America took place via Beringia, the land bridge that connected the two continents across the Bering Strait. The exact number that traveled across the land bridge is unknown, but it happened about 60- 25,000 years ago. The Native Americans believe they have a natural freedom and find abundant nourishment—people who live without laws, without police, or religion.

The Native Americans have undoubtedly played a pivotal role in shaping the history of the nation, and are deeply woven into the social fabric of American life. During the last three decades, scholars of ethnohistory of Native American studies fully demonstrated the importance of including Native Americans to understand US history.

George Washington advocated the advancement of Native American society and "harbored some measure of goodwill towards the Indians." A treaty of the Six Nations of 1784 brokered an end to all hostilities between the United States and the Iroquois Confederation

As America progressed, the Native Americans also helped to secure our victory during the Civil War. Their participation included individuals, bands, tribes, and nations. In total, 28,693 Native Americans served, mostly in the Confederate military and a minority in the Union. They participated in battles such as Pea Ridge, Second Manassas, Antietam, Spotsylvania, Cold Harbor, and in Federal assaults on Petersburg. At the outbreak of the war, most Cherokees sided with the Union, but soon allied with the Confederacy. Many were concerned with losing their land if they were on the wrong side of the war effort. Some high-ranking officers came out of the war. General Stand Watie, a leader of the Cherokee Nation and Confederate Indian Cavalry Commander, was the last Confederate General to surrender his troops.

Ely Parker was a Union Civil War General who wrote the terms of surrender between the United States and the Confederate States of America. Parker was one of two Native Americans to reach the rank of brigadier general during the Civil War. By fighting with the Whites, Native Americans hoped to gain favor with the prevailing government by supporting the war effort.

Ulysses S. Grant was once rejected for Union military service because of his race. He is said to have remarked to Parker, "I am glad to see one real American here."

Parker replied, "We are all Americans."

One forgotten area of Native American History in the US is women veterans. However, the

Women for Military Service is trying to overcome that lack of knowledge among society.

A more unknown woman was an Oneida woman, **Tyonajanegen**, at the battle of Oriskany during the American Revolution (1775-1783). Tyonajanegen fought at her husband's side on horseback during the battle. She was injured while loading her husband's gun.

Sacajawea was an incredible woman, but much of the common stories are a myth. In reality, she served as an interpreter for members of the expedition. They were unfamiliar with Native American languages. In their journals, they referred to her as "Bird Woman."

The war department hired four Native American Catholic Sisters from Fort Berthold, South Dakota, to work as nurses during the Spanish-

American War (1898). One of the nurses, Sister Anthony, died of disease in Cuba and was buried with military honors.

Charlotte Edith (Anderson) Monture of the Iroquois Nation served as an Army nurse in France.  Fourteen Native American women were serving as members of the Army Nurse Corps during World War I, two of them overseas. Charlotte was born in 1890 in Ohsweken, Ontario, Canada. In 1917, she left her job as an elementary school nurse to join the Army Nurse Corps. She later referred to her service in France at a military hospital as "the adventure of a lifetime." She passed away in 1996, at the age of 106.

Charlotte Edith (Anderson) Monture

Mrs. Cora E. Sinnard was a member of the Oneida Tribe and a graduate of the Episcopalian School of Nursing in Philadelphia. She served eighteen months in France with a hospital unit provided by the Episcopal Church.

The war efforts of WWII were blessed to have nearly 800 Native American women serve.

Elva (Tapedo) Wale, a Kiowa, left her Oklahoma reservation to join the Women's Army Corps. She became an "Air WAC," and worked on Army air bases across the United States.

Elva (Tapedo) Wale

Corporal Bernice (Firstshoot) Bailey of Lodge Pole, Montana, joined the Women's Army Corps in 1945 and served until 1948. After the war, she was sent to Wiesbaden, Germany, as part of the Army of Occupation.

Beatrice (Coffey) Thayer

Beatrice (Coffey) Thayer also served in the Army of Occupation in Germany. Beatrice remembers being assigned to KP with German POWs, who were accompanied by armed guards. Beatrice was in Germany when the Berlin Wall went up, and remained in the Army until 1970.

Alida (Whipple) Fletcher joined the Army during World War II and trained as a medical specialist. After her assignment to Camp Stoneman, California, she was deployed to the Pacific. Alida was on duty the night two ships loaded with explosives collided at a nearby ammunition dump. The accident killed approximately 400 sailors and wounded many more.

She was quoted as saying, "That night was the most tragic of my life."

First Lieutenant Julia (Nashanany) Reeves, a member of the Potawatomie Indian Tribe of Crandon, Wisconsin, joined the Army Nurse Corps in 1942 and was assigned to one of the first medical units shipped to the Pacific.

Julia was transferred to the 23rd Station Hospital in Norwich, England, where she was stationed during the invasion of Normandy. During the Korean War, Julia mobilized with the 804th Station Hospital.

Private **Minnie Spotted-Wolf** of Heart Butte, Montana, enlisted and turned out to be the first female American Indian to enrol in the Marine Corps. Minnie had worked on her father's ranch doing such chores as cutting fence posts, driving a two-ton truck, and breaking horses. She commented, "Boot camp was dreaded but not too hard."

Ola Mildred Rexroat

Ola Mildred Rexroat, an Oglala Sioux from Pine Ridge Indian Reservation, South Dakota, joined the Women's Airforce Service Pilots (WASP) directly out of high school. She was assigned to tow targets for aerial gunnery students at Eagle Pass Army Air Base in Texas. After the war ended, Ola joined the Air Force and served for almost ten years.

When the Korean Conflict and Vietnam War broke out, the military was desperate for womanpower. So, recruitment created campaigns aimed at young women. Many Native American women answered the call. Sarah Mae Peshlakai, a member of the Navajo Tribe from Crystal, New Mexico, enlisted in the Women's Army Corps in 1951 and served until 1957. Peshlakai trained as a medical specialist and was assigned to Yokohama Army Hospital in Japan, where she helped care for casualties from the Korean battlefields.

Verna Fender

Verna Fender entered the Navy during the Korean Conflict and trained at Bainbridge, Maryland. During basic training she was severely injured and was sent to a Naval hospital for physical rehabilitation.

After therapy, Verna returned to Bainbridge and completed her training. The Navy assigned Verna to its base in San Diego, California, where she completed her three-year term of enlistment.

Shirley M. Arviso, a Navajo of the Bitter Water Clan, served in the Navy from 1953 through

1963. She was the Communications Officer in charge of a group of people who decrypted classified messages.

Pearl Ross, a member of the Arikara Tribe from the Fort Berthold Reservation, joined the Air Force in 1953, and trained as a medical specialist. During the Vietnam era, she saw many men who had been wounded in combat. Pearl volunteered for overseas duty, but was turned down because the Air Force was hesitant to send women to Vietnam.

Pearl Ross

Linda Woods enlisted in the Air Force in the late 1950s and was on duty when President Kennedy was assassinated. She remembers the airbase where she was stationed went on full alert. A later assignment took her to the southern United States during the Civil Rights movement. As a non-White, she found the environment somewhat difficult;

however, she retained pride in her uniform as a woman of color.

Barbara Monteiro joined the WAC in 1963 and took her secretarial training at Ft. McClellan, Alabama. Her first duty assignment was to Ft. Huachuca, Arizona, where she worked for three years in the travel office and motor pool in support of troop readiness during the Vietnam War. In 1966, Monteiro was assigned to Ft. Richardson, Alaska, where she served as an administration specialist at the Education Center for a year.

The number of women enlisting increased in the '70s, including Native Americans. **Patricia White Bear** joined the Navy in the 70s. She trained as an instrument man and served at sea repairing, adjusting, and calibrating the wide variety of mechanical measuring instruments used aboard ships.

Dolores Kathleen Smith, a Cherokee, graduated from the Air Force Academy in 1982. She completed navigator training and was assigned to a KC-135 unit. She served in the operational plan's division of her unit and also as an instructor before retiring as a captain from the Air Force in 1990.

Darlene Yellowcloud of the Lakota Tribe was inspired to join the Army because so many of the men in her family had served. Her grandfather, Bear Saves Life, was killed in action in France during World War I. Her father, brothers, brothers-in-law, uncles, and cousins were all veterans. Darlene was assigned to the US Army in Korea as a Specialist 4th Class.

Darlene Yellowcloud

Lawnikwa Spotted-Eagle joined the Army in 1988, and attended basic training at Ft. Dix, New Jersey. Acting as a guidon carrier, she was injured when another carrier grounded a guide iron through her foot into the ground. She still has the scar, and now serves as a member of the Virginia Air National Guard.

Not all the Native American women serving in the military came home from combat.

Katherine Matthews of Cherokee, North Carolina, joined the Navy in the late 1970s and trained as an aviation machinist's mate. She died while serving in California in 1985.

Terri Ann Hagen

Terri Ann Hagen, a former Army medic, was a member of the Army National Guard when she was killed fighting a fire on Storm King Mountain in Colorado in 1994.

Since 1994, the number of Native American women in combat has grown incredibly in the United States. The Women's Memorial has only 111 Native American women veterans registered to date. As more Native American women veterans are registered at the Memorial, their stories will be available to the interested public.

The list above was compiled by the Native American History month by registering a Native American veteran at the Memorial. If you have someone that needs to be listed on their site please go to Women's Memorial.

However, not all Native Americans who made a name for themselves in the world served in the military.

Maria Tallchief (Elizabeth Marie "Betty" Tallchief) of the Osage family was an American ballerina. She was considered America's first major prima ballerina. Plus, she was the first Native American to hold the rank and is said to have revolutionized ballet.

Sharice Lynnette Davids (born May 22, 1980), is an American attorney, former mixed martial artist, and politician serving as the U.S. Representative from Kansas's 3rd congressional district since 2019. Davids became the first Democrat elected to represent a Kansas congressional district in a decade.

Evelyn Frechette

Evelyn Frechette was born in Neopit, Wisconsin in the fall of 1907. Neopit, and the Menominee Indian Reservation.

My mother used to say, "When you know who you are; when your mission is clear and you burn with the inner fire of unbreakable will; no cold can touch your heart; no deluge can dampen your purpose. You know that you are alive." Her immortal words will always be a part of my soul.

I can still remember that day, the agony in her face. I could only imagine how she must have felt, watching me disappear out of sight. It was the first time I'd seen her cry since Daddy died. At the time, I had some idea of the horrible events taking place on the reservation, but no idea how bad things were until I headed off to the boarding school in Flandreau,

South Dakota. The experience exposed me to the real world beyond the confines of my childhood home. Now, I am not saying life on the reservation was easy, it wasn't. We faced hatred and bigotry every day, as travelers made their way around the county. Although not everyone was bad: I remember one such gentleman and his wife, their acquaintance touched my soul and allowed me to keep hope that not every human on the planet wanted all Native Americans dead, or confined to a cell like a criminal.

Mrs. Evelyn Wilson 61, of 131 North Main Street, Shawano, died at 5:35 a.m. this morning, Monday, January 13, 1969.

The former Evelyn Frechette, daughter of the late Mr. and Mrs. William Frechette, was born on September 15, 1907, at Keshena. She had lived in the Neopit area all her life and was a member of St. Anthony Catholic Church.

Survivors are two sisters and two brothers, Anna, Mrs. Joseph Brown, Neopit, and Miss Frances Frechette, Milwaukee, Charles Frechette, Neopit, and Sylvester Frechette, Chicago.

Funeral services will be conducted on Wednesday at 10:00 a.m. at St. Anthony Catholic Church. Neopit Father Marcellus will officiate, and internment will be in the parish cemetery at Neopit. Friends may call at the Born Funeral Home, Shawano after 2:00 p.m. Tuesday until the time of the service on Wednesday. The Rosary will be said at 8:00 p.m., on Tuesday at the funeral home.

Evelyn Frechette's grave marker was later added by the Tic family who had mistakenly inserted 1970 instead of 1969 as the year she passed away.

References

G. Russell Giradin, W. J. (1994). *Dillinger the Untold Stories* . Indian Unversity Press.

Magazine, T. (2006/1935, February 4). *Rev. Edward L. Brooks, Brooks Farm and Beulah Home*. Retrieved from http://genealogytrails.com/ill/cook/beulahhomestory.html

School, S. A. (2019). *St. Anthony School*. Retrieved from : https://stanthonymilwaukee.org/history

Wisconsin, T. M. (2019). *The Menominee Indian Tribe of Wisconsin*. Retrieved from http://www.menominee-nsn.gov/CulturePages/AboutUs.aspx

www.ingramcontent.com/pod-product-compliance
Lightning Source LLC
Chambersburg PA
CBHW042112100526
44587CB00025B/4021